The World of
the Image

OTHER TITLES IN THE LONGMAN TOPICS READER SERIES

The World of the Image

TRUDY SMOKE
Hunter College of the City University of New York

ALAN ROBBINS
Kean University

New York   San Francisco   Boston
London   Toronto   Sydney   Tokyo   Singapore   Madrid
Mexico City   Munich   Paris   Cape Town   Hong Kong   Montreal

Senior Sponsoring Editor: Virginia L. Blanford
Senior Marketing Manager: Sandra McGuire
Production Manager: Bob Ginsberg
Project Coordination and Design: Pre-Press Company
Electronic Page Makeup: Laserwords
Cover Design Manager: Wendy Ann Fredericks
Cover Photo: Courtesy of Alan Robbins
Senior Manufacturing Buyer: Dennis J. Para
Printer and Binder: RR Donnelley & Sons Company, Harrisonburg
Cover Printer: Phoenix Color Corporation

For permission to use copyrighted material, grateful acknowledgment is made to the copyright holders on pp. 217–220, which are hereby made part of this copyright page.

Library of Congress Cataloging-in-Publication Data

The world of the image : Longman topics reader / [edited by] Trudy Smoke, Alan Robbins. -- 1st ed.
    p. cm. -- (Longman topics reader)
    Includes bibliographical references.
    ISBN 0-321-38882-8
    1. College readers. 2. English language -- Rhetoric -- Problems, exercises, etc. I. Smoke, Trudy. II. Robbins, Alan.
    PE1417.W653 2006
    808'.0427 -- dc22

                                          2006025915

Visit us at www.ablongman.com

ISBN 0-321-38882-8

12345678910—DOH—09 08 07 06

Everywhere you look in the modern world, images are becoming more common, more present, and more pervasive. We are immersed in a world of images. From the earliest cave paintings to the latest in high-resolution images, every advance in technology, each innovation, has provided a novel means of *picturing* that fills the world with a new generation of images. The digital revolution is no different. Images can now appear everywhere and anywhere, and thanks to the computer they are uniquely reproducible, malleable, and disposable. Whether we are ready or not, from public displays to private screens, from building surfaces to cell phones, from the *New York Times* to the newest e-zines, images are increasingly a part of the world in which we live.

We are also coming to rely more and more on images to understand ourselves and the world around us. Just think about all the information you have gathered about society, nature, culture, history, and even life itself. Now consider how much of that information is based on images you have seen rather than on your direct experience. This gives you a hint at just how important images are to our attitudes, beliefs, and knowledge. Whether through personal communications, media presentations, or scientific publications, it is largely through images that we understand the world around us. Just as we know that reading a written text is more than simply knowing the meaning of words, we need to explore how the reading of a visual text is more than just identifying the elements of an image. We need to know how these elements work together to create meaning and how we can understand and make sense of that meaning.

Our natural visual system, amazing as it is, is actually rather limited by scale, size, and scope. We take in only a tiny sliver of the world through our eyes. If it is bigger than the planet, smaller than a pinpoint, inside the body, or outside the senses, our knowledge of it comes from images created using some type of technology. In addition to expanding our physical limitations, images can expand our mental limitations by telling us new things about ourselves. They tell us how we live in societies, as individuals, and as citizens. Images tell us how to look, how to behave, what to buy, and to which groups we should belong. The mirror of the media reflects back to us, accurately or not, our own values, fears, dreams, and attitudes. In many ways, the media magnifies and modifies these values—and can even end up coaxing or coercing our beliefs.

For all these reasons, the study of and investigation into images is crucial to modern life. Unless we understand how images are actually *becoming* our world—the world we live and believe in—there is always the danger that we will be overwhelmed and even victimized by the very images that surround us. The authors whose writings have been assembled for this collection are all fascinated by some aspect of the image, by its power, and by what we can learn by probing into it. We hope that their writings fascinate you, make you think, and give you ideas about which to write.

To help you make your way through this exploration of images, this book is organized into six chapters, each of which focuses on a key theme.

The first chapter, *The Act of Seeing,* deals with vision itself and its many mysteries and complexities. The readings in this section should give you a new respect for the delicate process of seeing and an insight into how we make visual sense of a multifaceted world. It will be helpful to keep this intricate process in mind as we probe deeper into the specific ways we understand images. If you keep this in mind, it will come as no surprise that the ways in which we encounter and cope with the world of the image are itself complex.

Chapter 2 is called *Mirroring Ourselves*. The selections in it deal with the ways in which we rely on the images we create to tell us who we are and what we should look like. Notions of beauty, health, body decoration, history, and even identity all rely on our faith that images accurately mirror our lives and concerns. As you will see, the attitudes that our images help mold can be overpowering and very hard to change.

In *The Visual Surround,* the third chapter, we look at the impact of the explosion of images in our environment, the world that surrounds us, and the effect that this explosion has on us as citizens and consumers. This chapter will help you become more aware of the power of life's daily images: visual symbols that replace words, web cameras that follow your every move, violence in the media, and icons that become reference points for a common language. These are all examples of the fact that images are becoming more and more common in our lives.

The fourth chapter, *Images and Their Uses,* explores the many purposes that images can serve and the wide range of reasons for which images have been created since the beginning of human existence. From cave paintings to tribal rituals to the private creations of unique individuals—and even dreams—images have many functions and fulfill many needs. All these uses, and many more, further explain the driving force behind the explosion of images with the emergence of every new technology.

In Chapter 5, *Pictures That Prod*, the readings look at a crucial aspect of the image revolution: the various ways in which images can alter our attitudes and change our behavior. The influence of advertising is certainly the most familiar of these, but propaganda images also have this effect. Even cartoons and reality television participate in the elevation of images from objects *in* the world to a comprehensive world of their own—one that molds us and influences the way we know ourselves and others.

In *The Image as Reality*, our final chapter, we address the slippery distinction between images and reality. Readings in this chapter look at such questions as the role of digital manipulation in photography, the fake environments of Las Vegas, the photo retouching that is a standard procedure at NASA, and how the advent of film once again altered our view of the world. These selections point to the various ways in which images can change what we think of as real.

Each of the chapters begins with a quote that lays the groundwork for the issues to come. An introduction outlines some of the basic themes and ideas presented in that chapter. All five selections in each chapter begin with a biography that gives you a background for each author, which should help you understand the context in which he or she is writing. This is followed by a brief section called "Getting Started," which poses a few questions relevant to the reading. By thinking about these questions before you start to read, you will be in the best frame of mind for considering the issues that the selection raises. A set of questions and suggestions for writing at the end of each selection will direct you to think and write critically about the topic and the points of view presented. And finally, each chapter concludes with "Making Connections," a section that suggests more integrated thinking about the links and connections between the various authors and their ideas.

People from many different fields including art history, psychology, anthropology, and semiotics have been writing an of thinking about images for a long time. But more recently of visual studies—that is, thinking and writing solely on images as a unique field of inquiry—has gained momentum. By bringing all these authors together, this book supports the goal of visual studies, which is to teach us to use the tools of analysis and description that we have at our disposal to explore the ways in which images affect us.

You may or may not agree with the positions and conclusions of the authors in this book. It is far more important that you absorb and consider what you read, remain open to new, different, or even controversial ideas, and think and write about how these ideas relate to your own experiences and impressions. The authors included come from many different disciplines and backgrounds, but they all have one thing in common: a fascination with images. We hope that this fascination, this desire to understand the world of images that surrounds you, is something you take from this book.

TRUDY SMOKE
ALAN ROBBINS

ABOUT THE AUTHORS

Trudy Smoke is Professor of English at Hunter College, City University of New York. In addition to teaching courses in writing, linguistics, and literature, Dr. Smoke directed the Freshman Orientation Seminar program at Hunter College that welcomed more than 1000 entering students, and for six years she served as director of the freshman writing program. From 1995 to 2001, Dr. Smoke was co-editor of *The Journal of Basic Writing*. Since 2000, she has also co-directed the Writing across the Curriculum and Writing Fellows programs at Hunter College. The author of six books on writing, language acquisition, and ESL, English as a Second Language, Professor Smoke's recent publications include *Language and Linguistics in Context* (2006) (co-edited with H. Luria and D. M. Seymour) and the fourth edition of her popular textbook *A Writer's Workbook* (2005). Her work has also recently appeared in *Crossing the Curriculum: Multilingual Learners in College Classrooms* (2004), edited by Vivian Zamel and Ruth Spack and in *Mainstreaming Basic Writers: Politics and Pedagogies of Access* edited by Gerri McNenny and Sallyanne H. Fitzgerald. Dr. Smoke has been a frequent presenter at the CCCCs, TESOL, and other professional conferences and is currently at work on a book about language and immigration.

Alan Robbins is the Janet Estabrook Rogers Professor of Visual and Performing Arts at Kean University in New Jersey and director of The Design Center, which produces exhibitions, publications, and products in the various fields of design. Articles about his innovative work with students have appeared in the *New York Times* and the *Chronicle of Higher Education*. Professor Robbins is also an award-winning graphic artist and the author of sixteen books ranging from mystery to science fiction to humor. His novel, *Blue Moon*, won a New York State CAPS award for fiction in 1984; his latest novel, *An Interlude in Dreamland*, recently won a Writer's Notes Award for new fiction; and his essays on technology and design have appeared in *Newsweek* magazine and the *New York Times*. His cartoons, illustrations, and graphic designs have appeared in numerous publications and exhibitions, and he is a nationally known writer and designer of interactive games and puzzles, as well as a former contributor to *Games* magazine. Professor Robbins is a frequent presenter and keynote speaker at national conferences on the subjects of creativity, design, technology, and visual studies and in 2000 won a New York State Council for the Humanities Speaker fellowship.

The World of
the Image

CHAPTER 1

The Act of Seeing

"We don't see things as they are; we see things as we are."
—Anais Nin

Before we can begin to explore a subject as complex as looking at images, we should try to understand something about the act of seeing itself. How we see and make sense of images depends to some extent on how we see anything at all—and this is a complex matter. Therefore, the readings in this first chapter all focus on vision: on how seeing works or, in some cases, does not work. As you will see, the recurrent theme is that vision or seeing is not as simple as you may think.

Most people assume that the act of seeing can be easily explained. Objects reflect light in through the lens of the eye, the light is transformed into electrical impulses, and the brain records and interprets them. In a very basic way, this is true. However, each of these steps—from recording to transforming to interpreting—is enormously complicated. Slight changes in any of them can profoundly alter the process of seeing.

The mechanism of the eye is one thing, but the way in which we build a mental picture of the world through seeing is another. Vision is central to the way we think about the world; a third of the brain seems to be devoted to neurons or nerve cells that deal with vision. In fact, rather than talk about eyeballs and impulses, it is probably much better to think in terms of what Deborah Curtiss, author of our first selection, "Seeing and Awareness," calls "the eye-brain mechanism." In spite of its sophistication. Curtiss believes that we can "improve and expand visual perception" through exposure and exercise. As examples she offers a few exercises meant to improve three particular aspects of vision . . .

1

foveal (seeing details), peripheral (seeing surroundings), and scanning (selective seeing). Trying these exercises will demonstrate her premise that the more effectively we use our eyes, the more attuned we become to what there is to see, images included. Or as she puts it, "Visual literacy begins with visual awareness."

In the second selection, called "The Vision Thing: Mainly in the Brain," Denise Grady asks us to consider how much we take for granted in seeing. She describes a researcher who wore goggles that reversed the colors of the world. Under these conditions, tiny little events (like a person blinking or glancing at the shadow under a car) became intense distractions to seeing in the usual way. Understanding that the brain has to actively construct or invent our visual world, she refers to seeing as a form of "sensory reasoning." The brain is constantly at work trying to make sense of what it sees, and can fail in some striking ways—such as people with "blindsight," who can actually see but are simply not aware of it. Grady also suggests that some aspects of seeing—color, motion, and form—are processed independently through different pathways in the brain, while others—motion, depth, brightness—are processed together. These connections can lead to some very tricky confusions.

In our third selection, "When Babies Become Aware of Themselves," author Mark Pendergrast discusses the profound implications of a very common aspect of seeing, the image we see in a mirror. He suggests that the simple act of recognizing oneself in a mirror is something learned, a result of increased self-awareness. His selection also points out that the act of understanding a mirror image relates to key human traits such as empathy, sexuality, and even spirituality. This is another example of how the complex interaction of the eye and the brain allows us to create a visual sense of the world and of ourselves.

The fourth selection is "Seeing" by Annie Dillard. In this fascinating essay, Dillard points out how difficult it can be for people to adapt to the world of sight, something most of us tend to take for granted. Her striking examples support the idea that vision is not a simple process at all but instead a complex set of subtle understandings about what we see. In fact, it is shocking to discover that the newly-sighted may find the world (the one we see all the time) "tormentingly difficult." Even little things—like the sense of space they are in, the size of the world, their own visibility to others, or the differences in people's faces—create great challenges for people who previously knew what they knew of the world through touch or hearing.

And finally, in "How to Look at Nothing," James Elkins focuses on an aspect of seeing that most of us never think about . . . seeing nothing at all. His selection points out that the mechanism of seeing itself is so delicate and sensitive that we never actually see *nothing*, even in total darkness. Our eyes and brains are not passive receivers of the visual but actually produce visual effects themselves. In fact, as Elkins describes in his essay, we are so used to these subtleties of vision that seeing nothing—that is, no details of any kind—is intensely uncomfortable and strange.

Some of the selections in this chapter point to more complex ways of understanding how seeing works, while others focus on the many surprising ways in which this process can fail. Both of these approaches can tell us a great deal about vision and how we see, and therefore about how images affect us. There are practical applications for these kinds of investigations. The study of the mechanism of seeing may help us to develop artificial vision for computers for face recognition, document scanning, and image analysis. It can also advance the development of devices to help people with impaired vision. But most importantly, it can begin to give you a better appreciation for vision itself—a deeper understanding of just how intricate the eye-brain mechanism is and how extraordinary ordinary seeing is. The readings in this chapter should make you aware of what goes on when you look at something and that, in turn, will make your looking at images a richer experience.

Seeing and Awareness
Deborah Curtiss

Deborah Curtiss is the author of Introduction to Visual Literacy, *from which the excerpt below was taken. She attended the Yale University School of Art, where she trained as a painter. She has had more than two dozen solo exhibitions of her work, which can be found in private and public collections throughout the world. She has taught painting, drawing, design, and visual literacy at the University of the Arts, Temple University, and other institutions.*

Getting Started

Most of us take our vision for granted. After explaining the physiology of the eye, Curtiss provides some exercises that can help us develop our eye-brain connection and, ultimately, visual literacy. Do you think that this is possible? Have you ever done any drawing and noticed that it increased your visual awareness? Have you ever had the experience of focusing on some detail while missing important information around it? Have you ever tried to scan a scene to get the broadest sense of it without focusing on details? Curtiss thinks these are crucial skills in visual processing. Can you see how and when this might be true?

───────────── ✦ ─────────────

Visual literacy begins with visual awareness. To become visually aware we need first to turn to the physiological means by which we receive visual messages, namely the eye-brain mechanism.

Vision is a profoundly complex process, about which much is known but about which there remain many questions. Neurophysiology, perception psychology, and ophthalmology are but a few of the professions seeking further understanding of how we see.

It is estimated that visual perception comprises 75 to 80 percent of our sensory input. Moreover, of our visual perception, about 10 percent is in the eye and 90 percent is mental. Clearly, if we expand that 10 percent, the 90 percent will expand accordingly!

PHYSIOLOGY OF THE EYE

Let us look at some of the basic physical features of the human eye. The eye is more or less spherical in shape. In the front is an opening, the **pupil,** protected by a clear, transparent **cornea.** Through the cornea and pupil, light enters the interior of the eyeball, passes through a flexible biconvex **lens,** and projects the image of what one sees onto the **retina** at the back interior of the eye.

The retina is composed of about 132 million nerve cells, of which 125 million are rod-shaped cells (called **rods**) that distinguish light and dark; and 7 million are cone-shaped cells (called **cones**) that perceive color. The **optic nerve** carries the information from the retina in the form of electrical impulses to the brain, which decodes the messages and processes the information as vision.

In a small area of the retina at the back of the eye near the optic nerve, the cones are packed together very densely. This is known as the **fovea,** and it is responsible for our ability to focus, to see detail. The remaining area of the retina is used for **peripheral** vision, vision which is necessary for our perception of a broad visual field.

The eye also has muscles. The **iris** is a muscle that regulates the diameter of the pupil, making it small in bright light and large in dim or dark circumstances (to allow as much light as possible to enter the eye). The pupil ranges in diameter from 1 to 8 millimeters. Muscles attached to the eye and connecting with the eye socket enable us to move our eyes up and down, left and right, and around. This mobility permits us to **scan** a broad visual field without moving our heads.

In perceiving the visible world, we use our two eyes. When we look at an object through one eye and then the other, we see slightly different things. This **binocular** vision enables us to perceive depth and distance. But when we make a representational drawing, we must resolve these two slightly different images into one point of view. The camera, with a single lens, is monocular.

Psychologists of human perception maintain, quite convincingly, that much of visual perception is *learned* and, moreover, that it is subject to modification through learning. Thus, one can improve and expand visual perception. We can strengthen and sharpen it through exposure and exercise.

When one is learning a new skill or activity, it is often part of the training to strengthen relevant muscles and improve coordination. No one would expect to be able to swim a mile or ski a slalom without preparation. Similarly, depending upon the extent to which we are accustomed to using our eyes, we may need to strengthen and sharpen our visual apparatus. The following are exercises for the improvement of foveal, peripheral, and scanning vision. It is recommended that one or more of them be practiced daily for three to six weeks, or until strength in focused, peripheral, and scanning vision has been achieved.

Please be advised that these exercises will not improve impaired vision. They assume that any visual impairment you might have has been corrected to the extent possible by corrective lenses.

EXERCISE FOR FOVEAL VISION

This exercise, adapted from *The Zen of Seeing* by Frederick Franck, (published by Knopf/Vintage in 1973) is known as "blind contour drawing." Since it requires total visual attention and is in the form of a guided meditation, it will help to have someone else read the exercise slowly and quietly. In addition to improving foveal vision, it also can aid eye-mind-hand coordination and, for some people, lead to the peaceful effects of an alpha state of meditative consciousness.

First, find an object of visual interest to you. It may be a flower, a crumpled tissue, a sleeping pet, a picture, or whatever. It should be complex—a simple form will not hold your interest for very long. Additionally, you will want a comfortable place to sit, a pen or pencil, and a piece of plain paper attached to a pad or taped to a table, desk, or lapboard.

To begin the exercise, close your eyes and become aware of yourself sitting in space. Allow yourself to relax while taking several slow, easy, and deep breaths. Feel your tensions gravitate downward and out of your body.

Think of a time in which you were dazzled or amazed by a visual experience. It may have been a sunset, your first flight in an airplane, a striking skyline, or whatever. Really sense the intensity of your total awareness at that time, the drinking in of everything you were seeing, free of any editing. In that original experience, you were really *seeing* with total and undivided attention. Permit that quality of seeing to dominate this exercise. 15

When you feel you are participating in that original quality of seeing, free of expectations and distracting thoughts, open your eyes and look at the object you have chosen. For the remainder of the exercise, keep your eyes on that object and look at nothing else.

Continue to look at the object, permitting your eyes to wander around it as if they are explorers in an uncharted land. Keep looking at the object until you feel that there is nothing in the world but you and the object.

With your eyes *continuously* on the object, take your pen in hand and allow it to follow on the paper whatever your eyes see. Feel as if, with the point of your pen, you are caressing the outlines of the object.

Do *not* look at your paper. For now, what you draw does not matter at all. Keep exploring with your eyes, in ever greater detail, all the subtle ins and outs of your object. Allow your pen to follow wherever your eyes go, and whatever they see.

Do not take your pen off the paper, but keep it constantly exploring just as your eyes are doing. Feel free to draw on top of parts you have already drawn. Do not expect the drawing to be at all recognizable. It is merely a record of a visual journey.   20

Don't let your eye wander from the object, and don't try too hard. There is no need to think about what you are drawing, but merely permit your hand to follow what your eyes see.

Let the pen explore the interior edges and shapes of your object. Let it stroke and caress and discover.

This is an exercise and an experiment—an experience in seeing with undivided attention. The goal of the exercise is to extend your duration and quality of seeing with your foveal vision. The experience is successful if you feel as if you have become the object regardless of what has appeared on the paper.

Work to extend the time and quality of this exercise, but don't get lost with it. Forty five minutes is a good cut-off time.

As a special reward, allow yourself to do a regular drawing of   25 the object you exercised with. This time, look at the paper as well as the object—and discover representational drawing.

Hint: See the forms as *abstract shapes,* not as known things.

EXERCISE FOR PERIPHERAL VISION

This exercise is the opposite and complement to the exercise for foveal vision. It is similar in that it is a meditative exercise, and you don't look at your paper. But in this exercise you do not move your eyes at all; you keep them on one point. The point should be a very clear one, and not particularly interesting: the center of a doorknob, the corner of a table, or the dot of an *i* on a magazine cover.

Again, assume a comfortable position with pen or pencil and have a secured piece of paper oriented horizontally. Close your eyes for a minute or two, and breathe slowly to relax and divest yourself of extraneous thoughts. When you have reached a state of clear-minded relaxation, open your eyes and look at your chosen point.

While looking at it, feel around the edges of your paper with the fingers of your drawing hand. Run your fingers around the perimeter again, this time (while keeping your eyes still focused on the point) be conscious of the outer edges of your visual field and relate them to the edges of your paper: left side to left edge, top of your visual field to the top edge of the paper, and so forth. (Your visual field is not exactly rectangular, but it is close enough for this exercise.)

Keeping your eyes fixed on your point, put your pen to the 30 paper and draw all that you are conscious of in your visual field. Approximate all the relationships of shapes and forms that you see. They won't be clear, so your drawing won't be either. But that doesn't matter. We are not making art, nor are we even trying to make a representational drawing. This is an exercise in strengthening peripheral seeing.

You are in good company if you feel a little helpless and foolish while doing this exercise. You may also feel an irresistible urge to sneak a peek in order to catch a detail. Instead, enjoy this opportunity to be informal, playful, and imperfect.

This exercise is successful when you discover that you can see much more and in greater detail than you ever realized, even when not looking at whatever you are drawing. The experiment is successful if you feel that you have embraced the entirety of your visual field and have expanded your awareness.

EXERCISES FOR SCANNING VISION

In essence, when we scan things with our eyes we are selecting discrete bits of information from a broad visual field. There are several ways to improve the speed and accuracy of scanning vision. Many games are excellent for this purpose: any fast game with a ball, such as squash or basketball, provides a wealth of visual information that is continuously processed and acted upon.

Card games, especially forms of solitaire that require laying out the whole deck face-up, also demand a great deal of scanning vision. An especially challenging one is to lay out the cards face-up in nine overlapping columns, having respectively 9, 8, 7, . . . 2, 1 cards in each. Seven cards are left over, and may be played at any time, but once put in play they must remain in play. The object is to get the four suits in sequence from Ace to King played above the card spread. The spread is reordered by moving only *one card at a time* into descending numerical sequence, alternating black and red suits. A card may be placed in this order or in an open column and may be moved any number of times to effect the objective. It is a difficult game, but it can be won. And regardless, you are getting in a lot of scanning exercise while strategizing.

Here is another scanning exercise you can do anywhere, one 35 guaranteed to shorten a wait in line or any boring situation. Pick a color or type of object in your immediate environment and, while keeping your head in a fixed position, roll your eyes to the fullest extent in all directions, counting as quickly as possible the objects of that color or shape or type which you see. This is a very quick exercise, so do it several times, changing the category, or even combining categories, to have more objects to enumerate.

Doing puzzles (500 or more pieces), mazes, seek-and-find word games, and so forth are all good scanning exercises. They not only engage foveal and scanning vision, but entice us to coordinate seeing with problem solving. They deal with complex and sometimes chaotic situations that require visual ordering and organization to make sense.

Can we ever again feel guilty for "wasting time" while engaged in these games?

Visual literacy begins with visual awareness. An expanded and strengthened use of our eyes to perceive the visual world with interest, breadth, and depth, can lead to expanded mental capacity as well.

Questions

1. Reread the introduction and the conclusion of this essay. What similar or key words and ideas do you find in each? What is the thesis or main idea of this essay? Where is the thesis located in the essay?

2. What in Curtiss' article suggests to you that there might be some benefit from playing computer games? Which type of vision might be exercised while doing this? What other activities can you think of that help you to exercise your vision?

3. Curtiss asked you to create your own images as a means of enhancing your ability to see. What was it like to be asked to do this or to actually do it? If you are not an artist, did you feel nervous about doing it or even thinking about it? If you are an artist, did this make you think about your own work in a different way? How did it make you feel to be asked to produce images?

4. Find a photograph in any book that interests you. Look at the photo for 60 seconds and then put it away. Describe what you saw in as much detail as you can. What was the most important part of the image? What was the most visually powerful part? What did you notice first, second, third? How do you think this experiment relates to the idea of foveal vision presented in the article?

5. Put a keyword in the Google images search engine. Then click on one of the thumbnail images to see a larger version of it. Look at this for no more than 5 seconds; then close the file and see how much of the image you can describe without looking at it. How does this relate to the scanning vision mentioned in the article?

The Vision Thing: Mainly in the Brain
DENISE GRADY

Recipient of a 1986 commendation from the Newspaper Guild for "choice and excellence of crusading journalistic contributions in the areas of science and medicine," Denise Grady is a science reporter who has written for many publications, including the New York Times, Scientific American, *and* Discover *, in which the article below was originally published in June 1993. Her bachelor's degree is in biology and her master's is in English, giving her an excellent background to write about science and health issues.*

Getting Started

What do you think would happen to the way you see if black and white were reversed? Using reversing goggles, that is exactly what one researcher did in order to understand how we see and process visual information. How do you think it made him feel about the world around him? Have you ever tried to find your own blind spot—and then discovered that your brain "filled in" the "empty" part of the visual field? Are you aware that some people experience "blindsight"? Have you ever been tricked by an optical illusion? This article describes research that is being done to better understand how important the brain is to processing and making sense of the visual impulses we receive. Before you read it, look around the space you are in and notice the brightness, the colors, the shapes, the shadows, and how objects appear under different conditions. Think about how your eyes have played tricks on you.

———————— ✦ ————————

S tuart Anstis sat in his living room in the dark, wearing a pink visor that held up a hood made of thick black paper with eye holes cut out. He couldn't see anything but the flickering images on the TV set, which he had rigged to play everything in negative. He'd been watching a movie for some time—"There was this fellow dancing and miming and flirting," he recalls—when a friend, who happened to know the film, stopped by. "Oh, Bob Hope," the friend said. "And I said, 'Bob Hope! Good Lord!' I'd been looking at him all that time and didn't know who it was."

Vision researchers like Anstis—along with photographers—have known for decades that faces are nearly impossible to identify when light and dark are reversed. But why that's so is not well understood.

Curious about the difficulty of interpreting negative images, Anstis, a perceptual psychologist at the University of California at San Diego, decided last year to plunge into a negative world. He connected a set of goggles to a video camera that reversed black and white and converted colors to their complements—green to purple, yellow to blue, and so on—then put them over his eyes. For three days Anstis saw nothing in positive. He removed the goggles only at night, and then he slept blindfolded; he showered in the dark. The experiment was a variation on earlier studies by researchers who had worn glasses designed to turn the world upside down or shift it sideways. They had found that a surprising degree of adaptation occurred; somehow the visual system compensated, put things right, and allowed a person to function. Anstis wanted to find out if the same thing would happen when he traded black for white.

Through the goggles, faces of his friends and colleagues took on a black-toothed, menacing quality. Their pupils became white; the light glinting off their eyes appeared black. "I went on falsely seeing the highlight as the pupil," Anstis says, "so I constantly misread people's eye movements." He could never be quite sure when they were looking at him. Their blinking became a "peculiar flicker" that he found depersonalizing. "Emotional expressions were hard to read," he says. Pictures of celebrities were unrecognizable. By daylight—when the sky was a very dark yellow, almost black—a woman's sharply etched shadow, now rendered in white, looked like a paper cutout or even another person. Fuzzier shadows—cast by a hand held over a table, for instance—translated into a vague, eerie glow.

Objects were no easier to deal with than people. Meals in complementary colors—blue scrambled eggs, for instance—became so unappetizing that Anstis puckishly recommends negative goggles to dieters. Outdoors, sunlight converted to shadow made a flight of stairs a frightening experience. The risers became confused with the treads. "I lost my sense of reality, as if I'd been up too late," he recalls. "At the curb, cars whizzing by didn't look real. They looked like toys coasting along on white platforms, which were actually their shadows. I would have been quite happy to walk in front of them if it hadn't been for the roaring sound of the traffic." He felt as if his other senses were taking over his consciousness, to compensate for the lack of meaningful visual input. The scent of a laundry room, for instance, became remarkably intense.

Over the course of three days, he says, there was very little adaptation. He did begin reinterpreting sharp shadows, but the

5

fuzzy, glowing ones continued to trick him. A postdoctoral student who wore the goggles for eight days reacted the same way. "I was amazed at how difficult it is to deal with," Anstis says. "All the information is still there, just like reversing the signs in an equation, so we're really surprised that the brain has so much trouble."

Vision, of course, is more than recording what meets the eye: it's the ability to understand, almost instantaneously, what we see. And that happens in the brain. The brain, explains neurobiologist Semir Zeki of the University of London, has to "actively construct" or invent our visual world. Confronted with an overwhelming barrage of visual information, it must sort out relevant features and make snap judgments about what they mean. It has to guess at the true nature of reality by interpreting a series of clues written in visual shorthand; these clues help distinguish near from far, objects from background, motion in the outside world from motion created by the turn of the head. Assumptions are built into the clues—for example, that near things loom larger, or that lighting comes from above.

"The brain must process an immense amount of information as fast as it can, using any shortcuts it can," says Anstis. "It has to find a minimum hypothesis to cover a maximum amount of data. So it's got to use any trick it can." His experiment reveals one of those tricks: "We think the brain is programmed to use brightness the way it is in the world. That means shadows are always darker, and light comes from above."

A negative world, with light pouring down from the sky like black paint, shatters those basic assumptions. And when we violate the assumptions, confusion reigns. Reverse brightness, as Anstis did, and critical clues about the world, such as facial features and expressions, and shape and depth, are subverted. The result is illusion.

Seeing, in short, is a form of sensory reasoning. When the assumptions on which that reasoning is based are destroyed, seeing becomes senseless. Even though all the necessary visual information is there, we are reduced to groping around.   10

Everyday vision encompasses an extraordinary range of abilities. We see color, detect motion, identify shapes, gauge distance and speed, and judge the size of faraway objects. We see in three dimensions even though images fall on the retina in two. We fill in blind spots, automatically correct distorted information, and erase extraneous images that cloud our view (our noses, the eyes' blood vessels).

The machinery that accomplishes these tasks is by far the most powerful and complex of the sensory systems. The retina, which contains 150 million light-sensitive rod and cone cells, is actually an outgrowth of the brain. In the brain itself, neurons devoted to visual processing number in the hundreds of millions and take up about 30 percent of the cortex, as compared with 8 percent for touch and just 3 percent for hearing. Each of the two optic nerves, which carry signals from the retina to the brain, consists of a million fibers; each auditory nerve carries a mere 30,000.

The optic nerves convey signals from the retinas first to two structures called the lateral geniculate bodies, which reside in the thalamus, a part of the brain that functions as a relay station for sensory messages arriving from all parts of the body. From there the signals proceed to a region of the brain at the back of the skull, the primary visual cortex, also known as V1. They then feed into a second processing area, called V2, and branch out to a series of other, higher centers—dozens, perhaps—with each one carrying out a specialized function, such as detecting color, detail, depth, movement, or shape or recognizing faces.

The goal of much current research is to find out not only how those individual centers function but also how they interact with one another. For now, no one even knows where the higher centers ultimately relay their information. "There's no little green man up there looking at this stuff," says Harvard neurobiologist Margaret Livingstone. "In a sense, your perception *is* what's going on in those areas." Researchers would like to know just where and how the "rules" for seeing are stored, how they're acquired, which assumptions are built up from experience and which are hardwired. Anstis thinks his failure to adapt to his negative world might be evidence that brightness clues are built in, but there's not enough evidence to say for sure. "I don't know what would have happened," he says, "if we'd gone on in negative for ages and ages."

There are several approaches to analyzing the visual system. Anatomical studies look at neural wiring to learn what's connected to what. Physiological studies determine how individual cells and groups of cells react when a particular segment of the visual field is presented with a certain type of stimulus. Perceptual psychologists like Anstis start at the behavior end: they show subjects doctored, tricky images, including optical illusions, and use the responses to figure out just what elements of the environment the brain is responding to and how it's sorting out those elements for processing.

During the past two decades the separate avenues of visual research have come together in a striking way. All point to a fundamental division of labor in the visual system: color, motion, and form appear to be processed independently, though simultaneously, through different pathways in the brain. Physicians and researchers have long suspected that the visual system broke down certain tasks, because strokes and head injuries can leave people with highly specific deficits: loss of color vision, motion perception, or the ability to recognize faces, for instance. It thus seems likely that there are a number of separate systems involved in analyzing visual information, but what's not clear is just how many exist. "Everybody will give you a different answer," Livingstone says. She suspects two or three, but Zeki suggests four.

One thing researchers do agree on is that motion is processed separately from form and color. The system that picks up motion also registers direction and detects borders as defined by differences in brightness. It reacts quickly but briefly when stimulated, and so it doesn't register sharp detail. Another system sees color, but whether it also recognizes shape is not clear. "There may be a pure color system," says Livingstone, "but it's not known." In addition, there may be a second color system, one sensitive to both shape and color but not concerned with movement. It would react slowly but be capable of scrutinizing an object for a relatively long time, thus picking up detail. Zeki believes there's still another system, which perceives the shape of moving objects but not their color.

These systems usually work in concert to give us a more or less accurate rendition of the visual world. But because they process information differently, they can sometimes lead to conflict in the eye-brain system about what's really going on. Clues can be misread or misinterpreted. At the same time, the joining of different kinds of clues in the same pathway—say, brightness, motion, and depth—can mean that depth is impossible to read correctly when brightness is absent, or vice versa. By manipulating the way the eye-brain receives information from these pathways, vision researchers have revealed a variety of interesting and instructive phenomena. We might call them illusions. But to the eye-brain system, they're merely the result of following sensory reasoning to its logical conclusion.

For example, proof that motion and color are processed separately can be derived from a clever experiment conducted several years ago at the University of Montreal by psychologist Patrick Cavanagh (now at Harvard) and his colleagues. He found that when a moving pattern of red and green stripes was adjusted so that the red and green were equally bright, or equiluminant, the motion became almost undetectable. In other words, when brightness differences between the stripes were eliminated, color alone was not enough to carry information about movement. The motion system, unable to perceive enough contrast between the stripes, had nothing to "see" move.

That experiment led Cavanagh and Anstis to devise a new test for color blindness, based on the knowledge that, depending on the type of color blindness, either red or green will appear brighter to a subject. By measuring the amount of brightness the subjects had to add to the red stripes to make the pattern stop moving—that is, to achieve equiluminance—the researchers were able to detect some forms of color blindness.

Similarly, it's relatively easy to prove that shading and depth are processed together by altering or eliminating brightness information and watching what happens to depth. In a portrait of President Eisenhower created by Margaret Livingstone, the shadows and highlights on his face have been replaced with patches of color; the brightness of the colors doesn't correspond to the relative brightness of shadows and highlights, however. Since shadows cast by the eyebrows, nose, and lips help define a person's face, putting bright color in the shadow regions effectively erases and even inverts all three-dimensional information. "The features become unrecognizable," says Livingstone. "You can barely even tell it's a person."

Perspective drawings lose their depth if rendered in colors of equal brightness, as do drawings of geometric figures. The color scale used on the Eisenhower portrait is the one commonly used to produce contour maps and CAT scans; it's based on the visible spectrum, which has red at one end. The color scale therefore also uses red at one end, to code for the brightest regions; it uses yellow for comparatively darker ones. This irritates Livingstone no end. "People who read these color-coded CAT scans think they can interpret them," she says. "They think they know red is highest. But really, yellow is brighter." What the brain does is see the red areas as darker and less prominent than the yellow ones; the result can be an image whose depth is difficult to interpret. "This is a hardwired system, and no matter how much you try to override it intellectually, tell it what it should see, it will tell you what it really does see."

Recently, Livingstone has begun to suspect that artists have unique ways of exploiting the fact that motion, depth, and brightness are processed by the same pathway. "If you stare at something for a while, something three-dimensional, it goes sort of flat," Livingstone says. That occurs, she suspects, because the pathway is geared to detect changes in the environment, such as movement, and to respond quickly and briefly. Fixed on one image, its response dies out, and the impression of depth disappears.

"I think some artists might be stereo-blind," Livingstone says, meaning that they lack binocular depth perception. "I've talked to several who are. Everything looks somewhat flatter to them already." That makes it easier, she says, to translate a three-dimensional object into a flat drawing that nonetheless conveys depth. Artists with normal vision have told her that they've trained themselves to stare at their subject, wait for it to go flat, and then draw it flat, or to close one eye and eliminate stereo-vision automatically. "A normal person gets totally screwed up trying to draw 3-D," she says. "There are so many perspective, stereo, and occlusion cues. You need to get rid of that level of processing or you can't draw a flat picture."

Cavanagh has also been studying paintings, but for insight   25
into how the eye-brain creates richly embroidered visual images from sparse clues. "Flat art is a treasure trove of information about how vision works," he says. "When we look at a flat picture, we recover the depth, the spatial arrangements of the objects depicted. We could easily make a 3-D model of what we're seeing in the picture."

That ability to translate between 2-D and 3-D suggests something about the way we process images. "We look around and see things that look reassuringly solid and three-dimensional, a nice euclidean world," Cavanagh says. "But it's likely that our internal representation is nowhere near that complete." What we store, he suspects, is more like a set of two-dimensional images of what we're looking at, seen from many different angles. "It's a more intelligent representation," he says, "because it's sparse, an abstraction of the real, solid world, and yet it can still give us the impression that it is real and solid. It's like getting CD-quality music from a hand-cranked phonograph."

Cavanagh thinks that even the most primitive art forms, such as the line drawings found in the Lascaux caves, have much to tell about how information is encoded—for example, by the use of lines. "You have to ask why lines would ever be sufficient to see the depth structure of an object that's being drawn," he says. "Even if you see a line drawing of something you've never seen before, you get it instantly. Infants get it. Why do lines work at all if they don't exist in the real world? No objects in the real world have lines drawn around them."

Somewhere in the visual system, he says, there must be a code for contours that separate objects from their backgrounds. The boundary could be a difference in texture or color or even motion. Sure enough, an area has been found in the brain that responds to contours. Cavanagh describes it as contour-specific and attribute-independent. "It ended up, maybe by chance, responding to lines," he says. "Which is lucky for artists, or otherwise all drawings would have to be filled in. Instead, the brain fills in for them."

Actually, filling in is a well-known strategy that the brain uses to see more than meets the eye. It's a form of shortcutting that deals not with the information that is present but with the information that is lacking. The best-known example occurs at the natural blind spot in each eye. At the point where the optic nerve is connected in a normal eye, there's a patch in the retina that doesn't respond to light. A blind spot results in the part of the visual field that would normally be monitored by that patch. The blind spot is off center, toward the side of the visual field, and it's big enough to swallow up a golf ball held at arm's length, or even, at a bit more distance, a person's head. But we're unaware of it. For one thing, when both eyes are open, they cancel out each other's blind spots. For another, the constant motion of the eye prevents the spot from lingering at any one place. The blind spot doesn't become apparent until we close one eye and stare; even then, we've got to resort to tricks to detect it.

The interesting thing about the blind spot isn't so much what we don't see as what we do. The fact that there's no visual information there doesn't lead the brain to leave a blank in your visual field; instead, it paints in whatever background is likely to be there. If the blind spot falls on a dragonfly resting on a sandy beach, your brain doesn't blot it out with a dark smudge; it fills it in with sand.

But how? It's long been a subject of argument among psychologists and philosophers. Some argue that the process is a cognitive one carried out by some brain region at a higher level than the visual cortex. That process might be called logical inference: since we know the background is sandy and textured, we assume the blank spot must be, too, just as we might assume that if there's flowered wallpaper in front of us, the wallpaper behind us will have the same flowered pattern.

But filling in is different from assuming, says neuroscientist Vilayanur Ramachandran of the University of California at San Diego. It's most likely carried out in the visual cortex, by cells near the ones that the blind spot is depriving of input. It is, he says, an active, physical process: "There's neural machinery, and when it's confronted with an absence of input, it fills it in." The brain, in other words, somehow creates a representation of the background and sticks it into the blind spot.

"We think there's a separate system in the brain for edges and contours, and then one for surface features," Ramachandran says, "and this is the one doing completion of texture. It says, 'If there's a certain texture on the edge, it must be everywhere.'" He refers to the process as surface interpolation.

Curiously, there's a visual phenomenon that's almost the converse of filling in. It's called blindsight, and it occurs in some patients who have gaps in their visual fields because of brain injuries. Whereas many of the people Ramachandran studies have blind spots they don't notice, these people have vision they don't notice. They are somehow able to identify objects presented to their blind areas—without being consciously aware that they are seeing. Blindsight suggests not only that aspects of vision are processed separately, but that vision is processed separately from awareness. Seeing, and knowing that we see, appear to be handled differently.

Blindsight has been most extensively studied by Lawrence   35
Weiskrantz, a psychologist at Oxford University. Twenty years ago Weiskrantz and his colleagues found that a young patient who had lost the left half of his vision because of damage to his visual cortex could nonetheless identify things in the blind field: he could distinguish between an X and an O and tell whether a line of light was vertical or horizontal; he could locate objects even though he couldn't identify them.

But the odd thing was that the patient didn't think he was seeing. He would guess at what was being presented only when the researchers urged him to, and then be astonished when shown how many of his answers were correct. In subsequent years Weiskrantz studied more patients with blindsight, as did other researchers. Again and again the patients appeared to have a primitive sort of vision in their blind fields but denied any awareness of it. "I couldn't see anything, not a darn thing," Weiskrantz's patient insisted.

How can a person see and not know it? The phenomenon of blindsight has raised as many questions about the nature of consciousness as it has about visual processing. Weiskrantz suggests that blindsight is produced in parts of the brain other than the primary visual cortex. He points out that fat bundles of fibers from each optic nerve never reach the visual cortex but instead travel to the midbrain, which controls involuntary, unconscious actions. Still other fibers bypass the primary visual cortex and enter different cortical regions. These regions may produce the unconscious vision that characterizes blindsight; if they do, it means that the visual cortex is essential not only for normal vision but also for awareness of what's being seen. If seeing takes place outside the visual cortex, it apparently doesn't register in our consciousness.

Late last year, however, a respected neuroscientist challenged the idea that blindsight is derived from visual pathways that are diverted to the mid-brain. Michael Gazzaniga, of the University of California at Davis, reported that he and his colleagues had discovered that a patient with blindsight actually had live, functioning neurons in the portion of his visual cortex that supposedly had been destroyed. Those islands of healthy tissue produce blindsight, Gazzaniga argues.

Asked why patients would remain unconscious of their vision if the processing is going on in the visual cortex, Gazzaniga suggests that because the preserved areas are so small, the signals patients get may just be too small to trigger a conscious reaction. Moreover, he doesn't find it surprising that we might be unaware of things going on in the cortex. "Lots of studies suggest that things we're not consciously aware of go on in the cortex, probably a good deal of our psychological life."

The debate over blindsight is simple, Gazzaniga says: 40 "Weiskrantz thinks it's an alternative pathway, and we think it's the original one. More studies will be done. I have three people working around the clock on it, and it will be worked out."

An extreme form of filling in that has eerie echoes of blindsight may have afflicted American writer James Thurber, known for his humorous essays, drawings, and stories, including "The Secret Life of Walter Mitty." Thurber's experience illustrates the lengths the visual system will go to in order to "see," vision or no. Thurber lost one eye as a boy when his brother accidentally shot him with an arrow; the remaining eye began gradually to fail. By the time Thurber turned 40, his world had become a blur—something he made light of his in work. Once he wrote about how he frightened a woman off a city bus by mistaking the purse in her lap for a chicken. As his eyesight worsened, the images he saw progressed from the slapstick to the surreal. Ordinary things underwent wild transformations. Dirt on his windshield looked like "admirals in uniform" or "crippled apple women"; he would whirl out of their way.

Thurber's fantastic visions, though not diagnosed at the time, fit the description of a disorder called Charles Bonnet syndrome, in which people who are blind or partly so—because of eye diseases or certain types of brain damage—see vivid, intensely realistic images of things that aren't there. Ramachandran and his colleague Leah Levi have taken a special interest in the syndrome. One of Ramachandran's patients, a 32-year-old San Diego man who sustained brain damage in a car accident several years ago, has lost the lower half of his visual field. He doesn't see a black band or sense a border between the sighted field and the blind one, any more than the rest of us detect boundaries at the periphery of our vision. The extraordinary thing about this patient, Ramachandran says, "is that he hallucinates constantly. These hallucinations occur only in the blind field. He sees little children, and zoo animals and domestic ones, creeping up from below. He might say to me, 'As I'm talking to you, I see a monkey sitting on my lap.'"

Charles Bonnet syndrome, Ramachandran says, "is a more sophisticated type of filling in. It's the next level up. It's a response to visual deprivation. These hallucinations are phantom visual images, analogous to phantom limbs." He believes they originate in portions of the brain that store visual memories and generate visual imagery. In other words, they are yet another example of the puzzling array of phenomena that emerge from the complex entanglement of eye and brain.

"Let me try to give you a sense of where we are," says Margaret Livingstone, in an effort to assess the status of visual research today. "Take form perception. Human beings are very good at it. We recognize contours, faces, words, a lot of really complicated things. What we understand is that in the retinas, the lateral geniculate bodies, and the first layer of the visual cortex, we code for changes in brightness or color. In the next stage, cells become selective for the orientation of the change—that is, they code for contours, or edges. In some places cells select for the length of the contour. Then, if you go up very high, you find cells selective for certain faces." Livingstone pauses. "We know remarkably little about what happens in between. It's frightening how big a gap there is. But we do think we understand a lot about visual processing in spite of that gap."

Questions

1. What was the goal of the visual experiments performed by perceptual psychologist Stuart Anstis? What did he find out? According to him, does color affect our appetite for food? What happened when he tried to climb stairs wearing his goggles? Why did smells become more powerful to him? How might these findings be used to create images or products that would help us lose weight, eat more, feel relaxed, nervous, etc.?

2. Grady writes, "Vision, of course, is more than recording what meets the eye: it's the ability to understand, almost instantaneously, what we see. And that happens in the brain." What does Grady mean by this? What are some examples in her article or in your own experience that illustrate this point?

3. What does neuroscientist Vilayanur Ramachandran's finding that some people "have vision they don't notice" mean? What evidence has Ramachandran found that supports the idea that these people do have vision? How does this relate to the idea of blindsight?

4. Change your perception of the world by wearing a pair of sunglasses at night for half an hour and then write about this experience. How difficult was it to adjust to this altered view of the world? How long did it take you to feel comfortable seeing this way? What was the most challenging aspect of this experience and what was easiest? How does your experience relate to those described at the beginning of Grady's article?

5. Watch a TV commercial with the sound turned off. Then describe what you have seen in terms of three aspects of seeing described in the article: Motion—did things go rapidly or slowly, smoothly or erratically, horizontally or vertically? Form—were there mostly smooth shapes or angular ones, organic forms or industrial ones? Color—were there bright colors or subdued ones, did any colors predominate? What does the article say about how the brain understands these three aspects of vision?

When Babies Become Aware of Themselves

MARK PENDERGRAST

Working as an independent journalist and science writer has enabled Mark Pendergrast to explore and write about subjects that have always aroused his curiousity. His books include Uncommon Grounds, Victims of Memory, *and* For God, Country & Coca-Cola. *He has written numerous articles for the* New York Times, *the* Philadelphia Inquirer, *the* Wall Street Journal, *and the* Sunday Times *(London) among others. The excerpt below is from his 2003 book,* Mirror/Mirror, *which covers the history and physics of mirrors as well as some of the mysteries associated with these amazing objects that most of us take for granted.*

Getting Started

Think about what you did today before you arrived in class. How many times did you look in the mirror? Do you have any type of mirror with you? Do you look different in different mirrors? What happens when a baby sees him- or herself in the mirror? How is our identity shaped by our experience with mirrors? How do animals act when they look into mirrors? Do you think they recognize themselves?

———————— ✦ ————————

In a 1972 issue of *Developmental Psychobiology,* Beulah Amsterdam published the first mirror-recognition study for human babies, "Mirror Self-Image Reactions Before Age Two." She described how she had tested eighty-eight children between the ages of three months and twenty-four months by putting a spot of rouge on one side of the nose and seeing if they touched it while looking in the mirror. Early on, babies seemed to recognize their mothers in the mirror, but not themselves. By six months, infants were smiling and playing with themselves in the mirror, but they treated the reflection as another child. At one year, they began to search behind the mirror for their mysterious playmate.

Finally, Amsterdam concluded that from twenty to twenty-four months, "65 percent of the subjects demonstrated recognition of their mirror images." Subsequent research has substantiated her findings, indicating that most children's brains first register that they are observing themselves sometime during the latter part of their second year, when they become coy, embarrassed, clownish, or self-admiring in front of the mirror.

What exactly does mirror self-recognition imply? Gordon Gallup believes self-recognition means self-awareness. "You become the object of your own attention. You are aware of being aware. And that, in turn, allows you to make inferences about comparable states of awareness in others." Gallup doesn't deny that other animals such as dogs or even fleas may have alternate forms of self-concept, but the brain's capacity to allow us to know we are looking at ourselves appears to place us—along with higher apes and perhaps elephants and dolphins—in a unique category, and this simple ability to recognize ourselves in a mirror seems to be essential to the human enterprise.

Can it be a coincidence that toddlers develop language and begin to say "I," "me," and "mine" about the same time they learn mirror self-recognition? Or that the frontal lobes develop dramatically in the second year of life? Or that they reach Piaget's level of understanding "object permanence" (remembering and seeking out hidden objects) and begin to engage in pretend play? Or that they begin to act like strong, self-willed individuals in the terrible twos? Or that they begin soon afterward to develop empathy for others and moral standards? Or that their autobiographical memories supersede the period of "infantile amnesia" around the age of three?

In the late 1800s, Charles Horton Cooley, a Michigan sociologist, theorized that the human sense of self is created in infants through social interactions. Cooley—who was himself a shy semi-invalid—called this the "looking-glass self" because he believed that our self-concept is a reflection of what we perceive others think of us.[1] His disciple, George Mead, concluded, "It is impossible to conceive of a self arising outside of social experience." Gallup, suspecting that Cooley and Mead were onto something, gave the mark test to chimpanzees that had been raised in complete isolation, after habituating them to mirrors. As he predicted, they failed to identify themselves.

5

---

[1]In 1949, Jacques Lacan, a French neo-Freudian, incorrectly theorized that infants go through a "mirror stage" between 6 and 18 months of age in which they discover their mirror image and believe it is themselves, thus dooming them to a life of alienation from their true selves. As Lacan put it: "This jubilant assumption of his specular image by the child . . . [exhibits] the symbolic matrix in which the *I* is precipitated in a primordial form, before it is objectified in the dialectic of identification with the other." Is that clear?

Similarly, the famed Wild Boy of Aveyron, captured in the French woods in 1799, reached behind a mirror to find the boy he thought was hiding there. The Wild Boy never learned mirror recognition or how to speak. Perhaps such abilities must be developed during the crucial developmental period when the brain is growing and establishing new branches, connections, and synapses.

Of course, mirrors are not necessary for self-awareness. Blind people know perfectly well who they are, for instance. Thus Sidney Bradford, blind before his first birthday, was an intelligent, self-assured fifty-two-year-old when his sight was restored by a cornea transplant in 1958. He was fascinated by mirrors, often preferring to see the world in their reflection rather than directly. But Bradford couldn't get used to his own face in the mirror and shaved by touch in the dark as he always had.[2]

The ability to recognize oneself in a mirror correlates with (but does not cause) essential human traits such as logic, creativity, curiosity, the appreciation of beauty, and empathy, leading directly to tool use, scientific experiments, storytelling, poetry, art, theater, lawmaking, philosophy, religion, and a sense of humor. In other words, as humans evolved, the ability to *think*—to ponder themselves in mirrors, among other things—helped them to survive. Gordon Gallup quips, "I am, therefore I think," an inversion of Descartes' most famous statement. "It is our ability to conceive of ourselves in the first place that makes thinking and consciousness possible, not vice versa," Gallup concludes.

"Without self-awareness," Emory University primatologist Frans de Waal observes in his 1996 book, *Good Natured*, "we might as well be folkloric creatures without souls, such as vampires, who cast no reflections. Most important, we would be incapable of cognitive empathy, as this requires a distinction between self and other and the realization that others have selves like us."

As one would expect, other species that display mirror self-recognition also show the capacity to empathize, which is the very essence of the Golden Rule—to treat others as you would be treated. Dolphins, for instance, are famed for helping injured people. Yet the ability to put oneself in someone else's shoes also permits deception and cruelty. What would sadists know about exquisite torture unless they could imagine what it felt like? As Jane Goodall discovered with her beloved chimps, they could murder as well as comfort one another.

---

[2]The story ends tragically. With his sight restored, Bradford became self-conscious, lost his self-confidence, and died within two years.

Sex also seems to be connected with mirror self-recognition, as we have seen throughout this history of human interaction with mirrors. Bonobos and dolphins are highly sexed animals always ready for intercourse. Pan and Delphi, two half-brother dolphins studied by Marino and Reiss, always enjoyed sexual play with one another, but when mirrors were available, their libido went wild, so that in one half-hour session they attempted to penetrate one another forty-three times. In all cases, they assumed positions so that they could watch themselves in the mirror, breaking off if their bodies drifted out of sight, then resuming sex play in front of the mirror.

Self-awareness may lead to more satisfying sex, but it also makes humans, and perhaps some other animals, aware of their mortality. Humans want to believe in a humanistic deity—a mirror image of sorts—who will guarantee us immortality in heaven. Fear of death, Gordon Gallup believes, may account for the religious impulse, but I think there's more to it. Our search for meaning and our innate reverence for this world in which we live are also probably related to self-awareness and mirrors.

Questions

1. Why do you think that when babies under six months of age look into mirrors they recognize their mothers but not themselves? What are the steps babies make toward self-awareness as described through their experience with mirrors? What connections do you make between toddlers' language development and mirror self-recognition? What experiences have you had with babies or young children and mirrors?

2. Pendergrast mentions the term "object permanence" in his essay. This is associated with the Swiss psychologist Jean Piaget's theory of the four stages of child development. Go online or to the library to find out what these four stages are. How does understanding Piaget's theory help you to better understand the Pendergrast article?

3. Pendergrast writes about the Wild Boy of Aveyron, who was not raised in a social environment, and who could not recognize himself in the mirror. Pendergrast suggests that there is a connection between these two events. How would you explain the connection?

4. Look at yourself in a mirror and imagine that you are looking at another person. Write a short essay describing what this other person looks like and how the person presents him or herself. What kind of personality does this "other" person seem to have? How does this sense of your mirror image representing "another" person relate to what Pendergrast writes about mirror images and one's sense of self?

5. Write an essay in which you explain why you agree or disagree with Frans de Waal's statement that "without self-awareness, . . . we would be incapable of cognitive empathy, as this requires a distinction between self and other and the realization that others have selves like us."

Seeing
ANNIE DILLARD

The following essay is from Annie Dillard's first book, Pilgrim at Tinker Creek, *written in 1974 when she was 29 years old and for which she won the Pulitzer Prize in nonfiction. Dillard has continued to write, teach writing, and is presently Professor Emeritus at Wesleyan University. Her process for writing this book began with four seasons spent living near Tinker Creek in the Blue Ridge Mountains of Virginia. There, surrounded by forests, creeks, mountains, and animal life, Dillard, followed Thoreau's path and spent her time walking, camping, living with, and deeply observing nature. She kept a journal of her experiences that grew to be more than 20 volumes. She revised the journal writing into note cards, and then spent an additional 8 months turning the note cards into the beautifully written* Pilgrim at Tinker Creek. *In "Seeing," Dillard focuses on the act of seeing as experienced by people whose vision has been restored and on her own personal experiences.*

Getting Started

Think about what it might mean to see for someone who has never seen before. Think about the enormity of visual sensations experienced by an infant. How do we make sense of light, color and shapes? How do we understand depth, height, and distance? Dillard writes, "In general, the newly sighted see the world as a dazzle of color patches. They are pleased by the sensation of color, and learn quickly to name the colors, but the rest of seeing is tormentingly difficult." Why might this be so?

───────────── ✦ ─────────────

I chanced on a wonderful book by Marius von Senden, called *Space and Light.* When Western surgeons discovered how to perform safe cataract operations, they ranged across Europe and

America operating on dozens of men and women of all ages who had been blinded by cataracts since birth. Von Senden collected accounts of such cases; the histories are fascinating. Many doctors had tested their patients' sense perceptions and ideas of space both before and after the operations. The vast majority of patients, of both sexes and all ages, had, in von Senden's opinion, no idea of space whatsoever. Form, distance, and size were so many meaningless syllables. A patient "had no idea of depth, confusing it with roundness." Before the operation a doctor would give a blind patient a cube and a sphere; the patient would tongue it or feel it with his hands, and name it correctly. After the operation the doctor would show the same objects to the patient without letting him touch them; now he had no clue whatsoever what he was seeing. One patient called lemonade "square" because it pricked on his tongue as a square shape pricked on the touch of his hands. Of another postoperative patient, the doctor writes, "I have found in her no notion of size, for example, not even within the narrow limits which she might have encompassed with the aid of touch. Thus when I asked her to show me how big her mother was, she did not stretch out her hands, but set her two index-fingers a few inches apart." Other doctors reported their patients' own statements to similar effect. "The room he was in . . . he knew to be but part of the house, yet he could not conceive that the whole house could look bigger"; "Those who are blind from birth . . . have no real conception of height or distance. A house that is a mile away is thought of as nearby, but requiring the taking of a lot of steps. . . . The elevator that whizzes him up and down gives no more sense of vertical distance than does the train of horizontal."

For the newly sighted, vision is pure sensation unencumbered by meaning: "The girl went through the experience that we all go through and forget, the moment we are born. She saw, but it did not mean anything but a lot of different kinds of brightness." Again, "I asked the patient what he could see; he answered that he saw an extensive field of light, in which everything appeared dull, confused, and in motion. He could not distinguish objects." Another patient saw "nothing but a confusion of forms and colours." When a newly sighted girl saw photographs and paintings, she asked, "'Why do they put those dark marks all over them?' 'Those aren't dark marks,' her mother explained, 'those are shadows. That is one of the ways the eye knows that things have shape. If it were not for shadows many things would look flat.' 'Well, that's how things do look,' Joan answered. 'Everything looks flat with dark patches.'"

But it is the patients' concepts of space that are most revealing. One patient, according to his doctor, "practiced his vision in
a strange fashion; thus he takes off one of his boots, throws it
some way off in front of him, and then attempts to gauge the distance at which it lies; he takes a few steps toward the boot and
tries to grasp it; on failing to reach it, he moves on a step or two
and gropes for the boot until he finally gets hold of it." "But even
at this stage, after three weeks' experience of seeing," von Senden
goes on, "'space,' as he conceives it, ends with visual space, i.e.,
with color-patches that happen to bound his view. He does not yet
have the notion that a larger object (a chair) can mask a smaller
one (a dog), or that the latter can still be present even though it is
not directly seen."

In general the newly sighted see the world as a dazzle of
color-patches. They are pleased by the sensation of color, and
learn quickly to name the colors, but the rest of seeing is tormentingly difficult. Soon after his operation a patient "generally bumps
into one of these color-patches and observes them to be substantial, since they resist him as tactual objects do. In walking about
it also strikes him—or can if he pays attention—that he is continually passing in between the colors he sees, that he can go past a
visual object, that a part of it then steadily disappears from view;
and that in spite of this, however he twists and turns—whether
entering the room from the door, for example, or returning back
to it—he always has a visual space in front of him. Thus he gradually comes to realize that there is also a space behind him,
which he does not see."

The mental effort involved in these reasonings proves over-   5
whelming for many patients. It oppresses them to realize, if they
ever do at all, the tremendous size of the world, which they had
previously conceived of as something touchingly manageable. It
oppresses them to realize that they have been visible to people all
along, perhaps unattractively so, without their knowledge or con-
sent. A disheartening number of them refuse to use their new vision, continuing to go over objects with their tongues, and lapsing
into apathy and despair. "The child can see, but will not make use
of his sight. Only when pressed can he with difficulty be brought
to look at objects in his neighborhood; but more than a foot away
it is impossible to bestir him to the necessary effort." Of a twenty-
one-year-old girl, the doctor relates, "Her unfortunate father, who
had hoped for so much from this operation, wrote that his daughter carefully shuts her eyes whenever she wishes to go about the
house, especially when she comes to a staircase, and that she is

never happier or more at ease than when, by closing her eyelids, she relapses into her former state of total blindness." A fifteen-year-old boy, who was also in love with a girl at the asylum for the blind, finally blurted out, "No, really, I can't stand it any more; I want to be sent back to the asylum again. If things aren't altered, I'll tear my eyes out."

Some do learn to see, especially the young ones. But it changes their lives. One doctor comments on "the rapid and complete loss of that striking and wonderful serenity which is characteristic only of those who have never yet seen." A blind man who learns to see is ashamed of his old habits. He dresses up, grooms himself, and tries to make a good impression. While he was blind he was indifferent to objects unless they were edible; now, "a sifting of values sets in . . . his thoughts and wishes are mightily stirred and some few of the patients are thereby led into dissimulation, envy, theft and fraud."

On the other hand, many newly sighted people speak well of the world, and teach us how dull is our own vision. To one patient, a human hand, unrecognized, is "something bright and then holes." Shown a bunch of grapes, a boy calls out, "It is dark, blue and shiny. . . . It isn't smooth, it has bumps and hollows." A little girl visits a garden. "She is greatly astonished, and can scarcely be persuaded to answer, stands speechless in front of the tree, which she only names on taking hold of it, and then as 'the tree with the lights in it.'" Some delight in their sight and give themselves over to the visual world. Of a patient just after her bandages were removed, her doctor writes, "The first things to attract her attention were her own hands; she looked at them very closely, moved them repeatedly to and fro, bent and stretched the fingers, and seemed greatly astonished at the sight." One girl was eager to tell her blind friend that "men do not really look like trees at all," and astounded to discover that her every visitor had an utterly different face. Finally, a twenty-two-year-old girl was dazzled by the world's brightness and kept her eyes shut for two weeks. When at the end of that time she opened her eyes again, she did not recognize any objects, but, "the more she now directed her gaze upon everything about her, the more it could be seen how an expression of gratification and astonishment overspread her features; she repeatedly exclaimed: 'Oh God! How beautiful!'"

I saw color-patches for weeks after I read this wonderful book. It was summer; the peaches were ripe in the valley orchards. When I woke in the morning, color-patches wrapped round my eyes, intricately, leaving not one unfilled spot. All day long I walked among shifting color-patches that parted before me like the Red Sea and closed again in silence, transfigured, wherever I looked back. Some patches swelled and loomed, while others vanished utterly, and dark marks flitted at random over the whole dazzling sweep. But I couldn't sustain the illusion of flatness. I've been around for too long. Form is condemned to an eternal danse macabre with meaning: I couldn't unpeach the peaches. Nor can I remember ever having seen without understanding; the color-patches of infancy are lost. My brain then must have been smooth as any balloon. I'm told I reached for the moon; many babies do. But the color-patches of infancy swelled as meaning filled them; they arrayed themselves in solemn ranks down distance which unrolled and stretched before me like a plain. The moon rocketed away. I live now in a world of shadows that shape and distance color, a world where space makes a kind of terrible sense. What gnosticism is this, and what physics? The fluttering patch I saw in my nursery window—silver and green and shape-shifting blue—is gone; a row of Lombardy poplars takes its place, mute, across the distant lawn. That humming oblong creature pale as light that stole along the walls of my room at night, stretching exhilaratingly around the corners, is gone, too, gone the night I ate of the bittersweet fruit, put two and two together and puckered forever my brain. Martin Buber tells this tale: "Rabbi Mendel once boasted to his teacher Rabbi Elimelekh that evenings he saw the angel who rolls away the light before the darkness, and mornings the angel who rolls away the darkness before the light. 'Yes,' said Rabbi Elimelekh, 'in my youth I saw that too. Later on you don't see these things any more.'"

Why didn't someone hand those newly sighted people paints and brushes from the start, when they still didn't know what anything was? Then maybe we all could see color-patches too, the world unraveled from reason, Eden before Adam gave names. The scales would drop from my eyes; I'd see trees like men walking; I'd run down the road against all orders, hallooing and leaping.

Seeing is of course very much a matter of verbalization. Unless I call my attention to what passes before my eyes, I simply won't see it. It is, as Ruskin says, "not merely unnoticed, but in the full, clear sense of the word, unseen." My eyes alone can't solve analogy tests using figures, the ones which show, with increasing elaborations, a big square, then a small square in a big square, then a big triangle, and expect me to find a small triangle in a big triangle. I have to say the words, describe what I'm seeing. If

Tinker Mountain erupted, I'd be likely to notice. But if I want to notice the lesser cataclysms of valley life, I have to maintain in my head a running description of the present. It's not that I'm observant; it's just that I talk too much. Otherwise, especially in a strange place, I'll never know what's happening. Like a blind man at the ball game, I need a radio.

When I see this way I analyze and pry. I hurl over logs and roll away stones; I study the bank a square foot at a time, probing and tilting my head. Some days when a mist covers the mountains, when the muskrats won't show and the microscope's mirror shatters, I want to climb up the blank blue dome as a man would storm the inside of a circus tent, wildly, dangling, and with a steel knife claw a rent in the top, peep, and, if I must, fall.

But there is another kind of seeing that involves a letting go. When I see this way I sway transfixed and emptied. The difference between the two ways of seeing is the difference between walking with and without a camera. When I walk with a camera I walk from shot to shot, reading the light on a calibrated meter. When I walk without a camera, my own shutter opens, and the moment's light prints on my own silver gut. When I see this second way I am above all an unscrupulous observer.

It was sunny one evening last summer at Tinker Creek; the sun was low in the sky, upstream. I was sitting on the sycamore log bridge with the sunset at my back, watching the shiners the size of minnows who were feeding over the muddy sand in skittery schools. Again and again, one fish, then another, turned for a split second across the current and flash! the sun shot out from its silver side. I couldn't watch for it. It was always just happening somewhere else, and it drew my vision just as it disappeared: flash, like a sudden dazzle of the thinnest blade, a sparking over a dun and olive ground at chance intervals from every direction. Then I noticed white specks, some sort of pale petals, small, floating from under my feet on the creek's surface, very slow and steady. So I blurred my eyes and gazed toward the brim of my hat and saw a new world. I saw the pale white circles roll up, roll up, like the world's turning, mute and perfect, and I saw the linear flashes, gleaming silver, like stars being born at random down a rolling scroll of time. Something broke and something opened. I filled up like a new wineskin. I breathed an air like light; I saw a light like water. I was the lip of a fountain the creek filled forever; I was ether, the leaf in the zephyr; I was flesh-flake, feather, bone.

When I see this way, I see truly. As Thoreau says, I return to my senses. I am the man who watches the baseball game in silence in an empty stadium. I see the game purely; I'm abstracted and dazed. When it's all over and the white-suited players lope off the green field to their shadowed dugouts, I leap to my feet; I cheer and cheer.

But I can't go out and try to see this way. I'll fail, I'll go mad. 15 All I can do is try to gag the commentator, to hush the noise of useless interior babble that keeps me from seeing just as surely as a newspaper dangled before my eyes. The effort is really a discipline requiring a lifetime of dedicated struggle; it marks the literature of saints and monks of every order East and West, under every rule and no rule, discalced and shod. The world's spiritual geniuses seem to discover universally that the mind's muddy river, this ceaseless flow of trivia and trash, cannot be dammed, and that trying to dam it is a waste of effort that might lead to madness. Instead you must allow the muddy river to flow unheeded in the dim channels of consciousness; you raise your sights; you look along it, mildly, acknowledging its presence without interest and gazing beyond it into the realm of the real where subjects and objects act and rest purely, without utterance. "Launch into the deep," says Jacques Ellul, "and you shall see."

The secret of seeing is, then, the pearl of great price. If I thought he could teach me to find it and keep it forever I would stagger barefoot across a hundred deserts after any lunatic at all. But although the pearl may be found, it may not be sought. The literature of illumination reveals this above all: Although it comes to those who wait for it, it is always, even to the most practiced and adept, a gift and a total surprise. I return from one walk knowing where the killdeer nests in the field by the creek and the hour the laurel blooms. I return from the same walk a day later scarcely knowing my own name. Litanies hum in my ears; my tongue flaps in my mouth Ailinon, alleluia! I cannot cause light; the most I can do is try to put myself in the path of its beam. It is possible, in deep space, to sail on solar wind. Light, be it particle or wave, has force: you rig a giant sail and go. The secret of seeing is to sail on solar wind. Hone and spread your spirit till you yourself are a sail, whetted, translucent, broadside to the merest puff.

When her doctor took her bandages off and led her into the garden, the girl who was no longer blind saw "the tree with the lights in it." It was for this tree I searched through the peach orchards of summer, in the forests of fall and down winter and spring for years. Then one day I was walking along Tinker Creek thinking of nothing at all and I saw the tree with the lights in it. I saw the backyard cedar where the mourning doves roost charged and transfigured, each cell buzzing with flame. I stood on the grass with the lights in it, grass that was wholly fire, utterly focused and utterly dreamed. It was less like seeing than like being for the first time seen, knocked breathless by a powerful glance. The flood of fire abated, but I'm still spending the power. Gradually the lights went out in the cedar, the colors died, the cells unflamed and disappeared. I was still ringing. I had been my whole life a bell, and never knew it until at that moment I was lifted and struck. I have since only very rarely seen the tree with the lights in it. The vision comes and goes, mostly goes, but I live for it, for the moment when the mountains open and a new light roars in spate through the crack, and the mountains slam.

Questions

1. Dillard writes, "For the newly sighted, vision is pure sensation unencumbered by meaning." What are some of the difficulties people experience when they see for the first time as adults? What are some of the pleasures of this experience? In what ways do you think it is different for adults and children to experience visual sensations for the first time? How do you explain the differences?

2. Take a familiar object from your desk and hold it in your hands. Then close your eyes and try to experience and explore it with your sense of touch alone. When you are done, write about what this experience was like. What did you notice, discover, or get a sense of through touch alone that was different from looking at the object? How does this relate to the people in Dillard's article who did the reverse, who saw things they had only touched before?

3. At the end of this essay, Dillard tries to describe her own powerful experience of looking and seeing by using poetic and expressive language. Which parts of her description are most successful to you? Why? What has your experience been in looking at something and then trying to describe it in words? Write about a place that matters to you and try to include not only the sights but the sounds, smells, and textures as well.

4. Take a look at a photograph that you have taken and think about the experience of actually being there when you took it. Write about what the photograph catches and what it misses. How does your experience connect with Dillard's ideas about how we observe something with a camera and without one?

5. Write an essay in which you choose one sentence from Dillard's writing that has some meaning for you. Write that sentence at the top of your page. Use the sentence as an inspiration for your writing. You may decide to include the sentence in your writing as part of the title or as part of the body. Remember to use quotes whenever you use an author's words.

How to Look at Nothing
JAMES ELKINS

Visual studies expert and art historian, James Elkins is a Professor at the School of the Art Institute of Chicago and also teaches at University College in Cork, Ireland. He has written books that focus on art history and on images in science, art, and nature, including The Domain of Images, On Pictures and the Words that Fail them, *and* How to Use Your Eyes, *from which the excerpt that follows is taken. In the Preface to that book, Elkins writes, "Our eyes are far too good for us. The show us so much that we can't take it all in, so we shut out most of the world, and try to look at things as briskly and efficiently as possible. What happens if we stop and take the time to look more carefully?"*

Getting Started

Elkins asks us to "stop and take the time to look more carefully," something that most of us rarely take time to do as we rush through our busy lives. In his essay, he discusses how and whether or not it is possible to "look at nothing." Do you think it is possible to see absolutely nothing? What happens when you close your eyes and turn out the lights? Think about being in a deeply dark room or outdoors on a dark, moonless night. Think about being in the dark in a place where you have never been before. What do you see? How do your eyes respond to darkness? Is it ever totally dark? How do you feel when you are in the dark?

———————————— ✦ ————————————

Is it possible to see absolutely nothing? Or do you always see something, even if it is nothing more than a blur or the insides of your own eyelids?

This question has been well investigated. In the 1930s, a psychologist named Wolfgang Metzer designed an experiment to show that if you have nothing to look at, your eyes will stop functioning. Metzer put volunteers in rooms that were lit very carefully so there was no shadow and no gradients from light to dark. The walls were polished, so it was impossible to tell how far away they were. After a few minutes in an environment like that, the volunteers reported "gray clouds" and darkness descending over their visual field. Some experienced an intense fear and felt as though they were going blind. Others were sure that dim shapes were drifting by, and they tried to reach out and grab them. Later it was found that if the room is illuminated with a bright color, within a few minutes it will seem to turn dull gray. Even a bright red or green will seem to turn gray.

Apparently the eye cannot stand to see nothing, and when it is faced with nothing, it slowly and automatically shuts down. You can simulate these experiments at home by cutting ping-pong balls in half and cupping them lightly over your eyes. Since you can't focus that close, your eye has no detail to latch on to, and if you're sitting in a place with fairly even illumination, you won't have any shadows or highlights to watch. After a few minutes, you will begin to feel what the people in those experiments experienced. For me, it is a slow creeping claustrophobia and an anxiety about what I'm seeing—or even *if* I am seeing. If I use a red lightbulb instead of a white one, the color slowly drains out until it looks for all the world as if the light were an ordinary white bulb.

(This experiment won't work, by the way, if you close your eyes. The slight pressure of your eyelids on your corneas and the tiny flicker of your eye muscles will produce hallucinations, called entoptic lights, which will give you something to look at. The only drawback to using ping-pong balls is that your eyelashes get in the way. The experimenters recommend using "a light coating of nonirritating, easily removed, latex-based surgical adhesive" to fasten the eyelashes to the upper lid—but it's probably better to get along without it.)

These experiments are interesting but they are also artificial. It takes something as contrived as a polished white wall or halves of a ping-pong ball, to create a wholly uniform visual field. There is another way to see nothing that I like much better, and that is trying to see something in pitch darkness. In recent decades scientists have figured out that it takes only between five to fifteen photons entering the eye before we register a tiny flash of light. That is an unimaginably tiny quantity, millions of times fainter than a faint green flash from a lightning bug. Unless you have been in a cave or a sealed basement room, you have never experienced anything that dark. And yet the eye is prepared for it.

It takes at least five photons to produce the sensation of light, instead of just one, because there is a chemical in the eye that is continuously breaking down, and each time a molecule breaks, it emits a photon. If we registered every photon, our eyes would register light continuously, even if there were no light in the world outside our own eyes. The chemical that emits the light is rhodopsin, which is the same chemical that enables us to see in dim light to begin with. So as far as our visual system is concerned, there is no way to distinguish between a molecule of rhodopsin that has broken down spontaneously and one that broke down because it was hit by a photon. If we saw a flash every time a rhodopsin molecule decomposed, we would be seeing fireworks forever, so our retinas are designed to *start* seeing only when there is a little more light.

Five to fifteen photons is an estimate and there is no way to make it exact, but the reason why it can't be exact is itself exact. It has to do with quantum mechanics, the branch of physics that deals with particles like photons. According to quantum physics, the action of photons can be known only statistically and not with utter precision. The precise theory shows that the answer is imprecise. There is also a second reason why we can never know exactly how little light we can see. The human visual system is "noisy"—it is not efficient and it fails a certain percentage of the time. Only cave explorers and volunteers in vision experiments have ever experienced perfect darkness, and even then they see spots of light. Those are "false positives," reports that there is light when there isn't. We see light when we shouldn't and we fail to see light when, by the laws of physics, we should. Also, the two eyes take in different photons and so they never work in perfect harmony. In extremely low light, a report of light from one eye might be overruled by a report of darkness from the other. Many things can happen along the complicated pathway from the rhodopsin in the retina to the centers of visual processing.

These phenomena of false positives are called by the wonderful name "dark noise" and the not-so-wonderful technical term "equivalent Poisson noise." Then there's the light generated inside the eye itself, called the "dark light of the eye." It may have a photochemical origin, such as the light from rhodopsin; wherever it comes from, it contributes to the sensation of light.

Entoptic light, the dark noise, the dark light of the eye—this is the end of seeing. But they are wonderful phenomena. To see them, you have to find a perfectly dark spot—a windowless basement room or a hallway that can be entirely closed off—and then you have to spend at least a half hour acclimatizing to the dark. Where I live, in the city, it is impossible to find real darkness. There is a bathroom in our apartment that opens onto an interior hallway, but even if I close all the curtains, close off the hallway, and shut the bathroom door behind me, light still comes in under the doorway. I don't see it at first, but after ten minutes my eyes pick out a faint glow. Real darkness is elusive.

In the end, when there is nothing left to see, the eye and the   10
brain invent lights. The dark room begins to shimmer and with entoptic auroras. They seem to mirror my state of mind—if I am tired I see more of them, and if I rub my eyes they flower into bright colors. In total darkness, entoptic displays can seem as bright as daylight, and it takes several minutes for them to subside. Looking at them, it is easy to be sympathetic with anthropologists who think that all picture-making began with hallucinations. Some entoptic displays are as lovely and evanescent as auroras, and others as silky and seductive as a ghost. Pure dark, in the absence of entoptic colors, is still alive with dark noise. If I try to fix my gaze on some invisible object—say my hand held up in front of me—then my visual field starts to sparkle with small flashes of dark noise, the sign that my neurons are trying to process signals that aren't really there. They can also become quite strong, like the sparks that come off bedsheets on a cold winter night. I can also try to erase all sense of illumination by letting my eyes rest or wander wherever they want. When I do that, I am still aware of the sensation of light—really it is too dim to be called light; it is more the memory of light. Perhaps that is the "dark light of the eye," the chemicals splitting and reforming in the eye in the normal processes of molecular life.

So I am left with this strange thought: even though we overlook so many things and see so little of what passes in front of us, our eyes will not stop seeing, even when they have to invent the world from nothing. Perhaps the only moments when we truly see nothing are the blank, mindless stretches of time that pass unnoticed between our dreams. But maybe death is the only name for real blindness. At every other moment our eyes are taking in light or inventing lights of their own: it is only a matter of learning how to see what our eyes are bringing us.

Questions

1. Try doing the ping-pong ball experiment that Elkins describes in paragraph 3. As soon as you remove the covers from your eyes, write for ten minutes about your experience. What did you see? How did you feel? Were you relaxed or nervous? You may want to try the red light bulb experiment as well and compare your feelings after each of the two experiments. What are you finding out about how you see?

2. Reread paragraphs 5–8 and then write an explanation of why it is impossible for the eye to see nothing.
3. Close your eyes and write a description of what you see. What colors appear to you? Are there lights or reflections? Shapes or patterns? Does what you see with your eyes closed change as you continue to look? How does what you see in this way relate to what Elkins refers to as "dark noise"?
4. What does Elkins mean at the end of his essay: "it is only a matter of learning how to see what our eyes are bringing us"?
5. How did you feel about darkness when you were a child? Write about a memorable personal experience with darkness. Remember to tell your reader where you were, how old you were, and exactly what you saw and felt. Add as many sensory details as possible to bring the experience alive for your reader.

Making Connections

1. Concentrate on the way the readings in this chapter relate to the way you see the world. Which authors in this chapter have described an aspect of seeing that seems familiar or significant to you? What is your personal experience of seeing and how do these writers help you understand it better?

2. Most of the writers in this chapter refer to vision as something that happens in both the eye and the brain. What are the best or most vivid examples of this relationship in any of these readings? Can you think of other examples that you know or have read about that reinforce the idea that *seeing* is also a process of *thinking?*

3. In "Seeing and Awareness," Deborah Curtiss writes about how active it is to focus visually on something. In "How to Look at Nothing," James Elkins writes about how active it is to look at nothing at all. What is the connection between these two seemingly opposite processes? Could both of them be true?

4. In "When Babies Become Aware of Themselves" Mark Pendergrast suggests that a sense of self is key to seeing oneself in a mirror, while in "Seeing," Annie Dillard writes about the psychological challenges to one's sense of self when seeing for the first time. What role do you think a sense of self, feelings of confidence, or the comfort of habit play in seeing and vision? Are there any examples in your own experience when seeing was affected by your psychological state?

5. Do you think that artists (Curtiss, for example, is a painter, and Dillard is a writer) actually see the world differently from non-artists? Or are they simply able to express what they see differently from non-artists? Explain the reasons for your answer.

6. In "The Vision Thing," Denise Grady probes into the many factors we process to be able to see at all . . . motion, color, form, depth. In "Seeing," Annie Dillard discusses the fact that many people given sight are actually unable to cope with this new information. What is the connection between these ideas, that is, between being able to see and struggling to see?

7. What role do you think science plays in understanding how we see and how we know the world? Using the articles in this chapter as references, write about what science can tell us about understanding vision. Include in your essay one example from each of the readings in which a specific scientific approach or method helped explain some aspect of vision.

Mirroring Ourselves

"If we are to change our world view, images have to change."
—David Hockney

More and more we rely on images to tell us about the world. Think about all you know of the universe and then notice how much of that information comes from pictures you have seen as opposed to direct experience. In fact, the range of events we have all experienced directly is rather small, limited by the narrow slices of time and size and distance and speed that our eyes and brains can record. Our understanding of anything smaller than a pinpoint or bigger than the sky, faster than a fastball or slower than candle, comes to us through the images we make. But perhaps images are most powerful in what they tell us about ourselves . . . where we come from, who we are, what we look like. And how we, in turn, often think of ourselves as images to be seen and known by others.

Our first selection in this chapter treats the human face itself as an image. "Equation for Beauty Emerges from Studies" is a report by Daniel Goleman about research into the subject of beauty. The study he describes is based on the idea that the beauty men seek out in women is related to the perception of reproductive health. In this sense a woman's face becomes an image that can be studied for information. The study finds, surprisingly, that the features that convey this information are remarkably consistent—even mathematically quantifiable—and that those who are perceived as beautiful often get preferential treatment. This is an idea, of course, supported and promoted in the media.

"Never Just Pictures" by Susan Bordo looks at the dark side of our obsession with ourselves as images of beauty. In this selection Bordo takes a look at the relationship between the images of beauty in our culture and the eating disorders that this relationship supports. As reflected in her title, the author points out the power that images can have over our behavior, attitudes, and desires and just how profound our reliance on images is for feelings of self-worth.

In "The Body Jigsaw," Philippe Liotard focuses on a different aspect of the body as image. In his essay, Liotard considers the appeal of tattoos, piercings, scarring, and other forms of body decoration as homage to tribal aesthetics, as a challenge to the standard ideals of beauty, or simply as a way of playing with one's identity. Liotard points out just one of the ways in which we turn ourselves into images in order to have a visual impact on those around us.

The next selection, "Visual History and the African-American Families of the Nineteenth Century" by Donna M. Wells, takes a look at the role of photography in creating the image of the African-American family. Photography's effect on this image was profound since it made having a family portrait possible for the first time. She demonstrates the notion by referring to a series of photographs of Frederick Douglass, and illustrates the way in which images—photos, in this case—can be seen as a kind of visual text that discloses historical, social, and emotional truths to the careful viewer.

In our final selection, "New Jersey Trying a New Way for Witnesses to Pick Suspects," the whole issue of understanding the image of a face is called into question. Authors Gina Kolata and Iver Peterson discuss a new method for showing mug shots and lineups to crime victims that increases the potential for identifying suspects. That a new method is needed suggests that even something as simple as face recognition is not as straightforward as it would appear. According to the new research, forcing victims to look at one face at a time in a so-called sequential lineup decreases the number of false judgments. The study and the article also point out how dangerous it can be to rely too heavily on an ability we take for granted: our skill at being able to recognize and match images with faces.

Our theme in this chapter, then, is the power of images to influence, appeal, and misguide. Rather than being simple visual records, images form the foundations of what we consider to be true about the world. They help us create our sense of ourselves as faces, bodies, families, even as victims.

Equation for Beauty Emerges in Studies

DANIEL GOLEMAN

Daniel Goleman was born in Stockton, California in 1946. He has a Ph.D. in clinical psychology from Harvard and has also taught there. Dr. Goleman is the author of several books, including The Creative Spirit *(1992),* Emotional Intelligence: Why It Can Matter More Than IQ *(1995), and* Destructive Emotions: How We Can Overcome Them: A Scientific Dialogue with the Dalai Lama *(2003). "Equation for Beauty Emerges in Studies" was written during the many years during which Goleman was a writer for the* New York Times, *where he edited the science page and wrote articles on psychology and brain sciences.*

Getting Started

Could there be an equation that accurately measures out the dimensions of a beautiful woman's face? And could that equation hold true across cultures? Do physically attractive men and women get treated differently from less attractive people? Which are more likely to succeed? Do cute babies get treated differently from not-so-cute babies? What matters more to us in finding a mate—attractiveness, or kindness and intelligence? Before you read the essay, think about your own ideas about the importance of physical attractiveness and its relationship to success in life.

────────────── ✦ ──────────────

The beauty of the female face, it appears, is mathematically quantifiable. Moreover, new research is identifying why the emerging equation can attempt to define what has for so long been thought of as strictly subjective.

In the last two decades, psychologists have come to realize that physical attractiveness, in males as well as females, carries with it an impressive array of social and psychological benefits—from getting more attention from teachers in childhood, to earning more money in adulthood.

Researchers are now attempting to determine precisely what constitutes attractiveness, and what makes it so compelling.

While much of this research has thus far focused on the female face, psychologists are now also studying the features that make a man's face attractive. But, in mating, a man's looks matter less than his social status and wealth, according to David Buss, a psychologist at the University of Michigan, who has studied characteristics most commonly sought in a mate by men and women and has studied the role of attractiveness in human evolution.

In an article in *The American Scientist,* Dr. Buss reported that   5 the sexes agree for the most part on what they seek in a mate. In general, men and women say they value kindness and intelligence most, and agree on the importance of an exciting personality, good health and creativity. But for men, the physical attractiveness of a partner is significantly more important than it is for women, according to Dr. Buss. And for women, generally, a mate's earning capacity is a greater consideration than it is for men.

One explanation for these differences, in Dr. Buss's view, lies in the evolutionary advantages those preferences hold for each sex. In evolution, signs of beauty in a woman are cues that she is young and healthy—thus at the peak of her reproductive ability—and therefore desirable, according to Dr. Buss. These factors were of great importance through most of human history; in the past more women died in childbirth than do now.

For a man, physical appearance is not as great a signal of his reproductive value, however; age imposes fewer constraints on a man's capacity for reproduction. But a man is in a better position to further the survival chances of his offspring if he has access to resources or power, and so it has been to women's advantage to seek mates who had this access, Dr. Buss argues.

"So there is a selective advantage in evolution for those men who can best distinguish among women to find a mate who is at her peak reproductive powers," says Dr. Buss. "There would be an advantage to women whose physical make-up most closely resembled the signs by which men recognized a woman's health and fertility."

The attractive female face is just such a sign, according to research reported recently in *The Journal of Personality and Social Psychology* by Michael Cunningham, a psychologist at the University of Louisville in Kentucky. In a series of experiments, Dr. Cunningham asked 150 white, male American college students to rate the attractiveness and social attributes of 50 women from pictures of their faces. Twenty-seven of the women were finalists in the Miss Universe contest. Though most of the women were white, seven were black and six were Asian.

Dimensions and proportions of what was regarded as attrac-   10
tive emerged with remarkable consistency and precision from
Dr. Cunningham's research.

Elements of the perceived ideal of the attractive female face
included: eye width that is three-tenths the width of the face at
the eyes' level; chin length, one-fifth the height of the face; distance from the center of the eye to the bottom of the eyebrow,
one-tenth the height of the face; the height of the visible eyeball,
one-fourteenth the height of the face, the width of the pupil, one-
fourteenth the distance between the cheekbones; and the total
area for the nose, less than 5 percent of the area of the face.

Dr. Cunningham's data describe an ideal, not an actual face.
Nor can they be regarded as anything suggesting absolute beauty;
rather they are measures of a developed standard, a way to describe the images that a culture, in this case the American culture, defines as attractive.

Very small differences in these ratios made a large difference
for attractiveness. For example, the ideal mouth, Dr. Cunningham
found, was half or 50 percent the width of the face at mouth level.
If that percentage varied by as little at 10 points, his research subjects found the face much less attractive.

PERSONALITY AND DIMPLES

Of course, a woman's personality and intelligence may matter to
an individual man far more than her face in whether he will find
her attractive. Moreover, any given man may be drawn to a particular feature—dimples and freckles, say, or a strong, classical
nose—that the ideal lacks.

But the purport of the Cunningham research is that there is   15
strong agreement on what constitutes facial attractiveness, though
the specifics of the ideal may vary from culture to culture.

Dr. Cunningham believes his research holds clues to just why
the specific facial patterns of female beauty he identified hold
such social and psychological power. The large eyes, along with a
small chin and nose, he says, are facial features that typify a new-
born. The high wide cheekbone and narrow cheeks, though, are
signs that a woman has reached puberty. And the high eyebrows,
dilated pupils and wide smile are all signals of positive emotions:
interest, excitement and sociability.

"The infantlike features draw out in them the same caretak-
ing response a baby would; they make a woman seem cute and

adorable," said Dr. Cunningham. "But the signs of maturity signal that a woman has reached childbearing years, which adds a sexual dimension. And the sociable emotions signal personality traits that people are drawn to."

A 'COMPELLING' COMBINATION

"The sum total of the features signify someone who is slightly young and helpless, though sexually mature and friendly," Dr. Cunningham added. "And men find that combination compelling."

Research continues to show that being attractive carries a pronounced psychological advantage in life, that a powerful stereotype applied to attractive people equates their beauty with goodness. "Most people assume that good-looking men and women have nearly all the positive traits," according to Elaine Hatfield, a psychologist at the University of Hawaii who has reviewed the research on the social psychology of attractiveness in her book *Mirror, Mirror. . .* published in 1986 by the State University of New York Press.

Other people, for example, tend to assume that beautiful women and handsome men are warm, sensitive, kind, interesting, poised, sociable and outgoing, and will have good jobs and fulfilling lives.   20

These social perceptions are one of the benefits of cosmetic facial surgery, according to judgments made of photographs of men and women before and after their surgery. Those who underwent the surgery were seen by others afterward as more self-assertive, intelligent, likable, and able to succeed than they were before the surgery, according to research reported in the journal *Plastic and Reconstructive Surgery.*

The positive treatment of those with an attractive face begins from infancy, with parents tending to give more attention to cuter babies, and continues through life. The teachers of attractive children tend to assume they are more intelligent and popular than their peers. Such expectations, psychologists believe, become part of a self-fulfilling prophecy.

Whatever the reason, good-looking people have been found, on average, to end up in jobs with higher pay and prestige than do their less attractive competitors.

In one study, girls in high school were rated for attractiveness and 15 years later the more attractive women were found to be in families with significantly higher net incomes than were their less attractive classmates.

Of course, looks alone do not guarantee success. For in-   25
stance, the more handsome men in the West Point Class of 1950
rose to higher ranks while at the Academy than their less attractive classmates did, according to a report in the *American Journal
of Sociology*, by Allan Mazur, a sociologist at Syracuse University.
However, as the cadets' careers continued in the military after
graduation, looks helped less and less in promotions and other
factors came to the fore.

While there is no sure evidence that the specific features
identified in his research have been seen as attractive through
history, Dr. Cunningham believes that in cultures as ancient as
that of classical Egypt women were using cosmetics to mimic or
emphasize these features, just as modern cosmetic facial surgery
does today.

Some experts disagree with the arguments for the evolutionary
advantages of attractiveness. "I'm skeptical of these evolutionary
arguments because there is a huge leap from the data to the explanation," said Ellen Berscheid, a social psychologist at the University of Minnesota, who is a leader in the research on attractiveness.

Attractiveness in women should matter less in dating and
marriage as women gain more equal footing with men in positions of power and success, according to Dr. Berscheid.

Questions

1. According to the Goleman article, what are some of the benefits of physical attractiveness? When do these benefits start to accrue?
2. In seeking a life partner or even a date, there seem to be differences in what matters for men and what matters for women. Which of these differences does Goleman describe? What explanation does he provide, and do you agree with it? Do the findings of the studies he presents agree with your own experiences? Explain your answers.
3. Goleman writes: "Research continues to show that being attractive carries a pronounced psychological advantage in life, that a powerful stereotype applied to attractive people equates their beauty with goodness" (paragraph 19). Has this been your experience in life? What books, movies, or other types of entertainment support this point of view? Which ones counter it? Do you think that people on reality TV shows who go through physical transformations will be viewed or treated differently by their friends and family as a result of their new looks?
4. Social psychologist Ellen Berscheid is quoted as saying that as women gain more equal footing in positions of power and success, physical attractiveness will matter less for women (paragraph 28). Do you think this is true and if so, why do you think this would be the case? If not, why not?

5. Find a picture of a woman's face in a magazine or online that you feel shows beauty. Do the features in the image you picked seem to conform to the studies of beauty that Goleman mentions? In what ways is your choice the same, in what ways different? You might also use a ruler to see if the proportions match those found in Dr. Buss's study.

6. Write an essay in which you take a position on the following: A society where everyone is beautiful is an ideal society. All people who are not physically attractive should be given plastic surgery, paid for by the government, so that they can be made as physically attractive as possible. Explain your position with examples from your own experience and/or from popular media.

Never Just Pictures
SUSAN BORDO

Susan Bordo, who received her Ph.D. in English and Women's Studies from State University of New York at Stonybrook, is Professor of English and Women's Studies and holds the Otis A. Singletary Chair in the Humanities at the University of Kentucky. Among her many books are Unbearable Weight: Feminism, Western Culture, and the Body *(1993), and* The Male Body: A New Look at Men in Public and in Private *(1999). She is also co-editor (with Alison Jaggar) of* Gender/Body/Knowledge: Feminist Reconstructions of Being and Knowing *(1989). She is known for her work on culture and the body, especially in relation to eating disorders, cosmetic surgery, beauty and evolutionary theory, racism and the body, masculinity and the male body, sexual harassment, and the impact of contemporary media. "Never Just Pictures" is excerpted from Bordo's book* Twilight Zones: The Hidden Life of Cultural Images from Plato to O.J. *(1997).*

Getting Started

When we look at models and actresses, what are we admiring? Does the extreme thinness that characterizes many models present a healthy look to impressionable young people likely to buy the products the models advertise? Why do we think extreme thinness is glamorous, beautiful, and sexy? Why, when surveyed, do most girls say that they have a weight problem, or that they do not like their own bodies because they're too fat? Why are younger and younger children going on diets? What role does body weight play in our society? Do the issues related to being fat or thin pertain only to females?

———————— ✦ ————————

BODIES AND FANTASIES

When Alicia Silverstone, the svelte nineteen-year-old star of *Clueless,* appeared at the Academy Awards just a smidge more substantial than she had been in the movie, the tabloids ribbed her cruelly, calling her "fatgirl" and "buttgirl" (her next movie role was Batgirl) and "more *Babe* than babe."[1] Our idolatry of the trim, tight body shows no signs of relinquishing its grip on our conceptions of beauty and normality. Since I began exploring this obsession it seems to have gathered momentum, like a spreading mass hysteria. Fat is the devil, and we are continually beating him—"eliminating" our stomachs, "busting" our thighs, "taming" our tummies—pummeling and purging our bodies, attempting to make them into something other than flesh. On television, info-mercials hawking miracle diet pills and videos promising to turn our body parts into steel have become as commonplace as aspirin ads. There hasn't been a tabloid cover in the past few years that didn't boast of an inside scoop on some star's diet regime, a "fab-ulous" success story of weight loss, or a tragic relapse. (When they can't come up with a current one, they scrounge up an old one; a few weeks ago the *National Inquirer* ran a story on Joan Lunden's fifty-pound weight loss fifteen years ago!) Children in this culture grow up knowing that you can never be thin enough and that being fat is one of the worst things one can be. One study asked ten- and eleven-year-old boys and girls to rank drawings of children with various physical handicaps; drawings of fat chil-dren elicited the greatest disapproval and discomfort, over pic-tures of kids with facial disfigurements and missing hands.

————————

[1] I give great credit to Alicia Silverstone for her response to these taunts. In *Vanity Fair* she says, "I do my best. But it's much more important to me that my brain be working in the morning than getting up early and doing exercise . . . The most important thing for me is that I eat and that I sleep and that I get the work done, but unfortunately . . . it's the perception that women in film should look a certain way" ("Hollywood Princess," September 1996, pp. 292–294). One wonders how long she will manage to retain such a sane attitude!

Psychologists commonly believe that girls with eating disorders suffer from "body image disturbance syndrome": they are unable to see themselves as anything but fat, no matter how thin they become. If this is a disorder, it is one that has become a norm of cultural perception. Our ideas about what constitutes a body in need of a diet have become more and more pathologically trained on the slightest hint of excess. This ideal of the body beautiful has largely come from fashion designers and models. (Movie stars, who often used to embody a more voluptuous ideal, are now modeling themselves after the models.) They have taught us "to love a woman's pelvis, her hipbones jutting out through a bias-cut grown . . . the clavicle in its role as a coat hanger from which clothes are suspended."[2] (An old fashion industry justification for skinniness in models was that clothes just don't "hang right" on heftier types.) The fashion industry has taught us to regard a perfectly healthy, nonobese body as an unsightly "before" ("Before CitraLean, no wonder they wore swimsuits like that"). In fact, those in the business have admitted that models have been getting thinner since 1993, when Kate Moss first repopularized the waif look. British models Trish Goff and Annie Morton make Moss look well fed by comparison,[3] and recent ad campaigns for Jil Sander go way beyond the thin-body-as-coat-hanger paradigm to a blatant glamorization of the cadaverous, starved look itself. More and more ads featuring anorexic-looking young men are appearing too.

The main challenge to such images is a muscular aesthetic that *looks* more life-affirming but is no less punishing and compulsion-inducing in its demands on ordinary bodies. During the 1996 Summer Olympics—which were reported with unprecedented focus and hype on the fat-free beauty of muscular bodies—commentators celebrated the "health" of this aesthetic over anorexic glamour. But there is growing evidence of rampant eating disorders among female athletes, and it's hard to imagine that those taut and tiny Olympic gymnasts—the idols of preadolescents

---

[2]Holly Brubach, "The Athletic Esthetic," *The New York Times Magazine,* June 23, 1996, p. 51.

[3]In early 1996 the Swiss watch manufacturer Omega threatened to stop advertising in *British Vogue* because of *Vogue*'s use of such hyperthin models, but it later reversed this decision. The furor was reminiscent of boycotts that were threatened in 1994 when Calvin Klein and Coca-Cola first began to use photos of Kate Moss in their ads. In neither case has the fashion industry acknowledged any validity to the charge that their imagery encourages eating disorders. Instead, they have responded with defensive "rebuttals."

across the country—are having regular menstrual cycles. Their skimpy level of body fat just won't support it. During the Olympics I heard a commentator gushing about how great it was that the 1996 team was composed predominantly of eighteen- and nineteen-year-old women rather than little girls. To me it is far more disturbing that these nineteen-year-olds still look (and talk) like little girls! As I watched them vault and leap, my admiration for their tremendous skill and spirit was shadowed by thoughts of what was going on *inside* their bodies—the hormones unreleased because of insufficient body fat, the organ development delayed, perhaps halted.

Is it any wonder that despite media attention to the dangers of starvation dieting and habitual vomiting, eating disorders have spread throughout the culture?[4] In 1993 in *Unbearable Weight* I argued that the old clinical generalizations positing distinctive class, race, family, and "personality" profiles for the women most likely to develop an eating disorder were being blasted apart by the normalizing power of mass imagery. Some feminists complained that I had not sufficiently attended to racial and ethnic "difference" and was assuming the white, middle-class experience as the norm. Since then it has been widely acknowledged among medical professionals that the incidence of eating and body-image problems among African American, Hispanic, and Native American women has been grossly underestimated and is on the increase.[5] Even the gender gap is being narrowed, as more and more men are developing eating disorders and exercise compulsions too. (In the mid-eighties the men in my classes used to yawn and pass notes when we discussed the pressure to diet; in 1996 they are more apt to protest if the women in the class talk as though it's their problem alone.)

---

[4]Despite media attention to eating disorders, an air of scornful impatience with "victim feminism" has infected attitudes toward women's body issues. Christina Hoff-Sommers charges Naomi Wolf (*The Beauty Myth*) with grossly inflating statistics on eating disorders and she poo-poos the notion that women are dying from dieting. Even if some particular set of statistics is inaccurate, why would Sommers want to deny the reality of the problem, which as a teacher she can surely see right before her eyes?

[5]For the spread of eating disorders in minority groups, see, for example, "The Art of Integrating Diversity: Addressing Treatment Issues of Minority Women in the 90's," in *The Renfrew Perspective*, Winter 1994; see also Becky Thompson, *A Hunger So Wide and So Deep* (Minneapolis: University of Minnesota Press, 1994).

The spread of eating disorders, of course, is not just about im-   5
ages. The emergence of eating disorders is a complex, multilay-
ered cultural "symptom," reflecting problems that are historical as
well as contemporary, arising in our time because of the confluence of a number of factors.[6] Eating disorders are overdetermined
in this culture. They have to do not only with new social expectations of women and ambivalence toward their bodies but also
with more general anxieties about the body as the source of
hungers, needs, and physical vulnerabilities not within our control. These anxieties are deep and long-standing in Western philosophy and religion, and they are especially acute in our own time.
Eating disorders are also linked to the contradictions of consumer
culture, which is continually encouraging us to binge on our desires at the same time as it glamorizes self-discipline and scorns
fat as a symbol of laziness and lack of willpower. And these disorders reflect, too, our increasing fascination with the possibilities
of reshaping our bodies and selves in radical ways, creating new
bodies according to our mind's design.

The relationship between problems such as these and cultural
images is complex. On the one hand, the idealization of certain
kinds of bodies foments and perpetuates our anxieties and insecurities, that's clear. Glamorous images of hyperthin models certainly
don't encourage a more relaxed or accepting attitude toward the
body, particularly among those whose own bodies are far from that
ideal. But, on the other hand, such images carry fantasized solutions to our anxieties and insecurities, and that's part of the reason
why they are powerful. They speak to us not just about how to be
beautiful or desirable but about how to get control of our lives, get
safe, be cool, avoid hurt. When I look at a picture of a skeletal and
seemingly barely breathing young woman, I do not see a vacuous
fashion ideal. I see a visual embodiment of what novelist and ex-
anorexic Stephanie Grant means when she says in her autobiographical novel, *The Passion of Alice,* "If I had to say my anorexia
was about any single thing, I would have said it was about living
without desire. Without longing of any kind."[7]

Now, this may not seem like a particularly attractive philosophy of life (or a particularly attractive body, for that matter). Why
would anyone want to look like death, you might be asking. Why
would anyone want to live without desire? But recent articles in

---

[6]See my *Unbearable Weight* (Berkeley: University of California Press, 1993).

[7]Stephanie Grant, *The Passion of Alice* (New York: Houghton Mifflin, 1995), 58.

both *The New Yorker* and the *New York Times* have noted a new aesthetic in contemporary ads, in which the models appear dislocated and withdrawn, with chipped black nail polish and greasy hair, staring out at the viewer in a deathlike trance, seeming to be "barely a person." Some have called this wasted look "heroin chic": ex-model Zoe Fleischauer recalls that "they wanted models that looked like junkies. The more skinny and fucked-up you look, the more everybody thinks you're fabulous."[8]

Hilton Als, in *The New Yorker,* interprets this trend as making the statement that fashion is dead and beauty is "trivial in relation to depression."[9] I read these ads very differently. Although the photographers may see themselves as ironically "deconstructing" fashion, the reality is that no fashion advertisement can declare fashion to be dead—it's virtually a grammatical impossibility. Put that frame around the image, whatever the content, and we are instructed to find it glamorous. These ads are not telling us that beauty is trivial in relation to depression, they are telling us that depression is beautiful, that being wasted is cool. The question then becomes not "Is fashion dead?" but "Why has death become glamorous?"

Freud tells us that in the psyche death represents not the destruction of the self but its return to a state prior to need, thus freedom from unfulfilled longing, from anxiety over not having one's needs met. Following Freud, I would argue that ghostly pallor and bodily disrepair, in "heroin chic" images, are about the allure, the safety, of being beyond needing, beyond caring, beyond desire. Should we be surprised at the appeal of being without desire in a culture that has invested our needs with anxiety, stress, and danger, that has made us craving and hungering machines, creatures of desire, and then repaid us with addictions, AIDS, shallow and unstable relationships, and cutthroat competition for jobs and mates? To have given up the quest for fulfillment, to be unconcerned with the body or its needs—or its vulnerability—is much wiser than to care.

So, yes, the causes of eating disorders are "deeper" than just 10 obedience to images. But cultural images themselves *are* deep. And the way they become imbued and animated with such power is hardly mysterious. Far from being the purely aesthetic inventions that designers and photographers would like to have

---

[8]Zoe Fleischauer quoted in "Rockers, Models, and the New Allure of Heroin," *Newsweek*, August 26, 1996.

[9]Hilton Als, "Buying the Fantasy," *The New Yorker,* October 10, 1996, p. 70.

us believe they are—"It's just fashion, darling, nothing to get all politically steamed up about"—they reflect the designers' cultural savvy, their ability to sense and give form to flutters and quakes in the cultural psyche. These folks have a strong and simple motivation to hone their skills as cultural Geiger counters. It's called the profit motive. They want their images and the products associated with them to sell.

The profit motive can sometimes produce seemingly "transgressive" wrinkles in current norms. Recently designers such as Calvin Klein and Jil Sander have begun to use rather plain, ordinary-looking, unmadeup faces in their ad campaigns. Unlike the models in "heroin chic" ads, these men and women do not appear wasted so much as unadorned, unpolished, stripped of the glamorous veneer we have come to expect of fashion spreads. While many of them have interesting faces, few of them qualify as beautiful by any prevailing standards. They have rampant freckles, moles in unbeautiful places, oddly proportioned heads. Noticing these ads, I at first wondered whether we really were shifting into a new gear, more genuinely accepting of diversity and "flaws" in appearance. Then it suddenly hit me that these imperfect faces were showing up in clothing and perfume ads only and the *bodies* in these ads were as relentlessly normalizing as ever—not one plump body to complement the facial "diversity."

I now believe that what we are witnessing here is a commercial war. Clothing manufacturers, realizing that many people—particularly young people, at whom most of these ads are aimed—have limited resources and that encouraging them to spend all their money fixing up their faces rather than buying clothes is not in their best interests, are reasserting the importance of body over face as the "site" of our fantasies. In the new codes of these ads a too madeup look signifies a lack of cool, too much investment in how one looks. "Just Be," Calvin Klein tells us in a recent CK One ad. But looks—a lean body—still matter enormously in these ads, and we are still being told how to be—in the mode which best serves Calvin Klein. And all the while, of course, makeup and hair products continue to promote their own self-serving aesthetics of facial perfection.

Questions

1. Bordo writes: "Children in this culture grow up knowing that you can never be thin enough and that being fat is one of the worst things one can be" (paragraph 1). Do you agree with this idea? What do you think accounts for your way of perceiving this issue?

2. Why is weight such a common topic of discussion, even among young children? How do you account for our culture's obsession with weight considering that there are millions of starving people in this world?

3. According to Bordo, why do fashion designers prefer to use extremely thin male and female models? Bordo claims that the image some fashion designers project with their ultrathin models are images of drug addicts, wasted people, and even death. Why do you think these designers present their work this way? What is "heroin chic"? Think about models whose looks you find appealing. Do you find thinner models more attractive? Do they display clothes better than other models?

4. Bordo claims "the causes of eating disorders are 'deeper' than just obedience to images. But cultural images themselves *are* deep" (paragraph 5). What does she mean? What examples does Bordo provide to support this idea?

5. Find a photo in a magazine or online that shows what you think of as a fashion ideal. How does the image you picked fit in with Bordo's ideas about thinness and ideal body types? How does it contradict them?

The Body Jigsaw: Borrowing Body Decoration from Other Cultures

PHILIPPE LIOTARD

Philippe Liotard was born in France in 1963. He is a Lecturer in the Faculty of Science of Sports at the Universities of Lyon and Montpellier. His particular areas of interest are the sports of France and lesbian and gay issues in sporting competitions. His article "The Body Jigsaw" was originally published in the UNESCO Courier. *In it, Liotard examines the use of the human body as a canvas: a site for images—tattoos, piercings, and so on.*

Getting Started

Liotard begins his essay by asking us to think of "the body as a canvas, a space to mix and match physical and cultural elements in defining who or what [we] want to be" (paragraph 1). Do people get tattoos or pierces for shock value? Do they decorate their bodies to make a personal statement? Is it part of trying to fit in—a kind of conformity? Or is it a kind of harkening to a type of "primitive body decoration and ritual"?

——————— ✦ ———————

I magine the body as a canvas, a space to mix and match physical and cultural elements in defining who or what you want to be. Here lies the great paradox. The scarring and piercing of tribal aesthetics are all the rage in rich countries, while in the South, western ideals are coveted by a monied few.

In 1976, the punks barged into the lives of the reserved British with a bang. Disrespect was their word of order, as they went about ranting against the predictable world mapped out by their elders. They insulted the Queen and heaped abuse on nuclear energy, the economy, pollution, work and the media.

For even greater shock value, they tapped the power of the image. They spat on staid English conventions by donning a revolting, yet carefully studied appearance. A skirt could no longer be called a skirt, and punks gleefully paraded in torn, stained and gaudy clothes, marrying colours against all the canons of good taste. They cut their hair into crests, horns and other shapes, plastered themselves with lurid make-up and wore chains. They covered their arms, faces, necks and heads with tattoos, reinvented piercing using safety-pins, studs and rings in their noses, eyebrows, lips and cheeks, and went so far as to deliberately scar themselves.

With their altered, rebel bodies, the punks quickly gave birth to a charged self-image. Their very own promoters conspired with the media they despised and turned them into symbols of decadence, before exporting their bodily aesthetics throughout Europe, North America and Japan.

Now, a quarter of a century later, the punks have spawned a loyal following. Top models, sporting personalities, singers and show-business stars jostle to display original hairstyles and body piercings. In rich countries, teenage girls show off their navel rings and stick out their bejewelled tongues, while boys wear rings in their eyebrows. Twenty-five years on, the socially-scorned practices of piercing or altering one's body have become musts for counting in the fashion scene. Young westerners have appropriated once "underground" practices to gain entry into the trendy but ultimately mainstream club.

There is, however, a paradox in all this. One would expect originality and innovation. In fact, what we are witnessing is a sweeping trend of cultural mix-and-match, drawing on body-altering techniques long used by non-western cultures for purposes of religion, aesthetics or identity. The American artist Fakir Musafar coined the term "modern primitives," giving rise to a new ideal, a patchwork that "tribalizes" the western body. For the past 50 years, he has explored alternative forms of spirituality incorporating primitive body decoration and rituals.

How did these alternative ways of changing the body travel so far afield? What drives young westerners to have tattoos from the South Sea islands or Japan? What do these "tribal" or "primitive" markings and decorations mean in a western society?

Certainly not a return to the rituals that originally produced them: most of those who go for such adornments know nothing about these distant practices. Moreover, the bodies now being used as models were those that were stigmatized and displayed during colonial exhibitions in Europe and the United States right up to the early 20th century. They were curiosity objects and more significantly, living symbols of the supposed "backwardness" of the colonized peoples. Seen through European eyes, piercing, body scars and elongated lips, necks and ears were evidence of "barbarism," justifying the West's self-appointed duty to civilize. Such practices incarnated the opposite of the ideal "civilized" body.

By way of homage to the civilizations the colonial powers seemingly sought to stamp out, the vanguard of the "modern primitives" set out to investigate these body rituals. The "tribal aesthetics" of Maria Tashijian, who owns a chain of body-alteration shops in the United States, is vaunted as a way to educate people by preserving the memory of extinct cultures and passing on their idea of beauty. Through piercing, stretching the ear-lobe and body scarring, we can thus create a jigsaw of ancient and modern aesthetics.

Others, such as Musafar. see these practices as the chance to 10 work on one's own profound sense of Self. "Body play," in his words, consists of experimenting with every known body-alteration technique. By willingly going through the initiation ordeals of traditional societies, one actually relives a primal experience that has long been forgotten in the industrialized world. It is the path towards rediscovering an original innocence.

FORGET ABOUT THOSE BLONDE SURFERS

What's important is not the markings left on the body, says Musafar. Instead, what matters is the confrontation with physical pain that takes one toward another plane of consciousness, shunned in western societies where all is done to combat suffering. But unlike the physical and symbolic violence of initiation rites in traditional societies, these bodily alterations are the fruit of a conscious personal choice.

Such discourse, however, will be rarely heard among the millions of people who flirt with body decorating. The vast majority are merely fulfilling the modern-day desire for self-knowledge and recognition from others. They might invoke aesthetics, spirituality, sex games or the desire to belong to a group, but whatever the reason, the process of altering the body and putting it to the test comes down to playing with identity. This reflects a profound cultural shift.

The urge to assert oneself goes hand in hand with a desire to challenge social norms and values, and to advocate different ways of experiencing, feeling and displaying one's body. Many fans of body-art, piercing and tattooing say they can no longer accept the western model of a sanitized, bland, alienated body.

The ideals of the blue-eyed blonde and the Californian surfer with the sleek and muscular bronzed body have to go. In this light, altering one's body becomes a battle against conventional appearance, a quest to give meaning to a life deemed otherwise insignificant.

To this end, it's not enough to go shopping for traditions. 15 Piecing together a body can also be done using modern materials, knowledge and techniques. By inserting foreign objects under their skin, some body artists are creating protuberances on foreheads, breastbones and forearms to radically challenge age-old perceptions of the physical self.

A BATTLE AGAINST CREEPING STANDARDIZATION

All these interventions can be seen as a quest to escape a destiny spelt out in terms of sex, age and social origin. In this sense, they have political implications. By shattering models, rejecting beauty standards circulated in the mass media and asserting the right to do, wear and display what they see fit, this avant-garde is holding up the body as one of the last bastions where individual freedom can be expressed.

Faced with the pressure to conform, to discipline one's body in order to meet economic and social demands, constructing an appearance becomes the royal road to upsetting normality. Everyone becomes an actor, capable of displaying their body in a unique way. Rather than sinking into the crowd, they spark a chain of reactions (grounded or not), from attraction and fascination to rejection and fear.

The refusal to comply with social norms, the awareness that looking different has an impact, is all part of a battle against creeping standardization. In this light, such a philosophy stands at opposite ends from the promise of cosmetic surgery, diets and the like.

Television and the Internet are giving play to all these trends. Day after day, we are exposed to a million ways of perceiving the body, culled from past and present, from the imagination and real experiments. Such depictions remind us that the body is not about a static anatomy, and that there is more than one way to signal membership to a group. They also remind us that culture is always on the move. What is exotic one day is undesirable the next and rediscovered later. The globalization of images has spawned multiple models of the "civilized" body, breaking with the western standard-bearer.

DRESSED TO KILL IN KINSHASA

In developing countries, however, those with money will go to   20
any ends to cling to the most common western model, plucked straight out of television soap-operas. South American immigrants in the United States go for breast implants, lighten their skin and bleach their hair. In southern Africa and among African Americans, skin-lighteners and hair-straightening products are all the rage. The famed sapeurs of Kinshasa in the Democratic Republic of Congo make enormous sacrifices to keep up with what they see as the latest in Parisian chic. Cosmetic surgery is as popular in the U.S. as in South America, where women have operations that bring them eerily close to the Barbie doll ideal. In Asia, they ask surgeons to attenuate the "slant" of their eyes. . . . Does a perceived or real context of political and economic domination lead some to hide their specific features? "Westernizing" the human body reads like a strategy to fit in with globalization.

For now, creating a hybrid ideal of the body is a game for the privileged. Among the poor, only a minority is going about removing the stigmas they have historically borne. But popularizing this new ideal is stirring debate. By hijacking appearance codes and adopting body-altering techniques that were originally designed for medical purposes, people are carving in flesh the rules of a new game. Their efforts will likely herald an all-round confusion over what norms, if any, govern the human body.

Questions

1. How do you describe the characteristics of "rebel bodies" (paragraph 4) among people your age today? What are people around you doing to their bodies to stand out or fit in with their peers?

2. In paragraph 7, Liotard asks the following questions: "What drives young westerners to have tattoos from the South Sea islands or Japan? What do these 'tribal' or 'primitive' markings and decorations mean in a western society?" What do you think about these questions?

3. As part of creating their own personal "images" people have used breast implants, skin lighteners, hair coloring, and hair straighteners. Some women have cosmetic surgery so they can look more like "the Barbie doll ideal." How do you compare these kinds of procedures with tattooing, piercing, cutting, and branding?

4. Liotard writes: "Creating a hybrid ideal of the body is a game for the privileged" (paragraph 21). How do you interpret this statement? What does he mean by a "hybrid ideal of the body"? What does he mean by "the privileged"? Do you agree with his assessment?

5. Write an essay in which you respond to the following situation: Your best friend wants to get a tattoo but does not have parental permission. (Or is not sure what to do if she/he is above the age when parental permission is required.) Your friend asks for your advice and asks you to accompany him/her getting the tattoo. In your essay explain how you would respond to the situation, what you would tell your friend, and how you feel about tattooing in general.

Visual History and African-American Families of the Nineteenth Century

DONNA M. WELLS

Donna M. Wells is the Prints and Photographs Librarian at the Moorland-Springarn Research Center at Howard University and has worked on photographic exhibits about Frederick Douglass and many other important African Americans. However, Ms. Wells is also concerned with the role of photography and the less well known role of family photography in capturing social history, especially as it pertains to African Americans. This article appeared in 1996 in the Negro History Bulletin *published by the Association for the Study of African American Life and History.*

Getting Started

Wells writes about the power of photography, not only to record individuals but also to provide a wealth of information about society in general. Think about the oldest photograph you have ever seen. What do you remember about that photograph? How much does your sense of a period in history rely on old photographs of it? Do you think that posed photographs can accurately reflect the realities of life? What can we learn about families, about social relations, and about race relations by looking at photographs? Consider your own family photos. What do they say about the individual members of your family? What do they say about your family as a whole or about its place in society?

———————— ✦ ————————

When photography was introduced to the world in 1839, it revolutionized the way in which Americans perceived themselves and how they would be perceived by others. Originally, the process of making photographs was only made known to artists and scientists. For scientists, photography became a tool for providing visual proof of findings and to support scientific theories about such issues as racial inferiority. Within the art world, photography provided artists a cheaper and faster medium for creating likenesses of their clients.

During the latter part of the nineteenth century, photography had developed into an important component of documentary work, especially for the new fields of study anthropology and sociology. The impact of photography on the African-American family, both as a means of livelihood and as visual record, has only recently received scholarly attention. Only within the last fifteen years have photo historians brought our attention to the contribution of African Americans to the photographic profession and only within the past ten years have publications been introduced that critique the way in which African Americans have been portrayed graphically throughout history.

The photograph collections in archival repositories focusing on African Americans cover the realm of images involving African Americans either as photographer or as the subject. One of the richest areas for study of African-American social history are the photographs contained in personal papers and manuscript collections. Yet photographs continue to be used mainly as illustration for text rather than as a stand-alone resource or as a supportive document. Genealogists have long recognized the value of photography as a stand-alone document for research, but that research usually centers around a single family history.

Genealogical research, when conducted within the context of African-American history using a variety of resources, offers a more encompassing perspective of the African-American family in American society. In other words, our individual family photographs can provide a wealth of information about society in general.

Contemporary research in African-American history examines topics such as women's history, labor, the middle-class, urban life, science and invention, and religion. Family collections are a major source of information about these topics.

Why people take photographs has not changed much since its invention. Family collections are full of individual portraits and photographs of family milestones. Typical images include pictures of graduations, weddings, birthdays, family gatherings, the birth of a child, or a photograph of the home. Daniel Freeman, a Washington, D.C. photographer who operated at the turn of the century, also mentions the popular vanity shots which people still take with the single objective of having a visual record of the self that can be given to others. Tabletop displays and photo albums in the home of the nineteenth century family included images of family, landscapes, foreign scenes and photographs of celebrated leaders of the day. African-American families living during the nineteenth century took photographs for much the same reasons. They were as much treasured then as they are now, which is why so many of them have survived.

Prior to photography's debut, only the wealthy and the powerful could afford the services of an artist to paint their portrait. Photography provided an affordable means for many to obtain likenesses. In an 1864 speech on pictures, Frederick Douglass discusses the impact that the early photographic formats made on society:

> This may be termed an age of pictures. The sun in his course having fumed artist has flooded the world with pictures. Daguerreotypes, ambro-types, engravings and drawings, good, bad and indifferent, adorn and disfigure, and as frequently the latter as the former, all our dwellings. A very pleasing feature of our pictorial relations is the very easy terms upon which all may enjoy them. The servant girl can now see a likeness of herself, such

as noble ladies and even royalty itself could not purchase fifty years ago. Formerly, the luxury of a likeness was the exclusive privilege of the rich and great, but now, like education and a thousand other blessings brought to us by the advancing march of civilization, such pictures are placed within easy reach of the humblest members of society.[1]

This is a powerful statement for several reasons. First, Douglass views photography as the great equalizer of race and class, in that a servant girl could now afford to have a likeness made of herself. Second, the observation illustrates the impact that images had on society more than 150 years ago. The access to such an affordable product encouraged many free blacks to have their portraits taken. Third, the speech is important because it represents an African-American perspective on photography.

The daguerreotype was the earliest commercial photographic format and was named for its inventor, Louis Jacques Mande Daguerre. It was popular from its invention in 1839 until around 1860. Daguerreotypes are unique and fragile and images of non-whites are somewhat rare. The daguerreotype of Frederick Douglass is one of the earliest known images of him and is unusual because of the profile pose said to symbolize nobility of character. The Douglass image represents the control that free blacks had over how they wished to be perceived by the public. In many of his early photographs, Douglass appears poised, cultured and sometimes defiant, as in the engraving of Douglass taken from the frontispiece of his second autobiography, *My Bondage, My Freedom*. This engraving was made from an original daguerreotype.

A comparison of the first two photographs of Douglass with a later drawing of him shows a startling difference, a difference which was noted by Douglass in a book review in the *North Star*. Douglass commented on this drawing of him by Wilson Armistead: "That of Frederick Douglass, we shall leave to others to criticize, begging only to remark that, it has a much more kindly and amiable expression, than is generally thought to characterize the face of a fugitive slave."[2]

10

---

[1]Douglass, Frederick. "Life Pictures," Microfilm, 1864, Frederick Douglass Papers.

[2]Douglass, Frederick. "A Tribute to the Negro; being a vindication of the moral and religious capabilities, of the colored portion of mankind; with particular reference to the African race; illustrated by numerous biographical sketches-facts-anecdotes, &cl, and many superior engravings." By Wilson Armistead, in *The North Star*, 7 April 1849.

Douglass' comment is based on his on-going criticism of the portrayal of African Americans by white artists. Possibly, Douglass did not pose for the Armistead drawing, but in the photographic portraits, he had much more control over how he wished to be portrayed. Douglass was one of the most photographed individuals of the nineteenth century, a fact which is reflected in his papers at the Library of Congress and in the Frederick Douglass Collection at the Moorland-Spingarn Research Center. Douglass is best known as a statesman, lecturer and abolitionist. Numerous portraits of Douglass, illustrative of his position and status, can be found in his papers and in other nineteenth century collections containing images of the prominent individuals of the time.

Less familiar are the photographs of Douglass as family man. The clothing and demeanor of his three sons, Charles, Joseph and Lewis, in a photograph suggest a prosperous African-American family. Like many learned men of Douglass' time, musical training was part of the Douglass children's upbringing. In one photograph, son Joseph is seen with his father holding a violin. Frederick Douglass was also a violinist.

The photographs in the Frederick Douglass Collection at Moorland cover many different photographic formats and photographic processes. This is typical of collections which span the nineteenth century. The name and location of the photographer, personal notations about the subject and the style of dress are all useful tools in identifying a photograph. The photographic process or format can help in dating the image.

The stereograph photograph (1856–1880) gave viewers a three-dimensional image when viewed through a stereoptic viewer. Stereographs are somewhat reminiscent of the tabletop photography books we see in homes today. Many families had them in their homes to entertain guests. Sometimes the commercially produced stereographs, mostly of foreign countries and foreign people, appear in family collections.

Cartes-de-visite and the cabinet cards were albumen prints 15 (1850–1900) mounted on a heavy card stock. They make up the bulk of the photographic formats found in nineteenth century family collections and in archival repositories. The color of the cardboard mounts are helpful in dating images because popular colors changed every decade or so. Card photographs often have a considerable amount of identifying information on them, mostly about the photographer. The photographer's name, address, prices and other advertising information is printed on the front and back of the card mount. Handwritten notations on the back of the card sometimes provide identifying information about the subject of the photograph. Many photographs from this time depict the Victorian tradition in African-American dress.

One aspect of family research that is sometimes overlooked in locating relevant photographs is that family members had a life outside of the family. Portraits are the dominant form of illustration used in research but related images may require additional interpretation. Supportive information may show up in other collections, including church archives and fraternal lodge records.

Photographer John B. Washington, possibly the first professional black photographer in Washington, D.C., became a member of the Felix Lodge after 1865. Based upon city directories and census records, Washington operated as a photographer between 1850 and 1880. His lodge membership probably brought him a considerable amount of business from fellow lodge members. Other local photographers later became members of the same lodge, and considering the nature of photographic training, may have apprenticed at some point under Washington. The photograph of Washington was not part of a manuscript collection but was discovered in an early twentieth century history of the lodge.

A tintype (1856–1900) of Clara T. Keaton has a fragile paper mat somewhat intact. Printed notations on the upper part of the mat indicate that she was born in 1798. The notation on the bottom of the paper mat states that Clara Keaton was the first depositor of the Baltimore National Savings and Trust Bank. Clara Keaton may have been mother, sister, daughter, aunt or cousin to other persons, but Clara Keaton was waiting for the doors to open at the Baltimore National Savings and Trust Bank on its first day in business. This photograph was not part of a manuscript collection, and, based on the printed notations, the bank was probably instrumental in having the photograph made.

Other aspects about Clara Keaton can be speculated. Taking into consideration the dates that the tintype process was popular, Clara's style of dress, and her probable age, the photograph may have been taken around the 1860s or 1870s. Even with so much information available on the paper mat, other questions arise in looking at this photograph, which place Clara in a larger historical context. Since Clara is making the deposit herself, is she the head of the household? Was she employed as a washerwoman, servant, or other major means of employment for black women at this time? Was she a slave? When did the bank open? How did she come into enough money to open an account? Some questions could be cleared up easily through census records, business directories and the archives, if it exists, of the Baltimore National Savings and Trust. The point is,

this photograph alone can lead to other information about
African Americans living in Baltimore.

Identification and preservation are key to ensuring the longevity   20
of our visual history and published information is readily available
from libraries and archival supply companies. Family collections
are valuable to the study of African-American society, yet no clear-
cut method exists for reading or interpreting photographs. A considerable amount of creativity is involved but it is not necessary to be
an expert in the history of photography.

Questions

1. What is genealogical research? What is the connection between genealogical research and photography? What part of understanding a family is found
   in photographs?

2. Go online or do another kind of picture research and find a "vintage" or old
   photograph of a family or group of people posing for a camera. Compare it
   to a modern one, like a snapshot of your own family. What are the differences between the two? What are the similarities? What might be some
   reasons for either, or both?

3. How did photography become "the great equalizer of race and class" (paragraph 4)? What examples are provided in Wells' essay that support this
   point of view?

4. What do you make of the differences Wells describes in the photographs of
   Douglass and the drawing of him made by Wilson Armistead? What does
   this suggest to you about the difference between photography and painting
   in rendering a likeness of a person?

5. This article suggests that finding, preserving, and exhibiting photographs of
   African Americans in the late 1800s is important in understanding American
   history. Do you agree with this? If so, why do you think this is the case? What
   other kinds of photographs do you think might help us understand our past?

New Jersey Trying a New Way for Witnesses to Pick Suspects

GINA KOLATA AND IVER PETERSON

Gina Kolata is a science writer for the New York Times. *She has also
written several books including* Clone: The Road to Dolly and the
Path Ahead *(1998),* Flu: The Story of the Great Influenza Pan-
demic of 1918 and the Search for the Virus that Caused It *(1999),*

and Ultimate Fitness: The Quest for Truth about Exercise and Health *(2003). Iver Peterson is also a writer for the* New York Times *who frequently writes about New Jersey issues. In this article, they describe a simple change in the way that witnesses view suspects that may reduce the number of false identifications and help to find the real criminals.*

Getting Started

Do you think a lineup is a fair way to narrow down the suspects in a crime? Why do you think this? What makes you think that eyewitness reports can or cannot be trusted? Do you think people can make mistakes in reporting what they have witnessed, even if they firmly believe in what they say? What examples of this do you know about? Have you seen the mug shots that victims search through to help identify the perpetrator of a crime? In what ways might these help or hinder law enforcement? Some people criticize the police drawings that are made from eyewitness reports by saying that racial and social biases can creep into those drawings. What do you think about that?

———————— ✦ ————————

Prompted by new insights into the psychology of eyewitnesses to crimes, New Jersey is changing the way it uses witnesses to identify suspects.

Starting in October, the state will become the first in the nation to give up the familiar books of mug shots and to adopt a simple new technique called a sequential photo lineup, said John J. Farmer Jr., New Jersey's attorney general. Sequential viewing of photographs has been shown to cut down on the number of false identifications by eyewitnesses without reducing the number of correct ones.

The difference between the old and new systems is subtle but highly significant, according to researchers who have studied the psychology of witness identification. At present, eyewitnesses browse through photographs of suspects, comparing, contrasting and re-studying them at will.

Under the new system, victims and other eyewitnesses would be shown pictures one after the other. They would not be allowed to browse. If they wanted a second look, they would have to view all the photos a second time, in a new sequence. Also, the pictures would usually be shown by a person who would not know who the real suspect was.

"It's just a reality that eyewitness identifications are made un- 5
der situations of incredible duress, when people are trying to recall what someone looked like, and they can be more or less accurate," Mr. Farmer said. "So what we're trying to do with these guidelines is to give law enforcement a way in which we think we can at least narrow the risk that a mistake will be made."

The new rules also change the way physical lineups, called showups, will be done, although the use of suspects and stand-ins is so rare in New Jersey these days that some prosecutors cannot remember the last time they were used. As in photo line-ups, the new rules require that in showups, individuals must be presented to the witness one at a time, usually through a one-way mirror.

The New Jersey program, which is already being used in Camden and Hunterdon Counties, grows out of a quarter-century of psychological research and is supported by recommendations published two years ago by the United States Department of Justice for police forces nationally.

The federal recommendations followed a 1998 study by the National Institute of Justice, a research arm of the Justice Depart-ment, which asked police officials, defense lawyers, prosecutors and researchers to review 28 criminal convictions that had been overturned by DNA evidence. The study found that in most of the cases, the strongest evidence had been eyewitness identification.

The Justice Department published a guide titled "Convicted by Juries, Exonerated by Science" in 1999, summarizing its rec-ommendations for change, saying, among other things, that se-quential lineups were an acceptable option.

New Jersey, working with a pioneer in the field, Gary Wells, a 10
psychologist and researcher at Iowa State University, soon began drawing up its own guidelines.

New Jersey's program was developed by Debra L. Stone, deputy director of operations and chief of staff in the state's Division of Criminal Justice. Ms. Stone said that the plan elicited howls of protest when it was introduced to county prosecutors, and local police departments and prosecutors, who feared that the new procedures would make it harder to win convictions because fewer suspects would be identified. They also expressed concerns that the procedures would impose additional burdens on the short-handed police departments.

"But we had a program for them where we had Professor Wells come in to tell them some of his horror stories about misidentifications, and about the way people's memories work, and in the end they were very supportive," Ms. Stone said.

Chief John Miliano of the Linden, N.J., Police Department said: "Every time you see something coming along that makes your job a little harder, you kind of cringe a little. It's going to take extra time and personnel, but if it's going to make a case a little more solid or if it's going to eliminate a bad identification or a situation where an officer may try to influence an identification, then it's beneficial."

Mr. Farmer and Mr. Wells said they believed that New Jersey will be the first state in the nation to use the new lineup techniques.

Over the years, researchers like Mr. Wells, and Rod Lindsay, a   15
psychology professor at Queen's University in Kingston, Ontario, have demonstrated that sequential lineups made a huge difference.

Professor Lindsay would stage a mock crime—like a purse-snatching—in front of a group of people who had agreed to participate in a study. He would then show the witnesses a traditional lineup of suspects, like a group of photographs or a number of people standing in a row, but he would not put the "purse-snatcher" in the lineup. About 20 percent to 40 percent of the witnesses mistakenly identified someone as the criminal.

When the same suspects were put in a sequential lineup, and the eyewitnesses were shown photographs one at a time, and only once, the rate of false identifications dropped to less than 10 percent.

Other experiments showed that witnesses who did remember the criminal were just as likely to pick that person out of sequential lineups as they were from traditional simultaneous lineups.

The reason that sequential lineups work is rather simple. In simultaneous lineups, Professor Lindsay said, witnesses are able to compare individuals, choosing one from the group who looks the most like the person they think they saw commit the crime. But a sequential lineup limits the ability to compare.

The psychologists think that the chance of misidentification is   20
reduced the most by allowing witnesses to view photos only once. New Jersey, however, plans to let witnesses see photos more than once, although the sequence would be changed between viewings. And even if witnesses declare a decision in midsequence, they are required to view the sequence through to the end, to assure that each picture has been seen the same number of times.

Harold Kasselman, deputy first assistant prosecutor in Camden County, which has been using the new system since December, said, "Our feeling is that if they request it, we shuffle all eight photographs again and show them again in random order." A witness who makes an identification is told to sign and date the chosen photo, and to initial the other seven. All eight photos become evidence in the case.

Another crucial innovation, the researchers found, was to be sure that a neutral third party conducted the lineup, in what is called a blind test. If the detective knows which person is the suspect, it could allow the detective, consciously or not, to guide the witness.

"Let's say you're the detective and you've got your person in position three" in the group of photographs, Professor Wells said. "You show this spread to the witness and the witness says, 'Well, No. 2.' A natural reaction is to say, 'Be sure you look at all the photos.' On the other hand, if the first words to come out of the witness's mouth are, 'No. 3,' then it's, 'Tell me about No 3.'"

"It's just a natural human reaction," he said.

The studies also showed that witnesses can be just as certain   25 about a mistaken identification as a true one. And being told that a false identification is correct makes witnesses even more certain.

"It is one thing to detect lying in court, but how do you figure out that one person made a mistake in identifying a suspect and the other didn't?" Professor Lindsay said. "Both are perfectly sincere in telling you the truth as they know it."

But even though the experts are confident that they have found a better way to conduct lineups, they have had a difficult time convincing law enforcement officials.

Attorney General Farmer said that New Jersey is unusual in that he has the power to order a change in lineup procedures statewide.

In New York's less centralized law enforcement network, however, officials say that a change to sequential lineups would most likely need to be spearheaded by district attorneys, but in cooperation with the police and the attorney general. District attorneys said that while they were interested in whether sequential lineups might improve identifications, the matter needed far more study and debate before a shift could be made.

George A. Grasso, the New York City Police Department's deputy commissioner in charge of legal affairs, said group lineups were based on long-established case law and could be particularly hard to change in New York's sprawling system.

New Jersey's new rules would allow an investigating officer to   30 conduct the lineup in cases where no neutral officer is available because the police department is so small, or because it is so late at night.

Still, as Chief Miliano pointed out, detectives talk among themselves about their cases all the time, so even a fair-sized department like his might have a hard time finding an officer with no knowledge of a given case to conduct the lineup.

But as Richard P. Rodbart, deputy first assistant prosecutor for Union County, said, police officials know that once the new guidelines have fully gone into effect, any other approach will become a liability that defense lawyers will pounce on.

"I don't want an officer getting on a witness stand after he's used the old way and being asked, 'By the way, sir, are you familiar with the order from the attorney general that there has been a new way to do identifications?'" Mr. Rodbart said. "And then the officer says, 'Yeah, I heard something about that.' And then the defense attorney's voice rises, 'Did you follow that order?' and bang, he's on track to knock the case down."

Questions

1. What was the original method for witnesses to view suspects for identification? What changes is the New Jersey Police Department making in how witnesses view lineups or groups of photographs? What is the role that psychology plays in making the new method more accurate than the previous method?

2. What is a sequential lineup? How do we see differently when we see something one at a time? Or in a group? What is a one-way mirror? How do you think that seeing someone through a one-way mirror is different from seeing them standing in front of you looking at you?

3. The authors write that "witnesses can be just as certain about a mistaken identification as a true one. And being told that a false identification is correct makes witnesses even more certain" (paragraph 25). How do you explain that? Have you ever made such a mistake in misidentifying someone? How did it happen? What does this suggest about vision, about how the external environment affects how we see and interpret what we see?

4. The article describes what happens when a mock crime is staged in front of a group of people participating in research. Witnesses often misidentified the person who actually did the crime. They even chose someone from a lineup or group of photographs when the actual criminal was not included in the group. Why do you think this might happen?

5. What does this article suggest about the attitude of law enforcement toward witnesses, suspects, and the judicial process itself? Why do you think there are cases of the wrong person being identified, convicted, and even jailed? How has DNA evidence been used in such cases? What is the difference between relying on DNA evidence and relying on human vision and recollection? If DNA evidence is so compelling, why are images still used?

Making Connections

1. When you compare some of the issues examined in the Goleman and Bordo articles, what do you think these two authors would have to say to each other? Imagine a conversation between them. Working with a partner, write out a question and answer session between the two of them.

2. What commonalities do you find between some of the issues Goleman, Liotard, and Bordo raise? What is beauty? How do we make ourselves attractive? Is beauty different across cultures? Across time? Do we think the same looks are beautiful today as we did even ten or twenty years ago? Why do we care so much about appearance? Should we?

3. What role does photography play in the Kolata and Peterson article and the Wells article? How is photography used in each case? Do photographs present a truer likeness of someone than any other form of image reproduction?

4. Liotard writes that body art is "a game for the privileged" (paragraph 21). What role does class and privilege play in the Bordo, Wells, Kolata and Peterson, and Goleman articles? To what extent does beauty connect with wealth and privilege?

5. Visit a photography exhibit in person, online, or through a book. Write a description of what you see in the exhibit. Connect this to at least three of the articles in this chapter. You might focus on definitions of beauty, on ideas about history or modern society, or on the practical uses of images of people.

6. Which do you think is more correct?: (a) The way we think about ourselves determines the kinds of images we create; (b) The images that we make influence the way we think about ourselves. Is one more accurate or more important than the other? Are they both equally true? Pick two of the authors in this chapter and explain how you think they would answer this question.

The Visual Surround

"There's no reality except the one contained within us. That's why so many people live an unreal life. They take images outside them for reality and never allow the one within them to assert itself."

—Hermann Hesse

The explosion of images throughout our environment is more than just numerical. While it is true that there are more pictures than ever before—both those being archived and the new ones being produced—the impact of this explosion goes far beyond the sheer amount of them. We are coming to rely more and more on images to help us understand the universe, to entertain ourselves, and to communicate with each other. Just think about how much you know, or think you know, about the world around you that comes directly from images as opposed to your direct experience. In science, medicine, politics, commerce, and many other fields, we are relying more and more on images to make sense of things.

Because of this, the images that we create with our expanding technology do not just fill up the world with their numbers; they create a new reality within the world. As the quote above from the German writer Hermann Hesse implies, we take the images outside us for reality. Although Hesse suggests that there is some danger in this, we cannot deny the attractive, compelling, even magical quality of images and their appeal as a kind of reality we feel comfortable in.

In this complex visual surround, images become the way we navigate our lives whether by preserving memories, watching the news, being entertained, investigating the world, or even making our way through the landscape of images on screens, walls, paper, cell phones, and buildings. But what does this mean for us as citizens, neighbors, and consumers? How is the expanding world of the image changing our attitudes, our understanding, even our relationships? This is a broad topic with important implications for all our lives and no book can hope to explore it fully. Yet the readings in this chapter hint at some of the issues involved.

In Read Mercer Schuchardt's essay called "The Perfect Icon for an Imperfect Postliterate World," the author discusses how powerful even the simplest of images can be. His examples are graphic symbols, those compact little pieces of visual communication that appear everywhere in our consumer culture. As a case in point, Schuchardt looks into the effect and impact of one of the most ubiquitous of these symbols, the Nike Swoosh. And he makes the compelling case that the textless icon is replacing language due to the icon's definitive potential for instant recognition in any language, written or otherwise. This one example indicates the power of the image to communicate and this power has important implications in commerce, language, and even religion.

In our second selection, "Eden by Wire: Webcameras and the Telepresent Landscape," author Thomas J. Campanella discusses another modern—and overpowering—innovation in the role images play in our lives. Although webcameras are only the most recent in a series of distance-collapsing technologies, Campanella points out that they are so ubiquitous they represent a revolution in their own right. Webcameras completely change our sense of the visual surround and our relationship to it. They allow us to see the world remotely, yet communicate intimately. They allow us to participate in and share adventures such as space exploration previously available to only the very few. But telepresence, Campanella's name for this phenomenon, also raises the question of surveillance—not only how constant watching but also how constantly being watched affects us. The key question is whether the presence of all these cameras enslaves or frees us?

In "Media Images and Violence," Ann Marie Seward Barry explores the role of violence as entertainment. She starts by citing a number of studies that show a link between watching violence on TV and violent real-world behavior, then moves on to the perhaps even more common and powerful video game. As Barry states, the cumulative effect of hours of violent TV and video games "cannot help but influence the perceptual process by which human beings incorporate the world around them into the essence of themselves, and in turn affect the social order as a whole." It is an idea that fits comfortably with the premise of this chapter, that visual technology does not just fill us with images but actually determines the way we perceive reality. And if it is true that, as Barry says, "media educates by informing people about their culture and themselves and their roles in that culture," then what we see becomes even more significant.

Our fourth selection is by the journalist Thomas Hine and is called "Notable Quotables: Why Images Become Icons." In this article, the author explores images (and other cultural ephemera) that, thanks to computer technology and media presence, have become part of the way we think about the world. In his assessment, key images become a kind of visual quotation, a set of clichés in the endless churn of culture, and a kind of quick reference for certain attitudes and statements. So complex and vast is our visual surround that the list of these becomes an "unlikely mix of high and low culture, tragedy and banality . . ." Yet we cannot escape the powerful way in which these icons become part of the way we think and catalog the world.

Finally, Robin Landa in "Speaking Brand" describes a new development on the visual scene, the success of branding. A successful brand represents a sophisticated effort to coordinate and create consistent and convincing identities for companies and products. A powerful visual strategy like branding creates another level of influence beyond the impact of single images, and suggests a new way in which the visual surround becomes a compelling force in our lives.

The Perfect Icon for an Imperfect Postliterate World

READ MERCER SCHUCHARDT

Read Mercer Schuchardt has a Ph.D. in Media Ecology from New York University. He is Assistant Professor of International Communications at Franklin College in Switzerland. Schuchardt has taught courses in communications history and theory, interpersonal communications, film, and media politics at Marymount College and expository writing at New York University. His publications have appeared in many journals. His 1997 article "The Perfect Icon for an Imperfect Postliterate World," reflects two of his interests: religious symbolism and contemporary corporate iconography.

Getting Started

Sometimes in advertising a symbol or icon becomes so well known that the name of the product does not even need to be mentioned for us to recognize it. How many examples of this can you think of? Do you think this is becoming more common or less? What do you think are the most effective "textless" icons and what makes these work so well? Are you attracted to familiar logos and do you prefer to wear them on your clothes? Schuchardt suggests that there is almost a religious power to icons like these. Do you agree and do you think this is a good thing or not?

———————— ✦ ————————

The early followers of Christ created a symbol to represent their beliefs and communicate with one another in times of persecution. The well-known icthus, or "Christian fish," consisted of two curved lines that transected each other to form the abstract outline of fish and tail. The word for fish also happened to be a Greek acronym wherein:

Iota = Iesous = Jesus
Chi = Christos = Christ
Theta = Theos = God
Upsilon = Huios = Son
Sigma = Soter = Savior

Combining symbol and word, the fish provided believers with an integrated media package that could be easily explained and understood. When the threat of being fed to the lions forced Christians to be less explicit, they dropped the text. Without the acronym to define the symbol's significance, the fish could mean anything or nothing, an obvious advantage in a culture hostile to certain beliefs. But to Christians the textless symbol still signified silent rebellion against the ruling authorities. Within three centuries, the faith signified by the fish had transformed Rome into a Christian empire.

Today, in an electronically accelerated culture, a symbol can change the face of society in about one-sixteenth that time. Enter the Nike Swoosh, the most ubiquitous icon in the country, and one that many other corporations have sought to emulate. In a world where technology, entertainment, and design are converging, the story of the Swoosh is by far the most fascinating case study of a systematic, integrated, and insanely successful formula for icon-driven marketing.

The simple version of the story is that a young Oregon design student named Caroline Davidson got $35 in 1971 to create a logo for then-professor (now Nike CEO) Phil Knight's idea of importing and selling improved Japanese running shoes. Nike's innovative product line, combined with aggressive marketing and brand positioning, eventually created an unbreakable mental link between the Swoosh image and the company's name. As Nike put it, there was so much equity in the brand that they knew it wouldn't hurt to drop the word *Nike* and go with the Swoosh alone. Nike went to the textless format for U.S. advertising in March 1996 and expanded it globally later that year. While the Nike name and symbol appear together in ads today, the textless campaign set a new standard. In the modern global market, the truly successful icon must be able to stand by itself, evoking all the manufactured associations that form a corporation's public identity.

In the past, it would have been unthinkable to create an ad   5
campaign stripped of the company's name. Given what was at stake—Nike's advertising budget totals more than $100 million per year—what made them think they could pull it off?

First, consider the strength of the Swoosh as an icon. The Swoosh is a simple shape that reproduces well at any size, in any color, and on almost any surface—three critical elements for a corporate logo that will be reproduced at sizes from a quarter of an inch to 500 feet. It most frequently appears in one of three arresting colors: black, red, or white. A textless icon, it nevertheless "reads" left to right, like most languages. Now consider the sound of the word *Swoosh*. According to various Nike ads, it's the last sound you hear before coming in second place, the sound of a basketball hitting nothing but net. It's also the onomatopoeic analogue of the icon's visual stroke. Reading it left to right, the symbol itself actually seems to say "swoosh" as you look at it.

However it may read, the Swoosh transcends language, making it the perfect corporate icon for the postliterate global village.

With the invention of the printing press, according to the Italian semiotician Umberto Eco, the alphabet triumphed over the icon. But in an overstimulated electronic culture, the chief problem is what advertisers call "clutter" or "chatter"—too many words, too much redundancy, too many competing messages. Add the rise of illiteracy and an increasingly multicultural world and you have a real communications problem. A hyper-linked global economy requires a single global communications medium, and it's simply easier to teach everyone a few common symbols than to teach the majority of non-English speakers a new language.

The unfortunate result is that language is being replaced by icons. From the rock star formerly known as Prince to e-mail "smileys" to the NAFTA-induced symbolic laundry labels, the names and words we use to describe the world are being replaced by a set of universal hieroglyphs. Leading the charge, as one would expect, are the organizations that stand to make the most money in a less text-dependent world: multinational corporations. With the decline of words, they now can fill the blank of the consumer's associative mind with whatever images they deem appropriate.

Some powerful modern logos manage to appropriate other images and their meanings. The Mercedes-Benz icon, for instance, is easily confused with the peace sign (an association that can only help). Pepsi's new symbol needs little or no verbal justification because it so clearly imitates the yin-yang symbol. In fact, a close look reveals it to be almost identical to the South Korean national flag, which is itself a stylized yin-yang symbol in red, white, and blue.

Never underestimate the power of symbols. Textless corporate symbols operate at a level beneath the radar of rational language, and the power they wield can be corrupting. Advertising that relies on propaganda methods can grab you and take you somewhere whether you want to go or not; and as history tells us, it matters where you're going.

Language is the mediator between our minds and the world, and the thing that defines us as rational creatures. By going textless,

Nike and other corporations have succeeded in performing partial lobotomies on our brains, conveying their messages without engaging our rational minds. Like Pavlov's bell, the Swoosh has become a stimulus that elicits a conditioned response. The problem is not that we buy Nike shoes, but that we've been led to do so by the same methods used to train Pavlov's dogs. It's ironic, of course, that this reflex is triggered by a stylized check mark—the standard reward for academic achievement and ultimate symbol for the rational, linguistically agile mind.

If sport is the religion of the modern age, then Nike has successfully become the official church. It is a church whose icon is a window between this world and the other, between your existing self (you overweight slob) and your Nike self (you god of fitness), where salvation lies in achieving the athletic Nietzschean ideal: no fear, no mercy, no second place. Like the Christian fish, the Swoosh is a true religious icon in that it both symbolizes the believer's reality and actually participates in it. After all, you have to wear something to attain this special salvation, so why not something emblazoned with the Swoosh?

Questions

1. What does the "icthus" or Christian fish look like? What was its original purpose? Is it still used today? For what purpose? What does the Nike Swoosh look like? For what purpose is it used? How does Schuchardt connect two such different icons?

2. Schuchardt writes: "However it may read, the Swoosh transcends language, making it the perfect corporate icon for the postliterate global village" (paragraph 7). What are the characteristics of the Swoosh that make it effective as a corporate logo? What does Schuchardt mean by the "postliterate" world? What is the "global village"?

3. What examples does Schuchardt provide to support the idea that some modern logos "appropriate other images and their meanings" (paragraph 10)? Can you think of other logos that do this beyond the examples he provides?

4. Think about the clothes that you and your friends wear. How many of them have logos on them? You may be surprised that many of them do. What do these logos communicate about you when you wear them in public? How do you feel about providing free advertising for these brands?

5. Focus on an icon or logo that you think is effective in getting a message across. Describe it and how it has been used. What does the consumer need to know about the icon or logo you've chosen in order to decide whether to buy or accept the product or idea it represents?

6. Read through the article again, this time underlining the various cultural referents—recognizable names and ideas that Schuchardt mentions. Identify the people and/or ideas at the source of those referents. How does Schuchardt use those referents to support the ideas in his article?

Eden by Wire: Webcameras and the Telepresent Landscape

THOMAS J. CAMPANELLA

Thomas J. Campanella received his Ph.D. from the Department of Urban Studies and Planning at the Massachusetts Institute of Technology. Presently he is an Assistant Professor in the Department of City and Regional Planning at the University of North Carolina at Chapel Hill. There he teaches courses in the Theory and Practice of Urban Design, Making the American Urban Landscape, and Site Planning and Sustainable Design, among others. His most recent books include The Resilient City: How Modern Cities Recover from Disaster *(2004) [co-authored with Lawrence J. Vale],* Republic of Shade: New England and the American Elm *(2003), and* Cities from the Sky: An Aerial Portrait of America *(2001). The following is an excerpt from Dr. Campanella's article "Eden by Wire,"which originally appeared in* The Robot in the Garden: Telerobotics and Telepistemology in the Age of the Internet *(2000), edited by Ken Goldberg and published by MIT Press.*

Getting Started

Have you ever looked up and noticed all around you—in and on buildings, on streets, in stores, banks, and lobbies—cameras or webcameras? Campanella refers to these cameras as "a set of wired eyes, a digital extension of the human faculty of vision." But what are these cameras looking at? Are they necessary for our security or are they an intrusion into our lives? Who is watching us and what records are they keeping for what purposes? What do these webcameras mean for privacy and individual rights? How important are these cameras in an age of terrorism and fear? How do you feel about constantly being watched?

———————— ✦ ————————

Hello, and welcome to my webcam; it points out of my window here in Cambridge, and looks toward the centre of town. . .[1]

Wake up to find out that you are the eyes of the World.[2]

The sun never sets on the cyberspatial empire; somewhere on the globe, at any hour, an electronic retina is receiving light, converting sunbeams into a stream of ones and zeros. Since the popularization of the Internet several years ago, hundreds of "webcameras" have gone live, a globe-spanning matrix of electro-optical devices serving images to the World Wide Web. The scenes they afford range from the sublime to the ridiculous—from toilets to the Statue of Liberty. Among the most compelling are those webcameras trained on urban and rural landscapes, and which enable the remote observation of distant outdoor scenes in real or close to real time. Webcameras indeed constitute something of a grassroots global telepresence project. William J. Mitchell has described the Internet as "a worldwide, time-zone-spanning optic nerve with electronic eyeballs at its endpoints."[3] Webcameras are those eyeballs. If the Internet and World Wide Web represent the augmentation of collective memory, then webcameras are a set of wired eyes, a digital extension of the human faculty of vision.

Before the advent of webcameras, the synchronous observation of remote places (those farther than the reach of mechano-optical devices such as telescope or binoculars) was impossible for the average person—even the computer literate. To watch the sun set over Victoria Harbor in Hong Kong would have required physically being in Hong Kong, unless you happened to tune in to a live television broadcast from the harbor's edge (an unlikely event, as sunsets generally do not make news). Now it is possible to log into one of several webcameras in that city and monitor the descendent sun even as the morning's e-mail is read. We can, at the same time, watch the sun rise over Chicago, or stream its noonday rays over Paris, simply by opening additional browser

———————————

[1]Caption on Sam Critchley's CamCam page, a webcamera site in Cambridge, UK (http://www.pipex.net/~samc/).

[2]Lyrics from the Grateful Dead anthem "Eyes of the World" by Robert Hunter.

[3]William J. Mitchell, *City of Bits: Space, Place, and the Infobahn* (Cambridge: MIT Press, 1995), p. 31.

windows and logging into the appropriate sites. As little as a decade ago, this would have been the stuff of science fiction.

Of course, remote observation through a tiny desktop portal will never approach the full sensory richness of a sunset over the South China sea; *telepresence* is an ambitious term. Webcameras may not cure seasonal affective disorder; yet, there is something magical—even surreal—about watching the far-off sun bring day to a city on the far side of the planet. That we can set our eyes on a sun-tossed Australian street scene, from the depths of a New England winter night, is oddly reassuring—evidence that the home star is burning bright and heading toward our window.

THE ABNEGATION OF DISTANCE

Webcameras enable us to select from hundreds of destinations, and observe these at any hour of the day or night. The power to do so represents a quantum expansion of our personal space-time envelope; webcameras are a relatively simple technology, yet they are changing the way we think about time, space and geographic distance. As byte-sized portals into far-off worlds, webcameras demonstrate effectively how technology is dwindling the one-time vastness of the earth.

The story of technology is largely one of abnegating distance— time expressed in terms of space. For most of human history, communication in real time was limited to the natural carrying range of the human voice, or the distance sound-producing instruments (drums, horns, bells, cannon, and the like) could be heard. Visual real-time communication over wide areas could be achieved using flags, smoke signals or, as Paul Revere found effective, a lantern in a belfry. However, such means were restricted by atmospheric conditions and intervening topography. Asynchronous messages—using the earlier innovations of language, writing, and printing—could conceivably be carried around the globe by the fifteenth century; but doing so took years. Transportation and communications remained primitive well into the nineteenth century, effectively limiting the geographic "footprint" of the average person to the proximate landscape of his birth. The space-time envelope of the typical peasant, for example, was restricted to the fields and byways of her village and surrounding countryside; that of the medieval townsman by the ramparts of the city in which he lived. Travel, even between settlements, was costly and dangerous; those who took to the roads were often criminals and outcasts from society. Indeed, the etymological source of the

5

word *travel* is the Old French *travailler* or "travail"—to toil and suffer hardship.

It was not until about 1850 that technology began to profoundly alter the spatial limits of the individual, collapsing distance and expanding the geography of daily life. The development of the locomotive and rail transport in this period had the greatest impact on notions of time and space. The railroad destroyed the tyranny of vastness and the old spatial order; it was a technology that, as Stephen Kern has put it, "ended the sanctuary of remoteness."[4] Once-distant rural towns suddenly found themselves within reach of urban markets, if they were fortunate enough to be positioned along the new "metropolitan corridor" (towns bypassed, conversely, often found themselves newly remote, a particularly tough fate for places previously well-served by canal or stage).[5] Rail transport also brought about a new temporal order: Countless local time zones made the scheduling of trains a logistical nightmare, and eventually led to the adoption of a uniform time standard in the United States.[6]

Subsequent advances in transportation technology—fast steamers, the Suez Canal and eventually the airplane—osculated the great distances separating Europe, Asia, and America. Circumnavigation of the globe itself, a dream of ages, became reality not long after Jules Verne's *Around the World in Eighty Days* was published in 1873. Inspired by the novel, American journalist Nellie Bly became, in 1890, the first to circle the earth in less than the vaunted eighty days.[7] In the following two decades, this figure—and the scale of the globe itself—progressively shrank. A journey to China—once an impossibility for all but the most intrepid seafarers—had become, by 1936, a two-day flight by Pan American "China Clipper." With the arrival of commercial jet aviation in the 1960s, traversing the earth was reduced to a day's travel and a middle-class budget.

The abnegation of distance by electricity was somewhat less romantic, but no less profound. Innovations such as the telegraph, "wireless" and radio neutralized distance by making

---

[4]Stephen Kern, *The Culture of Time and Space* (Cambridge: Harvard University Press, 1983), p. 213.

[5]See John R. Stilgoe, *Metropolitan Corridor: Railroads and the American Scene* (New Haven: Yale University Press, 1983).

[6]Kern, pp. 12–14. November 18, 1883, the day the new national standard was imposed, became known as "the day of two noons."

[7]Kern, p. 213.

communication possible irrespective of space and intervening geography. Immediate, synchronous, real-time communication could take place via "singing wires" or even thin air. The first electric telegraph line linked Baltimore and Washington in 1844, and two decades later the first transatlantic cable went into operation—the alpha segment of today's global telecommunications network. Marconi discovered that telegraphic signals could be transmitted via electromagnetic waves, and in 1902 succeeded in sending the first transatlantic wireless message. The telephone, which spanned the United States by 1915, brought the power of distant synchronous communication into the kitchen. It made the electronic abnegation of space routine, and prompted predictions of home-based work and "action at a distance" as early as 1914.[8]

The more recent development of the networked digital computer has further neutralized distance and geography. The globe-spanning Internet, described as a "fundamentally and profoundly antispatial" technology, has in effect cast a great data net over the bumps, puddles, and irregularities of the physical world. The "cyberspace" of the Net operates more or less independently of physical place, terrain, geography and the built landscape.[9] This was partly by design. The origins of the Internet may be traced to ARPANET, a Cold War initiative of the United States Department of Defense intended to create a multinodal knowledge-sharing infrastructure that could withstand nuclear attack; if any one part of the system was destroyed by an ICBM—for example New York or Washington—data would simply re-route itself around the blockage.

If the Net and the "mirror world" of cyberspace is spatially abstract, webcameras can be interpreted as mediating devices— points of contact between the virtual and the real, or spatial "anchors" in a placeless sea.[10] Webcameras open digital windows onto real scenes within the far-flung geography of the Internet. The networked computer enables the exchange of text-based information with distal persons or machines; webcameras add to that a degree of real-time visual knowledge. As Garnet Hertz put it, webcameras constitute an attempt "to re-introduce a

10

---

[8]"Action at a distance," *Scientific American*, 77 (1914): 39.

[9]Mitchell, *City of Bits*, p. 8.

[10]The term is from David Gelernter's *Mirror Worlds* (New York: Oxford University Press, 1991).

physical sense of actual sight into the disembodied digital self."[11] In a rudimentary way, they make us *telepresent*, in places far removed from our bodies.

VARIETIES OF TELEPRESENCE

The term *telepresence*, like its cousin *virtual reality*, has been applied to a wide range of phenomena, and often inaccurately. It was coined in 1980 by Marvin Minsky, who applied it to teleoperation systems used in remote object-manipulation applications. As Jonathan Steuer has defined it, telepresence is "the experience of presence in an environment by means of a communication medium." Put another way, it is the mediated perception of "a temporally or spatially distant real environment" via telecommunications. Telepresence is reciprocal, involving both the observer and the observed. In other words, the observer is telepresent in the remote environment, and the observed environment is telepresent in the physical space in which the observer is viewing the scene.[12]

The genealogy of visual synchronicity begins with the development of simple optical devices to augment sight, such as the telescope, binoculars, microscope, the *camera lucida*, and the *camera obscura* (*asynchronous* co-presence, on the other hand, can be traced back to scenic depictions by primitive cave painters, though its modern roots lie with the discovery of photography and the later development of the stereoscope. This latter technology provided an illusion of a third dimension, dramatically increasing the sense of immersion into the photographic scene; by the turn of the century, stereoscopic cards were immensely popular, and depicted such exotic landscapes as the Pyramids of Giza).[13]

Synchronous visual co-presence *by means of electricity* was a dream long before it became reality. One fanciful depiction, published in an 1879 edition of *Punch*, imagined an "Edison Telephonoscope" enabling family members in Ceylon to be telepresent in a Wilton Place villa.[14] The first experiments in transmitting still

---

[11]Garnet Hertz, "Telepresence and Digital/Physical Body: Gaining a Perspective" (http://www.conceptlab.com/interface/theories/reality/index.html).

[12]Jonathan Steuer, "Defining Virtual Reality: Dimensions Determining Telepresence," *Journal of Communications* 42 (Autumn 1992): 75–8.

[13]Don Gifford, *The Farther Shore: A Natural History of Perception* (New York: Atlantic Monthly Press, 1990), p. 31.

[14]See Mitchell, *City of Bits*, pp. 32, 46.

images via telegraph took place in the 1840s, with Alexander Bain's proposal for a transmission system based on the electro-chemical effects of light. Twenty years later, Abbe Caselli devised a similar system that used rotating cylinders wrapped with tin foil to transmit and receive photographs and handwritten notes.[15] As early as the 1880s, photographs had been transmitted via radio signal in England; by 1935, Wirephotos enabled the rapid trans-mission of photographs around the globe.[16]

The electrical transmission of live images was first explored by the German physicist Paul Nipkow in the 1880s. Nipkow under-stood that the electrical conductivity of selenium—itself discovered in 1817—changed with exposure to light, and that all images were essentially composed of patterns of light and dark. Based on this principle, he devised an apparatus to scan (using a rotating, perfo-rated "Nipkow disk") a moving image into its component patterns of light and dark, and converted this into electrical signals using se-lenium cells. The signals would then illuminate a distant set of lamps, projecting the scanned image on a screen. Nipkow's ideas, which remained theoretical, provided the basis for the early devel-opment of television, which by the 1920s was transmitting live im-ages overseas.

Until the advent of the Net, television remained the closest thing to telepresence most people would ever experience. Even with the development of videoconferencing technology in the last decade, access to the hardware and software required to experience even basic telepresence was limited to a privileged few. Proprietary videoconferencing systems were costly and required specialized in-stallation and service. The arrival of the World Wide Web, by pro-viding inexpensive and ready access to a global computer network, made telepresence a reality for anyone with a modem, a PC, and a video camera. The World Wide Web, enabling webcameras as well as simple desktop videoconferencing applications such as CUSeeMe, brought telepresence to the grassroots.

Admittedly, webcamera technology as it exists today affords only the most basic variety of telepresence. The simple observa-tion of distal scenes, even in real time, hardly satisfies most defi-nitions of telepresence. David Zeltzer has argued that a sense of "being in and of the world"—real or virtual—requires no less than a "'bath' of sensation," and this can be achieved only when we are receiving a high-bandwidth, multisensory stream of information

15

---

[15]Brad Fortner, "Communication Using Media."

[16]Gifford, *The Farther Shore*, p. 26.

about the remote world—something hardly provided by most webcamera sites.[17] According to Held and Durlach, "high telepresence" requires a transparent display system (one with few distractions), high resolution image and wide field of view, a multiplicity of feedback channels (visual as well as aural and tactile information, and even environmental data such as moisture level and air temperature), and a consistency of information between these. Moreover, the system should afford the user dexterity in manipulating or moving about the remote environment, with high correlation, between the user's movements and the actions of the remote "slave robot."[18] Sheridan similarly proposed three "measurable physical attributes" to determine telepresence: extent of sensory information received from the remote environment; control of relation of sensors to that environment (the ability of the observer to modify his viewpoint); and the ability to modify the telepresent physical environment.[19]

With sluggish images appearing in a tiny box on a desktop, webcameras hardly constitute full sensory immersion in a distant world, let alone mobility and engagement in that world. While it is true that some of the more sophisticated webcamera sites offer a modicum of telerobotic interactivity, these tend to be clumsy and difficult to use—particularly when a number of users are fighting for the controls.[20] Webcameras afford what might be described as "low telepresence" or "popular telepresence." But their limitations are at least partially compensated by the vast extent of the webcam network, which itself can be seen as enabling remote-world mobility simply by providing such a wide range of geographic destinations.

---

[17]David Zeltzer, "Autonomy, Interaction, and Presence," *Presence*, 1: 128.

[18]Richard M. Held and Nathaniel I. Durlach, "Telepresence," *Presence*, 1: 109–11.

[19]Thomas B. Sheridan, "Musings on Telepresence and Virtual Presence," *Presence*, 1: 120–22.

[20]For a collection of examples see http://mitpress.mit.edu/telepistemology. Some of the better known telerobotic webcamera sites include the Keio Mt. Fuji Server (http://www.flab.mag.keio.ac.jp/fuji/); the Virtual Artists Rundle Street VA RoboCam in Adelaide, Australia (http://robocam.va.com.au/); the SchoolNet Robotics Webcam at Carleton University (http://webcam.engsoc.carleton.ca/); the EyeBot Project (http://www.dma.nl/eyebot/); the Interactive Model Railroad (http://rr-vs.informatik.uni-ulm.de/rr/); and the Light on the Net Project (http://light.softopia.pref.gifu.jp/), which enables the user to turn on or off a panel of lights in real time.

COFFEE POT TO DEEP SPACE

The accessibility of the Net and the simplicity of webcamera technology produced, in less than a decade, a network of independent cameras spanning the globe. As networking technology evolved, it was discovered that a sensory device affixed to a server could distribute real-time visual information to a large number of people. In 1991 a pair of Cambridge University computer scientists, Quentin Stafford-Fraser and Paul Jardetzky, attached a recycled video camera to an old computer and video frame-grabber, and aimed it at a coffee pot outside a computer lab known as the Trojan Room. They wrote a simple client-server program to capture images from the camera every few minutes and distribute them on a local network, thus enabling people in remote parts of the building to check if there was coffee available before making the long trek downstairs.[21] Later served over the Internet (and still in operation) the Trojan Room Coffee Cam became the Internet's first webcamera.

Inspired by Coffee Cam, Steve Mann—at the time a graduate student at the MIT Media Lab—devised a wireless head-mounted webcamera unit in the early 1990s that fed a chain of images via radio to a fixed base station and server. His "experiment in connectivity" enabled anyone logged into his website to simultaneously share his field of vision, or trace his movements in space through the day by examining continuously archived images. Mann's unit evolved from early experiments by Ivan Sutherland, in which half-silvered mirrors in a head-mounted display enabled the wearer to see a virtual environment imposed upon actual scenes. The WearCam enabled Mann to in effect *become* a webcamera, blurring the line between reality and virtuality, presence and telepresence.[22]

Webcamera technology is simple enough to allow even individuals with minimal computer experience to set one up, and many have done so, displaying prosaic views of driveways, backyards, and streets. A simple "golfball" camera such as the ubiquitous Connectix Quickcam can be used to supply images to a frame-grabber at a predetermined interval or as requested by a

20

---

[21]Quentin Stafford-Fraser, "The Trojan Room Coffee Pot: A (non-technical) Biography." (http://www.cl.cam.ac.uk/coffee/qsf/coffee.html).

[22]Steve Mann, "Wearable Computing: A First Step Toward Personal Imaging," *Computer*, 30: 2 (February 1997).

client. Assigned a unique IP (Internet protocol) address, the captured frame is then served over the World Wide Web and made available to one or more websites. Most webcameras capture and send a single frame at a time, while more sophisticated sites "push" a continuous stream of images to the client, thus providing a moving picture. Most live-streaming webcamera feeds are sluggish and temperamental, but they offer a compelling near-live glimpse into a remote place.

By 1995, dozens of webcameras were feeding pixels to armchair voyeurs around the world. Following the geography of the Net itself, the early webcameras were located mainly in the United States, Europe, and Japan. More recently, such devices have appeared in places farther off the digital mainline—including Pakistan, Russia, Poland, Mexico, Chile, Brazil, Croatia, Colombia, South Africa, and the Czech Republic. The geography of webcameras now extends to space itself. A number of telerobotic webcamera-equipped telescopes are in operation in the United States and Europe. These include relatively simple units such as one developed by the Remote Access Astronomy Project (RAAP) at the University of California, Santa Barbara (allowing high school students to remotely observe the heavens for science projects), to more sophisticated devices such as the Bradford Robotic Telescope in the United Kingdom, and the powerful 3.5-meter Apache Point telescope in New Mexico—operated via the Internet by researchers at the University of Chicago and elsewhere. An interface program called Remark affords seamless control of the Apache Point instrument, replicating a sense of "being at the telescope" (and creating in effect two "piggybacked" sets of telepresent space—that of the telescope itself and that of the celestial world glimpsed by its lens and the attached camera).[23]

Near-real-time satellite images of the earth are available over the Net, generated by the geostationary GOES-8 and GOES-10 satellites operated by the National Oceanic and Atmospheric Administration.[24] Plans for an even more sophisticated earth-observing satellite were unveiled by [the then] vice president Al Gore in the spring of 1998. The satellite, to bear the name "Triana" in honor of Columbus's navigator, would provide "the ultimate

---

[23]See UC Santa Barbara Remote Access Astronomy Project website (http://www.deepspace.uc-sb.edu/rot.htm); Bruce Gillespie, Robert Loewenstein and Don York, "Remote Observing at Apache Point," 1995 (http://www.apo.nmsu.edu/NMOpaper/paper.html).

[24]See Geostationary Satellite Browser Server (http://www.goes.noaa.gov).

macro world view," feeding high-resolution images to three earth stations, where they would be compiled into a full-disk portrait of the home planet and made continuously available to viewers on the Net. Pointing out that the last full-round images of the earth came two decades ago during the Apollo mission, Gore urged support and Congressional approval for the orbiting webcamera, noting that the $50 million project would both afford "a clearer view of our own world" and encourage "new levels of understanding" of the planet and its "natural and cultural systems."[25]

One of the most spectacular moments in webcamera-enabled telepresence took place in July of 1997, during the Mars Pathfinder mission. A remarkable stream of images, transmitted from the spacecraft itself and continually updated to the Mars Pathfinder website, stunned the Net world. Though not real-time in the strictest sense, the images of the Red Planet and its rock-strewn surface were fresh and clear enough to afford a convincing spatial sense of another world. More than 45 million viewers logged into the Jet Propulsion Laboratory sites during the first week of the operation—an Internet record—and over 80 million hits a day were recorded in the first week of the operations. One writer described the Pathfinder landing as a "defining moment for the Net," and compared it to similarly definitive moments in the evolution of other media—the outbreak of the Civil War and newspaper; Pearl Harbor and radio; the Kennedy assassination and television. Had these images not been so readily available on the Internet, it is likely that the Pathfinder landing would have remained an abstraction; television coverage of the event was typically brief and superficial.[26]

· · ·

"I'LL BE WATCHING YOU"

Webcameras do not always generate such enthusiasm. The specter of surveillance and the violation of privacy are real and vexing issues, and the possibility of Orwellian over-exposure has made many people anxious and fearful of webcameras. Ubiquitous

---

[25]Douglas E. Heimburger, "Talking at Innovation Summit, Gore Calls for an Earth-viewing Satellite," *The Tech* (17 March 1998). Gore's proposal was summarily dismissed by some as an exercise in "planetary navel-gazing" and a waste of taxpayer money. See Gabriel Schoenfeld, "Machines with a High Calling," *Wall Street Journal,* 6 July 1998, and Joe Sharkey, "Step Right Up and See Grass Grow and Paint Dry," *New York Times,* 22 March 1998.

[26]See NASA press release 24 June 1997; Amy Harmon, "Mars Pathfinder Landing was Defining Moment for Net," *New York Times,* 14 July 1997.

surveillance was the subject of the popular 1998 film *The Truman Show*, in which the feckless hero (Jim Carrey) is, since birth, the unwitting star in his own quotidian drama. Tiny cameras, ingeniously concealed in dashboard radios, lawnmowers, and bathroom mirrors, relay a perpetual stream of images to voyeurs in televisionland unbeknownst to him. Unfortunately, the technological aspects of the film are well within reach. Remarkably small cameras are available from security supply houses, along with tiny transmitters and dummy appliances in which to conceal them (one company gleefully advertises a wall clock, concealing a tiny video camera, as an ideal solution for keeping an eye on employees).

Then again, surveillance is nothing new. Video cameras are a   25
ubiquitous part of the urban landscape, so much so that we scarcely notice them; we are watched constantly, and have been for years. Supermarkets, convenience stores, elevators, automated teller machines, and office lobbies are all monitored via camera by persons unseen.[27] Public spaces such as tunnels and bridges, toll booths, college campuses, streets and public squares are, increasingly, also being watched. In the United Kingdom, home of Bentham's Panopticon, dozens of town centers are patrolled by video cameras, and Liverpool police recently began using a system of 20 cameras to produce full color, highly magnified nocturnal images.[28]

Surveillance has also moved beyond the visual. In 1996 Redlands, California, installed an "Urban Gunshot Location System," consisting of a matrix of sound sensors at intersections in the city enabling police to instantaneously detect and locate gunfire.[29] Of course, such applications are intended to serve the interest of public health and safety; but surveillance is by nature a clandestine act, and the risks of abuse, of invasions of personal and group privacy, are very real. Astonishing abuses have already been committed. Several years ago a minuscule hidden camera was discovered in a locker room of Boston's Sheraton Hotel, recording employees in various states of undress (the hotel claimed it suspected employee drug use); in California a J.C.

---

[27]See Phil Patton, "Caught," *WIRED 3.01*, and John Whalen, "You're Not Paranoid: They Really Are Watching You," *WIRED 3.03*.

[28]"You Don't Have to Smile," *Newsweek*, (17 July 1995), 52.

[29]It should be noted that local community activists have praised the system, which appears to have had a positive impact. See "Gunfire Detection Sensor Tested," *Trenton Times*, 7 January 1996.

Penney clerk filed suit when she learned that a guard had been zooming a ceiling-mounted security camera on her breasts.[30]

The growing popularity of webcameras has raised the prospect of similar mischief. At first it would seem like anger misplaced—protest should be aimed at the "glass ceiling domes of wine-dark opacity" of institutional surveillance, rather than the innocuous home-rigged webcamera aimed out a kitchen window.[31] Steve Mann has argued, institutions and the government have for years been "shooting" cameras at us; what webcameras enable is a chance to "shoot back" at Big Brother.[32] Then again, when one considers the enormous potential audience at the receiving end of a webcamera, the seemingly innocent device on the window ledge becomes a threat indeed—Little Brother is also watching, and he is hitched to a global network, indeed, persons in webcamera view are *theoretically* exposed to millions of users on the Net, not just a half-awake night guard at a security desk. Even if no one is watching—and most of the time no one is—the mere presence of a webcamera compromises personal space. In a feedback thread on the Trinity Square Street-Cam site in Colchester, United Kingdom, one woman wrote: "Big brother is watching us and we don't like it! We have no choice but to be in view going to work. . . . We are ANNOYED!"

Questions

1. What is "telepresence" (paragraph 11) according to Campanella? What other examples can you think of that he does not mention in the article? What do you think is so compelling about this kind of "seeing at a distance" and in what ways do you think it can be a positive factor in the uncertain world in which we live?

2. In what ways are webcameras and the cameras on cell phones, PDAs, and laptops "changing the way we think about time, space, and geographic distance" (paragraph 4)?

3. In paragraph 22, Campanella mentions Al Gore's desire to create "a full-disk portrait of the home planet." What is Google Earth? What does this view of the earth give us as members of a global society? How have you seen these images used? How do you think a tool like this changes our understanding of the world?

---

[30]"You Don't Have to Smile," *Newsweek* (17 July 1995).

[31]Patton, "Caught," *WIRED 3.01.*

[32]See Steve Mann, "Privacy Issues of Wearable Cameras Versus Surveillance Cameras," 1995 (http://www.wearcam.org/netcam_privacy_issues.html).

4. Why might webcameras generate concern? How might individual privacy be violated by the use of such cameras? Is our sense of security worth the possibility of violating an individual's rights?

5. Most people do not look carefully at footnotes; you may have noticed that there are quite a few connected with this article. Many of them suggest interesting websites to investigate that support Campanella's thesis or idea. The Web changes constantly so some of these sites may no longer be active, but check out a few of them and write a short essay about how they relate to his thesis.

Media Images and Violence
ANNE MARIE SEWARD BARRY

Anne Marie Seward Barry received her Ph.D. in Perceptual Psychology, Literature, and Film from Boston University. She is Associate Professor in the Communication Department at Boston College where she teaches courses in Visual Communication Theory, Visual Design, and Film as Communication. She has written several articles on visual communication, as well as The Advertising Portfolio *(1990) and* Visual Intelligence *(1997), where "Media Images and Violence" first appeared. In this essay, Professor Barry discusses the effects of television and video games on crime rates.*

Getting Started

Does watching violence on television have a direct effect on people's behavior? Do you think that playing video games that involve violent actions actually influences behavior? Why or why not? Do you play video or computer games yourself and if so, do they include violent elements? If they do, what is appealing about this aspect of them to you? Do you think people easily separate entertainment violence from real violence? Barry presents evidence that participating in such violence whether by watching or actually by playing does increase violent behavior. What do you think?

———————— ✦ ————————

In 1973, Joy, Kimball, and Zabrack studied the effect on a rural community in Canada when the television was first introduced there that year. Using two other similar communities as control groups in the double-blind study, they found that over a two-year period, aggression evidenced by biting, hitting and shoving had increased by 160 percent in the community where television had just been introduced. The increase, which affected boys and girls equally, was generally distributed rather than attributable to specific groups with an explainable predisposition to violence. The rate of violence in the two control communities remained the same.[1]

Leonard Eron and Rowell Huesmann, who have done several of the most comprehensive long-term studies in this area, followed 875 children from 1960 to 1981, from the point when they were 8 years old. After controlling for baseline intelligence, aggressiveness and socioeconomic status, they found that at age 8, the children who watched programming with violence in it, including Saturday morning cartoons, were more likely to be cited as meaner and more aggressive in their play by teachers. At 19, they were more likely to be in trouble with the law. At 30, they were more likely to be convicted of violent crimes and to be abusive toward their spouses and children. The amount of television children watched at age 8 predicted the amount of violence they perpetrated later in life. Second- and third-generation effects also appeared, as children who watched more television were more likely to punish their own children more severely than those who had watched less television.[2] Summarizing his research findings as chairman of the Commission on Violence and Youth of the American Psychological Association, Eron testified before Congress in 1992: "There is no longer any doubt that viewing a lot of televised violence is one of the causes of aggressive behavior, which may lead to crime and violence in the society." If media

---

[1] L. A. Joy, M. M. Kimball, M. L. Zabrack, "Television and Children's Aggressive Behavior," in *The Impact of Television: A Natural Experiment in Three Communities*, ed., T. M. Williams (Orlando, FL: Academic Press, 1986), 303–360.

[2] L. Rowell Huesmann, "Psychological Processes Promoting the Relation Between Exposure to Media Violence and Aggressive Behavior by the Viewer," *Journal of Social Issues* 42, no. 3 (1986): 125–139.

See also: L. Rowell Huesmann and Leonard D. Eron, *Television and the Aggressive Child* (Hillsdale, NJ: Lawrence Erlbaum, 1986), 45–80; Leonard D. Eron and L. Rowell Huesmann, "The Control of Aggressive Behavior by Changes in Attitudes, Values, and the Conditions of Learning," *Advances in the Study of Aggression* (Orlando, FL: Academic Press, 1984), 139–171; Leonard D. Eron, "Parent-Child Interaction, Television Violence, and Aggression of Children," *American Psychologist* 37, no. 2 (1982): 197–211; Eron, Leonard D. and L. R. Huesmann. "Adolescent Agression and Television." *Annals of the New York Academy of Sciences* 347 (1980): 319–331.

violence is reduced, he testified, "fully 10 percent of interpersonal aggression would be eliminated within the society."[3]

Brandon Centerwall, in studying the relationship between the introduction of television and homicide rates among whites in the United States, Canada, and South Africa, used the advent of television and the rise in crime rates in the U.S. and Canada after the introduction of television to accurately predict homicide rates in South Africa. After the introduction of television in the 1950s, the homicide rate doubled in the United States and Canada within ten to fifteen years. During the same period in South Africa, where television was banned until 1975, the homicide rate dropped by 7 percent. After the introduction of television into South Africa, however, homicide rates increased 130 percent between 1975 and 1987.[4]

In explaining his findings, Centerwall notes that he found none of the alternative explanations of economic growth, civil unrest, age distribution, urbanization, alcohol consumption, capital punishment, or availability of firearms satisfactory. Recognizing that blacks in South Africa lived under very different circumstances from those in the United States, for example, Centerwall used statistics only for white crimes. Knowing statistics can be a murky business at best, he used only homicide figures, which are highly reliable. Antiwar unrest and civil-rights activity in the United States were not paralleled in Canada, yet the U.S. and Canada showed the same rise in violent crimes. South Africa was comparable in economic development, book, newspaper, radio and cinema industries, so that television could be isolated as a factor from other media influences. In all three countries homicides rose within five to seven years and doubled within fifteen to twenty years—the amount of time, Centerwall believes, required for television influence to come of age.

The pattern he uncovered has held up consistently in every   5
regional, racial, and international comparison Centerwall has made. Although he does not count out other factors that contribute to violence, his conclusion is that if "television technology had never been developed, there would today be 10,000 fewer

---

[3]Quoted in "Does TV Violence Cause Real Violence?" in Violence on Television: Special Report by the Editors of TV Guide (New York: *TV Guide,* 1992), 6; and in "The New Face of Television Violence," in Violence on Television: Special Report by the Editors of TV Guide (New York: *TV Guide,* 1992), 6.

[4]Brandon Centerwall, "Television and Violence: the Scale of the Problem and Where We Go from Here," *Journal of the American Medical Association* 267, no. 22 (1992): 3,060–3,061.

homicides each year in the United States, 70,000 fewer rapes, and 700,000 fewer injurious assaults."[5]

. . .

VIDEO GAMES

As socially destructive as television and film violence can be, many believe that they pale in comparison to video games, which reward a "penchant for control, competition and destruction," and which actively involve players—overwhelmingly males between 13 and 30 years old—within the violence. While research has found that girls do not enjoy video games, boys find them to be the most psychologically arousing medium. It is also the one on which they concentrate most intensely.[6] Unlike TV or film, video games are intentionally interactive, and players must participate in causing the violence, usually winning the most points for the most outrageously cruel acts.

Since 1990, video games have surpassed all toys as the most popular present for children, representing a $7 billion industry in the United States. Traditionally, the most violent ones are the most popular. In 1993, for example, it was estimated that 75 percent of video games relied on violent content: "Mortal Kombat," then America's top-grossing arcade game, featured heroes decapitating people, ripping out their hearts, or tearing off their heads. During that Christmas season under public pressure, Toys "R" Us, Bradlees, and FAO Schwartz pulled off the shelves Sega's "Night Trap"—which featured vampires who stalk women, drill holes in their necks, and hang them from meat hooks. Soon thereafter Nintendo put out a slightly sanitized version of "Mortal Kombat," but when it started to lose money, and when the company received thousands of telephone calls and letters from young people demanding the more graphic version where the winner can gain extra points by ripping out a victim's spinal column, they rereleased the more violent version. Even though video game makers have followed network and cable's lead in agreeing to label their games for violence and sex content, and have formed panels to monitor violence in their respective media, labeling signals only a forewarning of content, not a change in content itself.

---

[5]Ibid. See also Brandon Centerwall, "Exposure to Television as a Risk Factor for Violence," *American Journal of Epidemiology* 129 (1989): 643–652.

[6]Robert W. Kubey and Reed Larson, "The Use and Experience of the New Video Media Among Children and Adolescents," *Communication Research* 17 (February 1990): 107–130.

An important part of mental maps evolving from media, video games reinforce the concept of violent action as an appropriate response when threatened, and they condition the player to respond quickly and without hesitation by rewarding the most violent play alternatives. Research comparing more and less aggressive versions of video game play, television program content, and dart game play, has shown that any activity performed in a more aggressive mode increased reported hostility[7] —an observation that reconfirms what we learned in the Gulf War—that playing video games is very effective rehearsal for real-life responses. Childhood play is the best training ground for adult action.

Like violence or cigarettes, video games can also be addictive. "Doom," a multiplayer video game in which players can destroy monsters or each other with chain saws or shotguns, for example, was introduced to the market place in 1993 by giving away the first episode on the computer Internet, and then selling the subsequent ones once the customer got hooked. Acknowledging that their marketing strategy was similar to the way drugs are dealt, the Id software company increased profits from $1.5 million to $10 million within their first year, introducing "Doom II" in 1994.[8]

In 1993, it was estimated that on average, students with computers spent 1.5 hours a day interacting with computer games. By 1995, Nintendo had developed a 32-bit (the higher the bit the higher the resolution and the realism) game system called "Virtual Boy" with virtual reality technology which immerses players in a three-dimensional stereo-surround world with high-resolution images; concurrently, film elements also moved into interactive CD-ROM formats with titles like "Corpse Killer," directed by John Lafia who also did *Child's Play 2*, and *Under the Killing Moon*, which allowed viewers to use computers to direct the plot. By the end of 1995, "Mortal Kombat 3" was available on shelves in a 32-bit version, and Nintendo had developed a 64-bit system for release in 1996. As violent computer games become faster and more three-dimensional, as if players were actually participating in a movie, the line between fantasy and reality gets thinner, and the potential increases for developing a generation addicted to even higher resolution violence in reality.

10

---

[7]P. J. Favaro, *The Effects of Video Game Play on Mood, Physiological Arousal and Psychomotor Performance.* Hofstra University, New York, 1983.

[8]Peter H. Lewis, "Virtual Mayhem and Real Profits," *New York Times* 3 September 1994, 35, 37.

Although most of the impact of such visual media experience cannot be linearly correlated with specific violent acts, there can be little doubt that the cumulative influence of hours of television watching, video game play and movie mayhem cannot help but influence the perceptual process by which human beings incorporate the world around them into the essence of themselves, and in turn affect the social order as a whole.

CONCLUSION

Film and television are media particularly suited to emotional learning because their language is experientially based. Verbal language facility is cognitively based and takes a great deal of time to master—we learn to read gradually, becoming more and more proficient over years of practice, expanding our thinking into ever-widening circles of complexity and sophistication. As we grow in verbal ability and read more widely, we become aware of different perspectives, of differing philosophies, of false prophets and charlatans, of the multigrained complexity of truth seeking.

Visual media, however, presents a view of reality that simply seems to be there. The world of visual media announces itself to our senses as reality, so that before we are capable of understanding that it is a manipulated and artificially constructed world, before we become experientially sophisticated enough to judge the nuances of manufactured visual "realities," we accept these self-contained visual worlds as true.

As we add each media experience to our understanding of the world, an image of how the world works grows within us, and, as Boulding suggested, it is this image of the world that determines our actions. Everything we do is relative to this holistic image that acts as an open system, actively seeking invariance, searching for the patterns that will help us make sense of our environment.

There is at present a double norm within the society: one that respects human value, and one that dominates visual media. It is a very adult, very sophisticated thinker who can separate out these never wholly distinct worlds and understand the nuances of their interrelationship. For the child, as for the many adults who write to their favorite soap opera characters as if they actually existed in real life, these worlds begin as one and only gradually, with a great deal of help from thinking adults do they separate into alternate worlds.

Even films that seem tame and acceptable, like Spielberg's *Jurassic Park*, reflect society's double-think in relation to children and media violence. Despite the fact that the film was made clearly with a children's audience in mind, for example—as evidenced by its ubiquitous marketing tie-ins with McDonald's and toy manufacturers—the film carried a PG-13 warning because of several intensely violent scenes. Ironically, even the rating itself served to increase allure for the children's audience, always hungry to understand the "adult" world. Spielberg himself would not allow his own children to see his film; yet clearly other children's parents did: gross domestic earnings surpassed $300 million and made it one of the top-grossing films of all time.[9]

Even if the violent behavior of children and adults can in specific instances be directly traced to specific media effects, it is clear that the major contribution of media is to the way we see the world. This world image begins to be formed with our earliest experiences, as we read our parents' expressions and mimic them. When visual media is introduced into this world, it contributes to emotional memory, which is never erased. In this way, television and film have contributed substantially to a perceptual climate in which violence has come to be seen as normal simply by virtue of its ubiquity. It is this aspect of media's public trust that caused Ted Turner to observe to a congressional committee in 1993 that "television violence is the single most significant factor contributing to violence in America" and to proclaim himself and other media moguls as murderers.[10]

As our understanding of perceptual process becomes clearer and the preponderance of evidence correlating social and media violence grows, the argument over whether the consumption of violent images causes violence or whether the tendency to violence in people is merely legitimated and glamorized by the pervasiveness of violence in the media seems more and more naive. Both contribute substantially to the picture in our minds that determines the way we perceive reality, the way we interpret the past, and how we project our perception into the future through analogy.

Today the picture that millions of young people have in their minds is filled with a holistic view of violence both as entertainment and as an unavoidable fact of everyday life. In the end, the combination of the two pervasive attitudes—the entertainment value of violence and its inevitability—have both worked to desensitize people to violence and rob them of a sense of control

---

[9]*Entertainment Weekly,* 9 July 1995, 101.

[10]"TV's Turner," 12.

over their own behavioral options. At the same time, practical problem-solving skills are reduced to the lowest level by media's selling of violence as the preferred solution, and violence is glamorized and promoted as a number one entertainment option.

When we are tempted to shrug off the effects of media violence   20 because we ourselves have become inured to it by saying that violence has always been a part of the human scene, or by resigning ourselves to adapting to its pervasiveness in our everyday lives, it is wise to remember that we ourselves are responsible for this world. As Myriam Medzian points out, at least thirty-three different societies exist today in which both war and interpersonal violence are extremely rare.[11] Thus violence is far from inevitable, unless we choose to make it so by promoting it. The "New Violence" in media is the harbinger of a new American culture characterized by low interpersonal involvement and by the attitude that violence is an apparently suitable solution to interpersonal conflict, a source of entertainment and enjoyment, and an effective vehicle for personal and social expression. Acceptance of violence is now a deep, shared experience of the young and a way of seeing formed by repeated exposure to media.

Questions

1. Read Brandon Centerwall's conclusion as quoted in the Barry essay (paragraph 5). Is this an acceptable conclusion to his research? You may want to read more about his research before you make your decision. Do you think the study should have taken other factors into account? How does this study indicate how important many people think that images are in creating one's behavior and one's understanding of the world?

2. What evidence does Barry provide to suggest that video games may present an even bigger threat to society than television? In what ways are our interactions with video games different from our interactions with television?

3. Take an informal survey in your class to find out if more males than females play video games. What games do students in your class prefer? About how many hours a day/a week do they play video games? Do your findings correspond to those of the author? What do your findings tell you about the role of video games in our culture?

4. Barry says that "verbal language facility is cognitively based and takes a great deal of time to master" but that we accept the world of visual media to be

---

[11]Robert R. Holt, "Converting the War System to a Peace System," cited in Meriam Medzian, *Boys Will Be Boys* (New York: Doubleday Anchor Books, 1991), 76.

true before we can even understand it (paragraphs 11–12). Do you agree with this statement and do you think that we understand reading words or seeing images differently? Does either one seem more powerful to you?

5. Write an essay in which you take a position on the following issue: Laws should be passed restricting the amount of violence permitted on television and in video games. Material that does not meet the criteria should be prohibited from being sold in stores or on the Internet. Do you agree or disagree? Use your own experiences or those you have read about to support your position.

Notable Quotables: Why Images Become Icons
THOMAS HINE

Thomas Hine writes about history, culture, and design. He has taught at the University of Pennsylvania and Temple University. From 1973–1996 Hine was the architecture and design critic for the Philadelphia Inquirer. *He is a frequent contributor to the* Atlantic Monthly, Martha Stewart Living, *and the* New York Times. *Among Hine's many books are* I Want That: How We All Become Shoppers *(2002),* The Rise and Fall of the American Teenager *(1999/2000), and* The Total Package: The Secret History and Hidden Meanings of Boxes, Bottles, Cases and Other Persuasive Containers *(1997). His article "Notable Quotables: Why Images Become Icons" appeared in the* New York Times. *It deals with the ways in which "advertising, news and entertainment media have created and disseminated a stock of images whose potency transcends local boundaries. . ."*

Getting Started

When we think about the images that surround us through their use in advertising, news, and entertainment media, we usually do not think of high culture and images from art history classes, but that is exactly what Thomas Hines tells us are imitated, parodied, and alluded to all around us in our everyday lives. Where have you seen Leonardo's *Mona Lisa* outside of a museum or art book? How about Edvard Munch's *The Scream* or Auguste Rodin's *The Thinker?* What other works of art can you think of that have been used to sell a product or idea? What images from more recent times form a common "universal" experience? Which images do you think will last through time to define this decade? this century?

—————————— ✦ ——————————

Tired of the same old telephone ring? Now you can purchase, through a special television offer, a device that plays the first four portentous notes of Beethoven's Fifth Symphony, complete with lyrics. "AN-swer the PHONE," sings the electronic baritone. "AN-swer the PHONE!"

Not interested? Perhaps you would like a Mona Lisa liquid-soap dispenser. The plastic pump emerges from the top of her head. Or how about Michelangelo's David as a refrigerator magnet set, available at many museum shops. You can dress him in a cowboy hat and blue jeans. Then, as the mood strikes, you can remove the hat—or the blue jeans.

There are countless examples: Piero della Francesca computer-mouse pads, roly-poly toys based on "The Scream" by Edvard Munch, software that turns out print like Miro's handwriting. Bookstore ads feature a robot mimicking Rodin's "Thinker." The Shaker hymn "Simple Gifts" was adapted by Aaron Copland in "Appalachian Spring," whose version became the theme for television's "CBS Reports" and now is used to sell Oldsmobiles, probably not what the obsessively simplifying Shakers had in mind.

Using well-known images, snatches of music, movie scenes or news events isn't simply the province of schlock merchants, advertisers and art directors. Individuals do it too. You'll hear people sing the "dah-duh-dah-duh, dah-duh-dah-duh" theme of the television series "The Twilight Zone" to highlight a weird situation. Or, more than half a century after "Gone With the Wind," they'll imitate Rhett Butler's frank declaration that he doesn't give a damn. By making the statement in someone else's voice, the speaker usually hopes to evade some responsibility for what was said. What's happening here? The unintended consequences of Art History 101, along with too much television? The inability of our culture to say anything new? Did Forrest Gump have something to do with it?

Mostly, the answer is that imitating images, sounds and gestures is part of the way humans have always communicated. But this used to be local: a matter of copying the neighbor who sews well or parodying a cousin who walks funny. What's special now is that the advertising, news and entertainment media have created

5

and disseminated a stock of images whose potency transcends local boundaries, and computer technology has made it easier for people to use and manipulate them.

A few years ago, someone like Keith Haring could be writing on subway walls one moment, have his radiant babies and copulating crowds seen throughout the world soon after—and then see his work knocked off almost immediately. Now, someone with a low-end computer and no artistic skill can access and manipulate creations that range in time and medium from the cave paintings at Lascaux to last week's "Seinfeld."

Although we all use and understand this language of image, sound and gesture, few of us give it much conscious thought. Recently, I had to explore this dimension of our cultural literacy while working on a new CD-ROM version of Bartlett's Familiar Quotations. I was responsible for finding examples of predominantly nonverbal expression that are regularly used, reused, parodied and appropriated. There are 23,000 literary quotations in this edition, not all of them familiar ones, so my fewer than 500 nonverbal expressions probably had to be a lot more familiar than those.

It was time to round up, for the first time, the usual suspects.

Here was Botticelli's Venus, surfing on her scallop. And Marilyn Monroe, skirt flying high, above a subway grate in "The Seven Year Itch." (I categorized both under Women, Love and Sex and Transportation.)

Here are Whistler's Mother and Rembrandt's "Syndics" fresh   10
from the cigar box. And Brahms's Lullaby, Mendelssohn's Wedding March, Chopin's "Funeral March" and other music for all occasions.

Clearly, "high" Western culture is not dead. Quite the contrary. We're swimming in it. We live our lives in a great sea of communication and manipulation, where fragments of high culture are constantly being repeated, combined, repackaged and adapted.

But this iconographic reservoir is also multicultural. It contains the many-armed Shiva, doing his cosmic dance, several different images of the Buddha in contemplation, and Hokusai's wave breaking with Mount Fuji in the background.

Photographed from space, the blue-green Earth floated in the dark. Posed or not, Alfred Eisenstaedt's couple kissed spontaneously in Times Square as World War II ended. John Paul Filo's Kent State picture of a grieving girl sums up one Vietnam-era tragedy, and the endlessly analyzed Zapruder film of Dallas in 1963 remains at least as enigmatic as the Mona Lisa.

It was quickly apparent that though my list included its share of masterpieces, it was far from the best that had been painted, sculptured, composed and photographed over time. It's an un-likely mixture of high and low culture, of tragedy and banality, transcendence and kitsch. Stonehenge, a Cadillac tail fin, "Amaz-ing Grace," Monet's waterlilies, Ansel Adams's Yosemite—all these incomparables assume a sort of equality as popular icons.

Few of them have achieved this status for purely formal rea-   15
sons. Van Gogh's "Sunflowers" serves as an icon not merely of lonely, mad creativity but also of how much people are willing to pay for a picture.

Tchaikovsky's Piano Concerto was made familiar by the star power of Van Cliburn, while Rossini's "William Tell" Overture got a big assist from the Lone Ranger. For many, Wagner's "Ride of the Valkyries" evokes the flight of helicopters in Francis Ford Cop-pola's film "Apocalypse Now." Others think of Elmer Fudd vowing to "kill the wabbit" in the cartoon short "What's Opera, Doc?"

Nearly everyone I talked to mentioned Leonardo's portrait first. And this nomination was frequently followed by the round, yellow smiley face. Is this perhaps a distillation of what people see in Leonardo's painting? Moreover, the smiley face has had an unusually abrupt switch from being used sincerely to ironically. Part of the appeal of Mona Lisa may be that you don't know which of these attitudes is behind her smile.

The touch of fingers between God and Adam on the Sistine Chapel ceiling was, likewise, often linked with what seems an in-tentional imitation, the touch of boy and alien in "E. T. the Extra-Terrestrial." What people were remembering was not the film itself but the print advertisement, where the touch was superimposed on a full moon.

The current ubiquity of Munch's "Scream," painted in 1893, owes a lot to its mimickry by Macaulay Culkin in the advertising for "Home Alone." While many people knew of the painting be-fore the movie, it would not have been a familiar quotation 15 years ago. Now it is so popular that newspaper cartoonists feel as comfortable with it as Pinocchio's growing and branching nose, indicating dishonesty, and the Titanic tilting rakishly into its ice-berg, an emblem of complacency followed by disaster.

After the Oklahoma City bombing, Rob Rogers, a nationally   20
syndicated cartoonist, grafted the face of Munch's screamer to the body of the farm couple in Grant Wood's "American Gothic" and threw in the Grim Reaper for good measure. This iconographic triple play spoke powerfully of terror in the heartland.

Since its enlistment to sell a comedy film, "The Scream" is reverting to its original meaning as an expression of *fin de siecle* angst, though more as a pop icon than as a work of art.

Which works become icons is, to some degree, accidental. With paintings and sculptures, those in large or much-visited cities clearly have an advantage, though inclusion in a standard textbook can overcome an obscure location. Use in a memorable context makes a big difference. The opening fanfare from Richard Strauss's "Also Sprach Zarathustra," for example, was both popularized and transformed by its use in the film "2001: A Space Odyssey."

But these visual and aural quotations are not famous merely for being famous. They all say something, though not necessarily what the creator had in mind. What matters most is what those who quote a work find there.

Rodin's "Thinker," itself an allusion to Michelangelo, went through a complex evolution. And after seeing it mimicked by Sylvester Stallone on the cover of Vanity Fair, Dobie Gillis on Nick at Nite and a robot in a bookstore ad, we may have lost our ability to recognize the strangeness and originality Rodin's contemporaries saw in it. Yet its fusion of contemplation with potential energy still comes through. Its embodiment of muscular contemplation has helped shape the way we think about ourselves.

The famous wooden portrait head of Nefertiti is, for example, 25 one of the most familiar images to have come to us from ancient Egypt. But much of its appeal is that it departs from many of the conventions of Egyptian art and presents a woman who is, in 20th-century terms, glamorous. She speaks across three and a half millenniums, if not as the woman next door, at least as a model in Vogue.

Rubens, by contrast, is commonly judged a great artist, but neither his fleshy figures nor the epic compositions of which they are a part mirror contemporary concerns. His images are sometimes quoted to demonstrate changing standards of beauty but little else.

The Parthenon, perhaps the most quoted building in the history of architecture, surely meant something different to the Athenians who built it about 2,400 years ago than to the Americans who, during the second quarter of the 19th century, turned it into banks, schools and state capitols. But the architects of the Greek revival were not simply recycling an interesting look. They thought it had meaning for a second-generation democracy.

Works that are little more than irritating—Merv Griffin's theme for "Jeopardy," for instance—can become quotations if they fit the right situation. Because it is played on the program in the midst of a great thicket of commercials that precede the game's denouement, the jingle has been used by ballpark organists to complain about pointless delay. There's plenty of that in baseball games; the music provides an evocative analogue.

In a culture that uses up imagery incessantly, recycling is inevitable. Introductory art-history courses tend to consist of compendiums of familiar quotations. And even if you never took the course, the designers and art directors who are producing the imagery surely did.

Most designers keep illustrated source books of design history close at hand. One result is that a much-anthologized image like Herbert Matter's 1935 Pontresina travel poster—with a close-cropped, diagonally placed photograph of a skier in goggles—is frequently imitated in advertising and editorial layouts. The image itself is not really familiar to most people, but its evocation of a cold, modern sexiness has become so in countless variations.

Part of what's involved in quotation and appropriation is just plain laziness. The images that get quoted are often not the best, merely the closest to hand. John Bartlett had it right more than 140 years ago when he said he saw his work demonstrating the "obligations our language owes to various authors for numerous phrases and familiar quotations which have become 'household words.'" What familiarity breeds isn't contempt. It's reuse.

There are whole genres of quotations that constitute a kind of language of cliché. One important group consists of images that evoke specific locales, like the Eiffel Tower, the Manhattan skyline, Big Ben and the Houses of Parliament, the onion domes of St. Basil's and the Hollywood sign. These were popularized largely by old movies, which would often use the same stock footage of a landmark to signal the intended locale of a film that had been shot on the back lot in Burbank or Culver City. Now people travel largely to see the places they've seen in pictures.

Some of these are more than mere scene setters. The shield-like Beverly Hills sign speaks of great wealth defending itself against intruders. And John Ford transformed the dramatic rock formations of Monument Valley from a real place into an epic landscape where events assume a mythic scale. Today it's a great spot to sell a Toyota.

Even people can be turned into quotations if they acquire strong associations. Albert Einstein, for instance, epitomizes pure braininess, often as a figure of ridicule. Che Guevara in his beret with the star on it is literally an icon, a quasi-religious depiction of the romantic revolutionary. And Winston Churchill and Richard Nixon, with their distinctive V-for-victory hand gestures, offer contrasting visions of men trying to win.

While many of the most memorable news photos and documentary film segments are tied to a single, dramatic event, the ones that keep reappearing make universal statements. The scene of the lone protester confronting the tank in Tiananmen Square is indelibly associated with the 1989 uprising in China. 35

More than that, it was a striking image of the individual confronting power, and, at least momentarily, confusing it. Although the image has rarely been used outside its Chinese context, I included it on the CD-ROM because the situation is likely to be repeated over and over, though probably not in so visually powerful a way.

Likewise, I went out on a limb with the most recent image on the Bartlett's disk: footage shot from a helicopter of a white Bronco on a Los Angeles freeway, complete with television reporters speculating on what would happen next. The televised car chase was itself a kind of quotation of the many thousands of chases that have filled the television screen during the last half century. Like Jack Ruby's on-camera murder of Lee Harvey Oswald, it was a case in which something we've seen all our lives as fiction suddenly becomes real.

The O. J. Simpson case will not be the last media meltdown, but it does seem a definitive one. I included the car chase because it was as close as our society comes to a universal experience. When future generations talk about our time, the white Bronco will, I suspect, be one of the visuals.

Questions

1. Reread the article, underlining every cultural reference (art work, film, logo, piece of music, or news event) that Hine mentions. Identify them and discuss where they come from, what they look like, and where and how you have seen them used outside the context in which they were originally created.

2. Hine introduces the idea of a visual or aural quotation in this article. What is a visual quotation? What is an aural quotation? What examples of each does Hine provide?

3. Hine writes about images that evoke specific locales, like the Eiffel Tower, the Manhattan skyline, the Houses of Parliament, and the Hollywood sign, and suggests that people now travel largely to see the places that they have seen in pictures. Can you think of other visual quotations that become

clichés representing a specific locale? Have you ever traveled to see a place that you have seen only in pictures? Did the location live up to the image of it? Which experience, the image or the actual place, remained as a more vivid memory to you? Why?

4. In the last two paragraphs, Hine describes an event that he thinks will become iconic as a cultural reference that will last through time. Do you think he was correct in his assessment about that particular image? Why or why not?

5. Write an essay in which you choose a visual quotation that "when future generations talk about our time ... will ... be one of the visuals" (paragraph 38). Think of an image that could be thought of as "a universal experience." Describe the image and explain why you think this visual quotation will pass the test of time and to some degree define who we are today.

Speaking Brand
ROBIN LANDA

Robin Landa is Distinguished Professor in the Department of Design at Kean University in New Jersey, where she has coordinated the BFA in Visual Communications degree program and teaches courses in Graphic Design and Advertising. Ms. Landa has lectured widely on the subject of branding and on visual thinking and creativity. Among her many books are Graphic Design Solutions *(2000),* Advertising by Design: Creating Visual Communication with Graphic Impact *(2004),* and Designing Brand Experience: Creating Powerful Integrated Brand Solutions *(2005).*

Getting Started

Think about the following corporate names or products: McDonald's, Nike, iPod, MGM, Energizer batteries, or Columbian coffee. What corporate logos or images do you associate with each of them? What other brand logos or images come to mind as you think about this topic? How important do you think a brand's image is to its success? Look around you and notice how many people are wearing brand names where they can be seen? Why do you think that people often prefer to buy a branded product even if it is more expensive than a generic product?

◆

Lego™. Google®. Levi's®. Sony®. Hershey's®. Mr. Clean™. Juan Valdez™. It's hard to imagine a time when products or services didn't have brand names; people simply bought crackers from a cracker barrel, not knowing the name of the manufacturer. Before the U.S. Civil War, bulk goods were sold by weight from barrels and open containers. Most products, with the exception of some tobacco companies, were not offered as "brand names" as we know them today. They were simply sold as commodities.

The Civil War economy created a ripe climate for technological advances and for the start of a "packaged goods" society. Soldiers needed canned goods and uniforms. People began to buy ready-made clothing, packaged foods, and shoes. More and more, people were drawn away from commodities sold from barrels to attractively packaged goods that promised "sealed freshness" and more sanitary products.

To meet this need, companies had to find ways to promote their "brand names" to customers through more earnest visual identities using logos, pictorial icons, distinctive colors, and unique slogans. Attractive packaging from labels to boxes to wrappers supported the effort and allowed for more focused promotion through advertising. Patent medicine manufacturers and tobacco companies led the way with proprietary names and uniquely decorative labels and packaging.

The folding box was an innovation that enabled the cereal industry to flourish. By putting a commodity in a small box, manufacturers could now inject personality into the product by adding information to demonstrate its benefit and a story to increase its appeal. This turned raw goods into desirable products and proved highly profitable. Part of this success relied on the creation of a recognizable visual and verbal identity that could be associated with a particular product.

Uneeda Biscuit™, a packaged brand name cracker made by the National Biscuit Company (now Nabisco) hired the advertising agency N. W. Ayer & Son to create an integrated branding campaign for their product. The agency suggested the brand name, the "spokescharacter"—a little boy in a raincoat to suggest air-tight freshness and crispness—along with a slogan, "Lest you forget, we say it yet, Uneeda Biscuit." This historic campaign, launched in 1899, was the first multi-million dollar advertising campaign; it would change everyone's perception of the critical role of branding and advertising.

This approach appealed to corporate executives and owners who understood the role that visual communications played in driving consumers to their brands and creating a loyal customer base. Manufacturers quickly realized that using visual devices such as logos or unique characters might differentiate their goods and appeal to a burgeoning consumer class. In using a visual identity, any manufacturer's goal was threefold—to differentiate its product, to ensure a consumer would judge the product's value and good quality by the looks of its visual identity, and to endear its product in order to foster brand loyalty.

Whether it was the meticulously planned campaign of the launch of Uneeda Biscuit or the early advertising success story of Lydia Pinkham's Vegetable Compound, brand manufacturers realized how integrated branding programs could stimulate sales. Advertising for Lydia Pinkham's Vegetable Compound, a tincture of alcohol and roots for women's ailments, greatly increased sales. In the 1880's, when Pinkham's son decided that he did not need to spend any more money advertising since sales were very good, he stopped advertising. Sales precipitously dropped.

The overall effect of integrated images—logo, icon, symbol, label, package and advertising—was to create brand names that people wanted, names that were impressive and reliable, even names that they could *trust* to provide freshness, quality or sanitary packaging. An illustrated portrait of a man dressed in traditional Quaker attire is the registered trademark of one of the earliest American brands—Quaker® Oatmeal. According to the Quaker Oats' website: "It all started in the late 1800s when three different Midwest milling companies had independently begun to process and sell high-quality oats for the consumer, giving the American family a product that would be superior in quality to the oats sold in open barrels at general stores." To the impressionable American audience at the turn of the twentieth century, this Quaker icon symbolized the company's values of honesty, thrift and purity, and earmarked Quaker Oats as an authentic and appealing brand. People wanted brands that would make their lives easier and more pleasurable; they wanted brands that would make them more attractive and socially acceptable.

One might think that today, when consumers in all industrialized nations are so very sophisticated or perhaps even immune to advertising, utilizing advertising icons (or any advertising) might be a fruitless attempt to persuade consumers or influence their beliefs about a brand. Yet, that does not seem to be the case.

There is a universal appeal to well-conceived iconic images that can level economic and educational ranks, and communicate across language barriers. In the U.S., well over one hundred 10 languages are spoken. However, one language common to most every American resident is national visual communications: TV spots, brand images, logos, and web sites. Here, we all speak McDonald's™ golden arches, Nike's™ Swoosh, the Energizer Bunny™, or the image of Juan Valdez™. In the early 1960s, a print ad for the Volkswagen Beetle™ (created by the creative advertising agency DDB) simply depicted a Coca-Cola® bottle on one side of the two-page spread and a VW Beetle on the other with a headline declaring the Beetle and the Coke bottle as "2 shapes known the world over." The ubiquity of flourishing images makes them common to us all.

Even when people belong to different political parties, read different authors, practice different faiths, and have different income levels, we all see the same brand images and commercials; audiences are democratized by brand identities, brand advertising, and even social-cause advertising. We all know what Ronald McDonald™ or Smokey Bear looks like; we all feel compelled to "Just Do It"; and we now fully realize the urgency of the appeal: "Friends Don't Let Friends Drive Drunk." Brand and advertising visuals and icons are ubiquitous. To paraphrase James B. Twitchell, professor, advertising historian and critic, "The only way to avoid advertising is to close your eyes."

Speaking in shorthand, ad icons, brand logos and advertising taglines compress corporate identities and essences into singular visuals or catchphrases. When a viewer sees Tony the Tiger™, that viewer sees a friendly recognizable cartoon tiger, a drawn icon that represents a commodity—sugared cereal. Tony the Tiger's affable personality is transferred to the cereal.

Brand and advertising icons are no different, in theory, than other visual symbols; they represent something larger than themselves. Brand and advertising icons are *larger* than the products or services they signify. McDonald's golden arches can provide comfort to many and in a post 9/11 world provide the reassurance that business is running as usual. The portrait of Betty Crocker™ is intended to provoke an emotional response in a female homemaker by encouraging her to feel that she can be an efficient yet congenial homemaker. The iPod dancer can make us feel that our own musical choices are unique.

Even the most familiar trademarks are revised to stay current with the times, but we also constantly see new and effective brand personalities such as the iPod dancer. The creation of new brand identities is a dynamic process that reflects the wisdom in communications theorist Marshall McCluhan's statement: "Historians and archaeologists will one day discover that the ads of our time are the richest and most faithful reflections that any society ever made of its entire range of activities."

Certainly, not all "spokescharacters," advertising images, or brand logos capture their target audience's interest, or endear the brand to the audience. What makes some take that leap from brand language to common vernacular is, in great part, mysterious. Some images transcend their original functions, becoming universal and emblematic of emotions or ideas: for example, the iPod dancers, the Nike Swoosh or Rosie the Riveter.

15

When women workers were desperately needed in wartime industries, from 1942 to 1944, the War Advertising Council's Women in War Jobs campaign introduced Rosie the Riveter, a fictional character who symbolized "patriotic womanpower." (Rosie is illustrated as an attractive woman with hair covered by a red bandana, in a blue work shirt, flexing her bicep.) Until World War II, millions of American women (who could afford to stay home) had never worked outside their homes. Working outside their homes was a new concept that needed a powerful visual symbol and Rosie provided that. According to The Advertising Council, Rosie the Riveter is the most successful advertising recruitment campaign in American history, which helped to recruit more than two million women into the workforce. No longer used to recruit, images of Rosie the Riveter linger on T-shirts, lunch boxes, posters and many other surfaces, still symbolizing womanpower. Postwar, when American men returned home from war, a reverse campaign effort had to be utilized to push women out of the workforce; the campaign advised women to do the patriotic thing and return home, with headlines such as "Good Work, Sister."

What makes the "Michelin Man" appealing to a wide range of people from business tycoons to grocery clerks? Why is it that political pundits in statements and speeches still use Wendy's™ former 1984 catchphrase "Where's the beef?" as a metaphor for something short in substance? How could a simple sock-puppet, the Pets.com mascot, capture the hearts of so many demographically diverse Americans? Why do such a diverse group of people come to trust the Apple trademark? The answer is that whether from different religions or regions, with languages or experiences—we all speak brand.

When the Apple iPod dancer image "look" was co-opted for use in guerilla street posters to make political statements about the Abu Ghraib prison abuse, it was clearly a case of using commonly understood pop vernacular and distinctive images to increase the reach of communication. We recognize them; we know what they stand for. We all "get" them.

Besides offering us a common popular language, brand icons, brand identities, and advertising offer something else. We, the consumers, borrow some of a brand's panache when we buy it or use it. We share its values, as if it were a human being capable of a value system. We want the lifestyle a brand represents; whether it is the Betty Crocker lifestyle or the sexy freedom of the iPod dancers. We want to have fun like the people dancing in the ads, or be as patriotic as Rosie. As noted humorist Erma Bombeck once quipped, "In general, my children refused to eat anything that hadn't danced on TV."

Often, we may simply be attracted to the graphic impact of the brand identity or ad visual. (Class and cultural associations form, in part, due to celebrity endorsements and positioning of the brand in a particular television program or a film.) Certainly, there are class and cultural associations that lead to brand association and "membership." Buying luxury brands can signify that the owner has arrived, has status. Or, if one "wears" the white beauty of an iPod, then one can express his or her values and aesthetic taste through brand use. 20

If we fully understood why anything from an ad icon to a political candidate clicks with an audience, then every brand or candidate would be successful. People's behavior, as individuals or in groups—often inscrutable—is far too complicated to be fully understood. Of course, most branding professionals understand enough about their respective audiences to create numerous effective brand campaigns.

Then again, some brand identities and advertising visuals engage us more successfully than others. At times, they engage us so well that we fully *buy into* their spirited appeal, regardless of the danger of the product being glorified. One only need think of the highly unfortunate effectiveness of the Marlboro Man™ brand image that linked smoking with machismo and rugged independence. Leo Burnett, whose agency created the Marlboro Man campaign strongly believed in personifying brands with characters; they also created Charlie the Tuna for Star-Kist and Morris the cat for Nine Lives, among others.

With watchdog consumer groups and governmental disclosure regulations, in a sophisticated land and time beyond Marlboro Country™, do branding images move us? In today's competitive marketplace, we—the informed audience—decide which brands make it and which do not. For a brand to be a winner, people have to bestow stardom upon the brand, and for this to happen, it has to resonate with us. It's much easier to connect to a compelling visual than to an amorphous corporation. And it's much easier to connect to others in this diverse world when we all speak "Brand."

Bibliography

Boorstin, Daniel J. *The Decline of Radicalism: Reflections on America*. New York: Random House, 1969.

McDonough, John, and Karen Egolf, eds. *The Advertising Age Encyclopedia of Advertising*. 3 vols. New York: Fitzroy Dearborn, 2003.

Rothenberg, Randall. "The Advertising Century." *AdAge.com*. http://www.adage.com/century/rothenberg.html.

Twitchell, James B. *Living It Up: America's Love Affair with Luxury*. New York: Simon & Schuster, 2003.

Vanderbilt, Tom. "The 15 Most Infuential, Important, Innocuous, Inane, and Interesting Ad Icons of the Last 500 Years (In No Particular Order). *Print*. November/December, 2000, pp. 116–121.

Non-print sources

http://www.adage.com/century
Sell and Spin: A History of Advertising. A&E Home Video. 1999.
http://www.adcouncil.org

Questions

1. Landa writes: "Ad icons, brand logos, and advertising taglines speak in shorthand—compressing corporate identities and essences into singular visuals or catchphrases" (paragraph 12). Give an example of an ad icon. A brand logo. An advertising tagline. What message do you think each of these conveys to you about the product being advertised?

2. Do you prefer to buy products that have the brand name on the outside, or tucked away on the inside label? Why? Do you notice other people's brand items? What does seeing a brand that you like suggest to you about the wearer or user of the product?

3. What are some of the earliest brand names or companies that Landa mentions in her essay? What others can you think of? As a project, find how the Betty Crocker™ look has changed over the years. What differences do you see in her appearance today from the way she looked fifty years ago? Do

you find changes in the appearance of the Quaker™ Oats man? What do advertisers do to make us feel familiar with a product but also to freshen or liven up the look?

4. Do you agree that when we buy a brand product, to some degree we are buying into a life style and a value system? Think about examples that support your point of view about this.

5. Write an essay in which you agree or disagree with the following: Branding and advertising cannot sell us what we don't already want. Use examples from your own life or from that of people you know to support your point of view.

Making Connections

1. The Hine, Landa, and Schuchardt essays all mention icons—images and verbal messages. What common threads do you find among these three articles? What differences do you find? What are the most important ideas that emerge for you about the idea of icons and how we live with them?

2. Barry writes about the effects of media violence on us as spectators. Which of the other authors in this chapter express concern about violent or troubling aspects of media saturation in our "visual surround?" What connections can you make between Barry's article and others in this chapter?

3. All of the writers in this chapter suggest that the images we make have a profound influence on the way we construct the world, but they may disagree as to whether this is a positive or negative effect. Barry and Campanella, for example, seem to present differing views about this. What points of agreement or disagreement can you find and how do you feel about these issues?

4. Look at the photograph on the cover of this book that shows Times Square, an example of the visual surround in which we live. In fact, most public images are created by corporations for commercial purposes and one danger is that these kinds of images are so powerful in their influence on us that they might actually prevent us from thinking for ourselves. How do you think each of the writers in this section would respond to this statement?

5. In her article, Landa looks at the positive impact of images in branding while Barry, in her article, examines the negative consequences of images of violence. Write a short response to each article in which you take the opposite position by looking at the downside of branding and the possible benefits of violent images.

6. How much control do we have over the images that we see in the media? In what ways is it possible to regulate the types of images that children see on the computer and/or on television? Which of the articles addresses this problem most directly?

7. Imagine a panel discussion with Hine, Landa, and Schuchardt at your school. Think of five questions that you would like to ask them. How do you think they would answer them?

8. Every year at their annual meeting, the Linguistics Society of America votes to choose the top word or phrase for that year. The same thing could be done with images. What do you think the top *image* is for this year? What about it makes it so important?

Images and their Uses

"We are image makers and image-ridden."

—Philip Guston

Images are among the most important objects that we human beings, in our compulsive need to remake the world, have created. They are perhaps our most direct and powerful means of communication, cutting through the boundaries of time and language. Images may be among the oldest things we have made, as suggested by Paleolithic tools with markings that seem to record information in some way still not deciphered. And, as far as we know, the purposeful creation of images also seems to be unique to humans among all creatures. Bees may dance and dolphins may chatter and elephants may even be induced to paint, but humans are the only ones for whom image-making seems to emerge from powerful needs for self-expression and visual communication. As Philip Guston, a well-known painter, suggests above, images are deep within us, an essential part of who and what we are.

The images we create with our evolving technology have another function too. They transform the world we live in. Each mark, gesture, painting, or photograph forms a small part of a new world of images that influences the way we think, imagine, behave, and dream. And this influence, in turn, inspires the new images we create which again change the world. It is an endless cycle of creation and impact that has transformed the visual environment and our place in it.

Because of this, images emerge from a variety of different needs within individuals and even from within cultures as a whole. They also fulfill a wide range of different uses as public records, personal artwork, formal communication, and private expression.

Close your eyes for a moment and think about images that have had an effect on you. What needs do you think they fulfilled for their creators? for yourself? The selections in this chapter point out just a few of the various functions that images can serve.

In "Behold the Stone Age," our first selection, Robert Hughes discusses the discovery of one of the greatest archeological finds in the history of visual communication. These are the 20,000 year-old caves filled with images created by Cro-Magnons found in Europe, which challenge our common notion of our Paleolithic ancestors as primitive and simple—in fact, they show the opposite to be true. Hughes describes a complex Late Stone Age society filled with fashion, technology, architecture, and a very essential need to make pictures. Massive bison and graceful panthers have been drawn carefully to take advantage of the natural contours of the cave walls, which give them a sculptural quality. The essay raises more questions than answers about the who and why of these paintings, but in probing into the reasons that prehistoric people made these particular images in such inaccessible locations, Hughes points to the mesmerizing power image-making has always had, from the caves of Europe all the way up to the digital age.

Our second selection, "Silent Music and Invisible Art" by Edmund Carpenter, takes us on a different journey through image-making. An anthropologist, Carpenter looks at unique types of images created by certain societies. These are images that are deemed to be so powerful for the people who created them that they are intended only to be hidden and remain unseen. This is an unusual concept in our age, in which everything appears in all media instantly—with the power of the Web, we are used to the notion that everything is available and endlessly reproduced. Yet only a small portion of the art produced by the societies Carpenter mentions was meant to be publicly displayed; much of it was considered too important to become part of the commerce of art and design. As Carpenter explains, this is particularly true for art that relies on "visions," which were themselves thought of as too valuable for display or discussion. Pictures too important to be seen or so valuable that they should *not* last. . .this is a challenging concept to us, and the essay raises important questions about the specific roles and functions of images in society.

Our third selection is "Dreams on the Couch." In it, David Gelman focuses on a very different kind of image than our other authors, although it may be the kind of image with which we are most familiar. Gelman uses the term image not to refer to the artifacts of technology, but to dreams which have their very own, and very powerful, uses and functions. In this essay, the author probes into the impact of Sigmund Freud's study of dreams. The founder of psychoanalysis thought of them as the "'royal road' to the unconscious," meaning that hidden within their strange imagery were the secrets to understanding the personality of the dreamer. Also stressed is the power of dreams not simply as a form of communication, whether clear or coded, but as a spontaneous output of the mind. They are yet another example of how image-making is an essential component of human nature.

Next, Douglas S. Fox, in "The Inner Savant," focuses on images from an entirely different perspective, but an equally compelling one. His essay explores the intriguing world of drawings produced by autistic children. Fox describes the amazing ability of some autistic children to make detailed and precise drawings of the world completely from memory, a natural ability most artists would envy. These are complex processes of perception and skill, and Fox suggests the possibility that his subjects are recording what they see without interpretation, and that this gives them the ability to reproduce what they see with relative ease. Fox also describes some of the exercises artists use to try to mimic this capability—which we may all have hidden under complex layers of conceptualization. The essay suggests that we may all have much greater talents for seeing and image-making than we know.

The final essay in this chapter is "In the River of Consciousness," by Oliver Sacks, a neurologist, medical researcher, and well-known writer. Sacks focuses on the way our brains function to construct the world around us and organize our perceptions by exploring neurological disturbances that cause one patient's world to freeze and another to see life as a series of flickering images rather than as a continual flow of events as most of us do. In making an analogy between our ability to perceive movement and the way that a motion picture works, with its illusion of continuous motion, Sacks points out how technology influences how we describe and see the world.

Whether discussing ancient paintings, the drawings of a child, the dreams of the dreamer, or the construction of the perceiver, all the selections in this chapter suggest that the impetus to make images, imaginatively or physically, is deeply human. And the products of these urges can serve a variety of purposes, either for the culture as a whole or for the individual. It is an important suggestion, since it implies that all images are worthy of study—any one of them can tell us something about ourselves, the image-ridden animals that we are.

Behold the Stone Age

ROBERT HUGHES

The art critic Robert Hughes was born in Sydney, Australia in 1938. He studied art and architecture at Sydney University, during which time he made a name for himself within the Sydney "Push"—a progressive group of artists, writers, and intellectuals. While an undergraduate, Hughes was commissioned to write a history of Australian painting. After this, he moved to Britain in the early 1960's where he wrote for such publications as The Spectator, *the* Telegraph, *the* [London] Times *and the* Observer, *before landing the position of art critic for* Time *in 1970. In addition to his many articles for* Time, *he has written some of the most important books on art criticism in the last thirty years, including* The Shock of the New *(1981),* The Fatal Shore *(1987),* Culture of Complaint *(1993), and* American Visions: The Epic History of Art in America *(1997). In "Behold the Stone Age," Hughes analyzes the importance of Cro-Magnon art. He writes that with the cave paintings of Lascaux and Altamira "the whole history of human visual communication unfolds."*

Getting Started

Describing the discovery in 1995 of Chauvet, a Paleolithic cave named for its discoverer near Avignon, France, Hughes reflects on the purpose and function of cave art. Many of us know about the cave paintings at Lascaux and Altamira, discovered in the 1940s, but the art in Chauvet is different from these. Instead of depicting the relatively non-threatening animals (bison, horses, etc.) found in other caves, the art of Chauvet depicts dangerous ones—cave bears, panthers, and woolly rhinos. In considering these differences, Hughes asks us to think about the function of cave art. Did it serve a practical purpose? Did it serve a spiritual purpose? Did it bring aesthetic pleasure? Did it engender fear? Why is Chauvet located in an area that can only be reached with the utmost difficulty? Hughes asks the question, "When, how, and above all why did Homo sapiens start making art?"

✦

Not since the Dead Sea Scrolls has anything found in a cave caused so much excitement. The paintings and engravings, more than 300 of them, amount to a sort of Ice Age Noah's ark—images of bison, mammoths and woolly rhinoceroses, of a panther, an owl, even a hyena. Done on the rock walls with plain earth pigments—red, black, ocher—they are of singular vitality and power, and despite their inscrutability to modern eyes, they will greatly enrich our picture of Cro-Magnon life and culture.

[In 1995] when the French government . . . announced that a local official, Jean-Marie Chauvet, had discovered the stunning Paleolithic cave near Avignon, experts swiftly hailed the 20,000-year old paintings as a trove rivaling—and perhaps surpassing—those of Lascaux and Altamira. "This is a virgin site—it's completely intact. It's great art," exulted Jean Clottes, an adviser to the French Culture Ministry and a leading authority on prehistoric art. It has also re-opened some of the oldest and least settled of questions: When, how and above all why did Homo sapiens start making art?

In the span of human prehistory, the Cro-Magnon people who drew the profusion of animals on the bulging limestone walls of the Chauvet cave were fairly late arrivals. Human technology—the making of tools from stone—had already been in existence for nearly 2 million years. There are traces of symbolism and ritual in burial sites of Neanderthals, an earlier species, dating back to 100,000 B.P. (before the present). Not only did the placement of the bodies seem meaningful, but so did the surrounding pebbles and bones with fragmentary patterns scratched on them. These, says Clottes, "do indicate that the Neanderthals had some creative capacity."

Though the dates are vastly generalized, most prehistorians seem to agree that art—communication by visual images—came into existence somewhere around 40,000 B.P. That was about the time when Cro-Magnons, Homo sapiens, reached Ice Age Europe, having migrated from the Middle East. Some experts think the Cro-Magnons brought a weapon that made Neanderthals an evolutionary has-been: a more advanced brain, equipped with a large frontal lobe "wired" for associative thinking. For art, at its root, is association—the power to make one thing stand for and symbolize another, to create the agreements by which some marks on a surface denote, say, an animal, not just to the markmaker but to others.

Among the oldest types of art is personal decoration—   5
ornaments such as beads, bracelets, pendants and necklaces. The body was certainly one of the first surfaces for symbolic expression. What did such symbols communicate? Presumably the

wearer's difference from others, as a member of a distinct group, tribe or totemic family: that he was a bison-man, say, and not a reindeer-man.

The Cro-Magnons were not the inarticulate Alley Oops of popular myth. They were nomadic hunter-gatherers with a fairly developed technology. They wore animal-skin clothing and moccasins tailored with bone needles, and made beautiful (and highly efficient) laurel-leaf-shaped flint blades. Living in small groups, they constructed tents from skins, and huts from branches and (in what is now Eastern Europe) mammoth bones.

Most striking was their yearning to make art in permanent places—the walls of caves. This expansion from the body to the inert surface was in itself a startling act of lateral thinking, an outward projection of huge cultural consequence, and Homo sapiens did not produce it quickly. As much time elapsed between the first recognizable art and the cave paintings of Lascaux and Altamira, about 15 to 20 millenniums, as separates Lascaux (or Chauvet) from the first TV broadcasts. But now it was possible to see an objective image in shared space, one that was not the property of particular bodies and had a life of its own; and from this point the whole history of human visual communication unfolds.

We are apt to suppose that Cro-Magnon cave art was rare and exceptional. But wrongly; as New York University anthropologist Randall White points out, more than 200 late–Stone Age caves bearing wall paintings, engravings, bas-relief decorations and sculptures have been found in southwestern Europe alone. Since the discovery of Lascaux in 1940, French archaeologists have been finding an average of a cave a year—and, says professor Denis Vialou of Paris' Institute of Human Paleontology, "there are certainly many, many more to be discovered, and while many might not prove as spectacular as Lascaux or Chauvet, I'd bet that some will be just as exciting."

No doubt many will never be found. The recently discovered painted cave at Cosquer in the south of France, for instance, can be reached only by scuba divers. Its entrance now lies below the surface of the Mediterranean; in the Upper Paleolithic period, from 70,000 B.P. to 10,000 B.P., so much of Europe's water was locked up in glaciers that the sea level was some 300 ft. lower than it is today.

Why the profuseness of Cro-Magnon art? Why did these people, of whom so little is known, need images so intensely? Why the preponderance of animals over human images? Archaeologists

10

are not much closer to answering such questions than they were a half-century ago, when Lascaux was discovered.

Part of the difficulty lies in the very definition of art. As anthropologist Margaret Conkey of the University of California, Berkeley puts it, "Many cultures don't really produce art, or even have any concept of it. They have spirits, kinship, group identity. If people from highland New Guinea looked at some of the Cro-Magnon cave art, they wouldn't see anything recognizable"—and not just because there are no woolly rhinos in New Guinea either. Today we can see almost anything as an aesthetic configuration and pull it into the eclectic orbit of late-Western "art experience"; museums have trained us to do that. The paintings of Chauvet strike us as aesthetically impressive in their power and economy of line, their combination of the sculptural and the graphic—for the artists used the natural bulges and bosses of the rock wall to flesh out the forms of the animals' rumps and bellies. But it may be that aesthetic pleasure, in our sense, was the last thing the Ice Age painters were after.

These were functional images; they were meant to produce results. But what results? To represent something, to capture its image on a wall in colored earths and animal fat, is in some sense to capture and master it, to have power over it. Lascaux is full of non-threatening animals, including wild cattle, bison and horses, but Chauvet pullulates with dangerous ones—cave bears, a panther and no fewer than 50 woolly rhinos. Such creatures, to paraphrase Claude Lévi-Strauss, were good to think with, not good to eat. We can assume they had a symbolic value, maybe even a religious value, to those who drew them, that they supplied a framework of images in which needs, values and fears—in short, a network of social consciousness—could be expressed. But we have no idea what this framework was, and merely to call it "animistic" does not say much.

Some animals have more than four legs, or grotesquely exaggerated horns; is that just style, or does it argue a state of ritual trance or hallucination in the artists? No answer, though some naturally occurring manganese oxides, the base of some of the blacks used in cave paintings, are known to be toxic and to act on the central nervous system. And the main technique of Cro-Magnon art, according to prehistorian Michel Lorblanchet, director of France's National Center of Scientific Research, involved not brushes but a kind of oral spray-painting—blowing pigment dissolved in saliva on the wall. Lorblanchet, who has recreated cave paintings with uncanny accuracy, suggests that the technique

may have had a spiritual dimension: "Spitting is a way of projecting yourself onto the wall, becoming one with the horse you are
painting. Thus the action melds with the myth. Perhaps the
shamans did this as a way of passing into the world beyond."

Different hands (and mouths) were involved in the production, but whose hands? Did the whole Cro-Magnon group at
Chauvet paint, or did it have an élite of artists, to be viewed by
nonartists as something like priests or professionals? Or does the
joining of many hands in a collaborative work express a kind of
treaty between rival groups? Or were the paintings added to over
generations, producing the crowded palimpsest-like effect suggested by some of the photos? And so on.

A mere picture of a bison or a woolly rhino tells us nothing   15
much. Suppose, France's Clottes suggests, that 20,000 years from
now, after a global cataclysm in which all books perished and the
word vanished from the face of the earth, some excavators dig up
the shell of a building. It has pointy ogival arches and a long axial
hall at the end of which is a painting of a man nailed to a cross.
In the absence of written evidence, what could this effigy mean?
No more than the bison or rhino on the rock at Chauvet. Representation and symbolism have parted company.

Chauvet cave could be viewed as a religious site—a paleolithic cathedral. Some have even suggested that a bear's skull
found perched on a rock was an "altar." Says Henry de Lumley,
director of France's National Museum of Natural History: "The
fact that the iconography is relatively consistent, that it seems to
obey certain rules about placement and even the way animals are
drawn . . . is evidence of something sacred." Yet nobody lived in
the cave, and no one in his right mind could imagine doing so;
the first analyses of the contents have yielded no signs of human
habitation, beyond the traces of animal-fat lamps and torches
used by temporary visitors, and some mounds of pigmented earth
left behind by the artists.

Modern artists make art to be seen by a public, the larger
(usually) the better. The history of public art as we know it, across
the past 1,000 years and more, is one of increasing access—beginning with the church open to the worshippers and ending with
the pack-'em-in ethos of the modern museum, with its support-
system of orientation courses, lectures, films, outreach programs
and souvenir shops. Cro-Magnon cave art was probably meant to
be seen by very few people, under conditions of extreme difficulty
and dread. The caves may have been places of initiation and trial,
in which consciousness was tested to an extent that we can only

dimly imagine, so utterly different is our grasp of the world from that of the Cro-Magnons.

Try to imagine an art gallery that could be entered only by crawling on your belly through a hole in the earth; that ramified into dark tunnels, a fearful maze in the earth's bowels in which the gallery goer could, at any moment, disturb one of the bears whose claw marks can still be seen on the walls; where the only light came from flickering torches, and the bones of animals littered the uneven floor. These are the archaic conditions that, one may surmise, produced the array of cave fears implanted in the human brain—fears that became absorbed into a later, more developed culture in such narratives as that of the mythical Cretan labyrinth in whose core the terrible Minotaur waited. Further metabolized, and more basically misunderstood, these sacred terrors of the deep earth undergird the Christian myth of hell. Which may, in fact, be the strongest Cro-Magnon element left in modern life.

Questions

1. Imagine the situation, the materials available, and the people and animals living in the Paleolithic era described in Hughes' article. Why do you think they would want to create images of animals on the walls of caves? Which of Hughes's theories seems most acceptable to you? Explain your answer.

2. What evidence does Hughes provide to convince his readers that the Cro-Magnon people were "not the inarticulate Alley Oops of popular myth" (paragraph 6)? What picture of these people does Hughes present? How does the cave art at Chauvet fit with his idea of them?

3. What does Hughes mean by "sacred terrors" in the last paragraph? How does he connect this idea to cave art?

4. Hughes writes that the history of images has been one of increasing access. This is certainly true with the ever-expanding content of the Web which is making most of the images ever created instantly available to anyone with a computer. What do you think are the positive and negative consequences of having so many images instantly available to everyone? Do you think this kind of accessibility makes these images more or less valuable?

5. Write about an experience that you have had encountering a piece of art that surprised you. What was it? Where was it? Describe it carefully, so that your reader can imagine it clearly. How did you feel about the art itself? What made you decide it was art?

Silent Music and Invisible Art
EDMUND CARPENTER

*Edmund Carpenter was born in 1922 and received his Ph.D. from
the University of Pennsylvania. He has taught anthropology for 40
years at many universities, including Harvard and the Universities
of Toronto and California. He was one of the early pioneers in combining anthropology and film-making. He began doing fieldwork as
a boy in 1935 and has worked in New Guinea, Borneo, and Tibet,
as well as throughout the Arctic regions of Canada, Greenland,
Alaska, and Siberia. In 1951, he spent the winter in an Eskimo sod
hut. Among his publications are* Patterns That Connect *(1996), a
12-volume work called* Social Symbolism in Ancient and Tribal
Art *(1986–1988) and* They Became What They Beheld *(1970). The
essay, which originally appeared in* Natural History Magazine, *asks
some intriguing questions about "invisible art."*

Getting Started

Describing art created by diverse sources as Robert Matta, a Chile-
an surrealist painter, and tribal or community art created by Native
Americans and the peoples of Japan, Germany, Alaska, and Tibet,
Carpenter draws upon his global studies to illustrate what he calls:
"invisible art." Is there such a thing? Why might someone want to
create it? Carpenter writes, "Perhaps the real mystery of tribal art is
not its form or its beauty, but its reminder of the gift of privacy."
How might art ensure the gift of privacy? Why would someone create art only to destroy it or watch it wash away? Is someone whose
art is not shared truly an artist? Is there any value to temporary or
unseen art?

───────────── ✦ ─────────────

To Western man, "silent music" is a contradiction in terms. "Invisible art" seems equally absurd, impossible, like the child of
a barren woman. Even inaccessible art, although conceivable,
seems somehow wrong, especially if deliberately inaccessible.

Roberto Matta, the surrealist, once put a painting on the six
interior sides of a box, which he then sealed. And Walter de Maria
proposed that a great cylinder be buried in a mountain overlook-
ing Munich, its entrance concealed and never revealed. But Matta

found no buyer and de Maria no backer. Art, we feel, demands viewers, and music, listeners.

I heard of an incident in the 1950s when a number of drug patients, many of them jazz musicians, were deprived of their instruments as punishment for some minor infraction of hospital rules. They sat about listlessly until a saxophonist picked up his invisible instrument and began to play silently; soon all the others joined in.

We call this mime, not music. Music is something we hear and share. Yet in many tribal societies, silent music is cultivated, even institutionalized. Singers sometimes plug both ears, converting sound into inner vibration. Or they may play small musical instruments inside their closed mouths.

Among North American Indians, silent music was the essence 5
of the spirit quest. At puberty a boy went apart from his fellows and fasted for a time in the wilderness. If he was the proper sort, a spirit took pity on him, bestowing special powers, principally in the form of songs. These remained his personal property, never to be revealed, save just before death—and even then, not always.

In days of torment and doubt, he sang alone or silently to evoke his guardian's help, singing again when relief was granted. He also gave thanks by painting or carving images addressed to his guardian. These were hidden in inaccessible places—on cliff walls facing the sky or in forbidden caves facing darkness. They were never intended to be seen by the living.

Most were small, but a few—probably clan efforts—were immense, laid out on mountaintops or scraped from desert floors. One is reminded of the tale of the giant so huge he is invisible. From the ground nothing can be seen save meaningless lines of rock and earth. Only when seen from the sky do these lines become coherent. Now, from airplanes, we see what was once reserved for spirits.

In Canada, such earth sculptures are generally geometric, but along the Mexican–United States border, many are anthropomorphic, often depicting a male and female in coitus. Here, as elsewhere in the tribal world, such pairs probably represent the original tribal ancestors in "primordial copulation"; the monument thus represents the origin of the tribe and, by extension, the beginning of the world.

Such pregnant images were far too potent for mortal eyes. So were the contents of medicine bundles. Some medicine bundles were never opened, not even by their owners, who already knew what lay within. They had been entrusted with songs and formulas that now resided in fetishes concealed within the bundles. Any exposure, certainly any public exposure, could only diminish these powers.

We often think of communication as the transfer of knowl-   10
edge from a knower to a nonknower. In a tribe, where all who are entitled to know, already know, such transfer is meaningless; the sharing of knowledge threatens both its ownership and the very nature of that knowledge. Even when an object is brought forth publicly, it may be exposed in such a way it cannot really be seen. Among the Haida Indians, finely detailed rattles become mere blurs when rapidly shaken at crowded, firelit ceremonies. And among the Salish, when a spindle whorl is spun, its complex design disappears; when not in use, it is hidden away.

We Westerners treat art as public property. We display it with maximum clarity, in every possible medium, hoping for the largest possible audience. Our museums boast of crowds who come to see art and buy reproductions to take home.

American Indians treated art differently. Only a small part of their art was intended for public display. Clan and house objects were collectively owned, of course, but even they were displayed only on appropriate occasions, by appropriate persons, in appropriate ways, before select audiences. Residents in Indian villages spent their lives surrounded by hidden art; each saw only those treasures and heard only those songs he was entitled to see and hear.

Art inspired by visions was even less accessible. Private visions, like private songs, remained private. Public exposure diminished their power and made them vulnerable to theft, so they were carefully concealed.

Still, the possessor was tempted to hint about the visions. One method was pictorial shorthand, which produced abstract designs no stranger could decipher. Meaning was reserved for owners and when they died, was forever lost.

Among the Salish, according to anthropologist Wayne Sut-   15
tles, "the vision was the unique experience of the individual," a source of skill and status. Its owner kept its exact nature secret, perhaps until old age. But he might hint at it in the winter dance, by word or movement. Any other representation was "vague, ambiguous, covert."

"Clearly," Suttles reported, "there were limits on the representation of visions ('guardian spirits'). In native theory, everyone (or every male perhaps) ought to 'train' and have a vision. But it was dangerous to reveal too much about it. If you talked about it, you could 'spoil' it; it might leave you or even make you sick or it could be taken away from you by an enemy shaman. Yet eventually you wanted others to know that you 'had something.' Probably all [ethnologists who have worked on the Northwest Coast] have heard hints and half-revelations about what people 'have.' [Being possessed] by a song at the winter dance is, of course, evidence that you 'have something' and the words of the song and the movements of the dance may hint at what it is. But it must be tempting to hint in other ways, though dangerous to go too far."

In some tribes, visions were never concretely represented. Elsewhere they were portrayed, but with constraints that affected artistic expression. One effect was a tendency to make images that were essentially *in-visible*. When you look outward, you see nature. But when you look inward, you see those invisible forces that underlie nature, including human nature. This is the *in-sight* of the blind seer. It is also the method of the modern scientist who insists that reality is not in appearances, but in the laws that govern them.

Eskimo artists concern themselves with both natural appearances and inner realities. As hunters they observe nature carefully, and as artists they match their carvings with nature. Some carvings are so accurate, so detailed, that one can tell, say, a common loon from a red-throated loon.

But when these artists depict inner reality, art becomes making, not matching, and images become surrealistic. As one Netsilik woman said, "We believe that people can live a life apart from real life."

The Danish ethnographer Knud Rasmussen tells of asking   20
Anarqaq, an Eskimo shaman, to draw spirit visions: "He would sit for hours with closed eyes, solely intent on getting the vision fixed in his mind, and only when this was done would he attempt to put it into form. Sometimes the recollection of the event affected him to such a degree that he trembled all over, and had to give up the attempt."

Anarqaq consented to make these drawings on the condition that Rasmussen take them to his own country and not show them to Anarqaq's people.

Ritual words can be more important than visions. Sometimes they are a source of artistic inspiration or the basis for skill and status. And sometimes they are the power behind certain ceremonies, incantations, rites. The efficacy of ritual paraphernalia and protective designs often depends on them. Like visions and silent music, ritual words are privately owned by individuals who keep them to themselves.

How do you paint a song? How do you carve a word? One way is to use an acoustic model: make the eye subservient to the ear by patterning space acoustically. An essential feature of sound is that it fills space. We say, "The night shall be filled with music," just as the air is filled with fragrance. The concertgoer closes his eyes.

Auditory space has no favored focus. It is a sphere without fixed boundaries, space made by the thing itself, not space containing the thing. It is dynamic, always in flux, creating its own dimensions moment by moment.

Alaskan Eskimo mask makers were inspired by songs heard 25 in dreams. Each design, obedient to an inner impulse, creates its own dimensions, asserts its own identity, unhampered by external restraints. Used once, each mask was then burned.

Japanese and Tibetan Buddhism are full of esoteric paintings and images not supposed to be seen. Certain Buddhist mandala must be destroyed almost as soon as they are completed.

In the Japanese secular art of *bonseki*, the artist is required to destroy his sand paintings after about two weeks. Navaho sand paintings qualify as "sand mandalas" with the same requirements. In fact, sand paintings in many parts of the world are generally erased as a final step in their production. Chants associated with them are kept secret.

Rituals and sacred dances are impermanent art forms, and often the articles produced for them are destroyed at the close of the performances. This custom is so widespread as to suggest great antiquity.

Among the Eskimo, carvings are rarely saved. When spring comes and igloos melt, old habitation sites are littered with waste, including beautifully designed tools and tiny carvings, not deliberately thrown away, but with even greater indifference, just lost.

To the Eskimo, a carving, like a song, isn't a thing. When you 30 feel a song within you, you sing it; when you sense a form emerging from the ivory, you release it. As the carver holds the unworked ivory lightly in his hand, turning it this way and that, he whispers, "Who are you? Who hides there?" And then: "Ah, Seal!" He rarely sets out to carve, say, a seal, but picks up the ivory, examines it to find its hidden form, and if that is not immediately apparent, carves aimlessly until he sees it, humming or chanting as he works. Then he brings the form out; the hidden seal emerges. It was always there. He didn't create it, he released it; he helped it step forth.

Eskimo are more interested in the creative activity than in the product of that activity. Art to them is a transitory act, a relationship.

Hidden art takes many forms: an insignia on the inner side of an Elizabethan finger ring; entire Indonesian temples concealed beneath stone structures; paintings on the inside of a mummy case, facing the deceased.

I once saw a gold brooch whose form was abstract, until you blew on it, at which point its spinning parts formed the letters KKK, for Ku Klux Klan.

Small cabins on the banks of the Rhine belong to families whose fishing rights date from medieval times. During *Fastnacht*, a three-day winter festival, cabins are left unguarded. An unidentified artist selects one and covers its inner walls with pornography. When the owner returns, he may simply lock the door or he may invite friends. Either way, tradition requires that the paintings remain for one year; then they are eradicated. Such paintings generate wide speculation. Rumors abound. Old tales are revived. Yet only a few people actually see anything.

A tribe has been defined as a community where everyone   35
shares all information simultaneously. But surely not all information? Even the smallest band of tribesmen keeps secrets and enjoys mysteries, and art is a favorite hiding place for both. Tribal art is filled with puzzle pictures and visual puns and cryptic messages in cartoon shorthand. No stranger deciphers even the first layer of these many ambiguities.

Perhaps we should redefine a tribe as a group whose shared knowledge permits communication through secrecy. We, who have lost this ability, create instead the ultimate in accessibility as a substitute for the network of tradition.

We love to *solve* mysteries. Our children, when visiting their grandmother, head first for the attic, to open trunks. I was fascinated to learn that a safe deposit in Basel can be opened only by its owner, even if it lies dormant for a thousand years. Fascinated but skeptical: could any Westerner, even a Swiss, resist a mystery for a thousand years?

Recently a museum collection of African fetishes, each sealed in leather shrouds, proved too tempting; the curator X-rayed them, thus satisfying his curiosity while preserving their bindings.

If there is an Indian mound in the neighborhood, we open it. I doubt that a single known mound in North America has escaped violation. Nearly forty years ago, as an archeologist, I asked a landowner for permission to open a burial mound. He refused on the grounds that he respected the mystery. I was disappointed but I never forgot, or condemned, his decision.

When American Indians burn their sacred treasures, rather   40
than sell them to us, we are disappointed and puzzled, and that
puzzlement derives partly from respect.

Perhaps the real message of tribal art is not its form or its
beauty, but its reminder of the gift of privacy.

I accept that there are mysteries best left unsolved—that
some answers must forever elude outsiders. I was once very close
to several Eskimo friends but I gave up hope we could ever come
to know each other completely. If I had come to know them completely, I would have become an Eskimo; I would have lost my
own identity, and this I did not choose to do.

"We wed ourselves to the mystery," not to conquer it or be
conquered by it, but to greet it.

Questions

1. What is "inaccessible art," according to Edmund Carpenter? Do you think
   such art is "wrong" as he suggests it might seem to Westerners in paragraph
   one? or do you think that hidden art can be as important as public art? Why?
2. Carpenter writes about a variety of images that are not meant to be seen
   by the public because they have personal, spiritual, or ritualistic uses. Do you
   think that tongue piercings and hidden tattoos fit into this category? Why
   might some people want to display such private images and why might others
   want to keep them hidden?
3. In paragraph 27, we read about *bonseki*, a secular art of Japan, in which
   artists create sand paintings that they destroy after about two weeks. Have
   you ever created a sand painting or seen one made? Have you ever made a
   snow sculpture? A sand castle? How do you explain the satisfaction of creating a picture or sculpture that will likely be washed away with the tide or
   melt in the sun?
4. The kinds of things that might fit into the category of images intended only
   for limited viewing go far beyond those mentioned by Hughes in this article—
   the insignias of private groups, valuable works of art in the homes of the
   rich, photographs taken for intimate reasons. What other kinds of images
   can you think of that might fall under this heading and what are the reasons
   for their creation?
5. Go online and look at the art of Andy Goldsworthy, whose work is meant to
   disappear back into nature after it is photographed. What do you think of
   art like Goldsworthy's that is deliberately designed not to last? Can it be as
   important as work intended to last for centuries? Does it seem contradic-
   tory to you that Goldsworthy photographs his work so that it will not
   entirely disappear?

Dreams on the Couch
David Gelman

David Gelman is a former editor of Newsweek *from which the following article is taken. Gelman often writes on psychological issues and how they affect our daily lives. In "Dreams on the Couch," he writes about dreams and how they may be understood both from the Freudian perspective as well as from a variety of methods developed by later psychologists.*

Getting Started

Gelman describes dreams as "visual hallucinations of a sometimes bizarre order, full of obscure events and allusions." Think back to your own dreams. Do any of them stand out in your mind? Do you have any dreams that occur over and over again? Do you dream in color or in black and white? Do certain images seem especially vivid? Have you ever tried to explain or understand your dreams? Have you ever thought about dreams as a way of internally creating images?

———————— ✦ ————————

> *I do not know how dreams arise [but] I know that if we meditate on a dream sufficiently long and thoroughly—if we take it about with us and turn it over and over—something almost always comes of it.*
>
> —CARL JUNG

> *When the work of interpretation has been completed, we perceive that a dream is the fulfillment of a wish.*
>
> —SIGMUND FREUD

Our dreams often appear to us as a kind of derangement of the senses. They are visual hallucinations of a sometimes bizarre order, full of obscure events and allusions. Emotions can seem out of whack in the dream plot: a loved one dies, and we feel no grief, but a prosaic scene around the family table evokes a terrible, gnawing anxiety.

Dreams follow their own rules of logic. Freud called them "transient psychoses." Yet he was convinced that they were charged with meaning in every last, seemingly nonsensical detail. "They are not meaningless, they are not absurd," he insisted in "The Interpretation of Dreams," the groundbreaking masterwork that launched psychoanalysis. "On the contrary, they are psychical phenomena of complete validity, constructed by a highly complicated activity of the mind." That conviction has had to withstand an almost constant onslaught of doubters and debunkers arguing just as confidently that dreams are devoid of meaning.

Freud could pursue the hidden psychic messages of dreams with a tenacity equaled only by his fictional contemporary, Sherlock Holmes. Sooner or later, he was sure, the secrets would yield to his "collection of picklocks," as he once described his uncanny insights. To him, the effort seemed worthwhile; dreams, he said, were the "royal road" to the unconscious. Even so, later analysts found the going too rough. Many have switched to other pathways, mainly that of the "transference"—the phenomenon in which a patient unwittingly replays significant relationships of his life on the neutral figure of the analyst. But dreams continue to come up for discussion, and at times they can still provide the quickest entrée to the teeming, subterranean world of the unconscious.

For Freud the generating force of a dream was not the random brain activity that some now say it is, but rather a powerful unconscious wish. Most often, the wish appears in disguised form because it harbors forbidden thoughts—Oedipal longings for the parent of the opposite sex, for example. Thus there are two forces operating: the wish, and a defense against it, a censor. By a process of distortion that Freud called "the dreamwork," the censor transforms the hidden, or "latent," content of the dream into "manifest" content—the dream as it appears to the dreamer. By then, Freud emphasized, the wish may be "disguised to the point of being unrecognizable." Things might even appear as their opposites: pleasure as pain, desire as fear.

That point remains difficult for people to grasp. To this day 5 analytic patients reporting sad or frightening dreams will say, "How could that possibly be a wish?" Therapists themselves have wearied of trying to ferret out hidden wishes. Indeed, even Freud later acknowledged that dreams did not always represent wish fulfillments, although he continued to insist they were motivated by wishes. Nowadays there is an increasing tendency to interpret the manifest dream, without looking any deeper, a trend that parallels the general movement of psychotherapy itself to briefer, more superficial techniques. Many analysts now believe the surface details of a dream, along with the patient's associations to them, provide the information they need to make a useful interpretation. "There is no need to assume dreams have a latent content," says Harry Fiss, professor of psychiatry at the University of Connecticut. The most recent thinking is that dreams simply continue the conscious concerns of wakeful life, but in the "dream language" of visual metaphors.

As an example, Fiss tells of a newly married, middle-aged patient of his who was worried about pleasing his wife sexually, even though the wife didn't seem especially demanding. Fiss had established that when the patient was young, his mother often left him for extended periods with relatives or servants. A few months into therapy, the patient reported a dream in which he was a circus trapeze artist, performing spectacular midair somersaults. The analyst no longer recalls the exact dialogue that followed, but he says it might have gone something like this:

FISS: What comes to your mind when you have this dream about the acrobatic act?

PATIENT: I don't know . . . For some reason my mother comes to mind. When she came to visit once a year I used to show off.

FISS: Oh, that's interesting. You might have felt if you impressed her she would stay longer? . . . What about your wife, do you feel you have to impress her too?

According to Fiss, the interpretation became a turning point in the therapy—what is sometimes called an "Aha!" experience. The patient suddenly realized he didn't have to perform sexual heroics to satisfy his new wife. A strict Freudian, Fiss says, might interpret the dream in Oedipal terms, perhaps a repressed rivalry with the father for the mother's affections. But he insists there was nothing hidden in this patient's problem; he was fully conscious of it. The acrobatic feat was simply the "dream-language way of stating the fear of impotence in a pictured image, that made it more meaningful for the patient. There is no forbidden wish in this dream. The manifest dream says it all."

Analysts, nevertheless, remain sharply divided on that thesis, and there are still plenty of adherents to the "classical" approach of interpretation. One thing that has changed is that analysts seem less interested in the forbidden wish itself than in how the dreamer defends against it. The defense may show a pattern that helps explain the patient's real-life behavioral problems. Edward

Brennan, a psychoanalyst with a private practice in New York City and Greenwich, Conn., cites a hypothetical dream that illustrates a significant defense pattern. In the dream, a woman is stalked in some shadowy place by a man who finally confronts her and threatens her with a hunting knife. The traditional view might be that Oedipus is calling the tune here. The woman wants to be penetrated by her father, and because such a wish is morally unacceptable, the distorting dreamwork has turned it into its opposite: the object of her secret desire has become a stranger belligerently pushing himself on her, with a knife instead of a penis.

But Brennan offers a more updated reading. The dream, in his view, may reflect a perfectly "normal" wish to get close to a man. But a fantasy, or "mistaken idea," lurking in the woman's unconscious, has become attached to the wish—namely, that the encounter would be "not tender and gratifying but brutal, possibly fatal." The image of the man with the knife could have arisen from some forgotten early experience—the buried memory of a menacing, alcoholic father, for instance.

As the dream proceeds, either of two things might happen, 10 according to Brennan. The stalker may look like he's about to plunge the knife into her, and the woman's anxiety will escalate to panic. "At that point, where the defense is insufficient, you have a nightmare. She will have no choice but to wake up, and she may say to herself the most reassuring words in the world: 'It was only a dream.'" The other possibility, he says, is that the woman's defenses do spring into action, changing the course of the dream. The light grows stronger, showing that she is not on the street but at a fancy dress ball. Her attacker is just another guest, and instead of a knife, he is proffering her a couple of drooping asparagus spears from the hors d'oeuvres table. Her defenses have effectively quashed the threat, rendering her attacker impotent. "It's not a knife but some soft, wobbly thing," says Brennan. (The phallic symbolism is not unintentional.)

The dream thus ends on a comforting note. But the danger, says the analyst, is that in waking life this defensive strategy may continue to manipulate the woman's behavior, "so that when she looks to become involved with men, the likelihood is she will unwittingly but purposefully pick out men who are inept, impotent. And she will have often a series of tales to tell you about the bad luck she has had in finding men by whom she was disappointed." Indeed, says Brennan, one thing that makes dreams enormously useful is that they will "unfailingly" identify such unconscious conflicts. They will illuminate not only the wish, but the fear attached to it, as well as the characteristic defense the dreamer employs. And they will do so "over and over again until the analyst and the patient would have to be blind not to see it." Says Brennan: "The unconscious has only one technique: repetition."

That proposition was tested by Milton Kramer, a leading dream researcher based in Cincinnati. He collected 15 dream descriptions from each of five different experimental subjects, then scrambled them and gave them to a group of high-school students to sort out. He says the students had little difficulty figuring out who had dreamed what, by their repetition of certain themes.

Whatever approach they favor, analysts would probably agree that a dream interpretation, above all, must be a plausible scenario, a story that clicks into place for the dreamer. (In a sense, that is what analysis itself is about.) Jung said his sole test for an interpretation was that it "worked" for the dreamer. He made it "a rule," he said, "never to go beyond the meaning which has an effect upon the patient." Freud made a similar rule (one that he sometimes honored in the breach) not to analyze a dream without first hearing the patient's own associations to its contents. Most modern analysts still try to observe that rule.

Yet many dreams are so bewildering, so crowded with details that seem outside the dreamer's experience, that they defy association. Others work almost like poems, providing, in ways the dreamer had no idea he was capable of, uncanny distillations of a particular feeling or situation. And sometimes they employ devices that seem to suggest the dream has a mind of its own.

A 40-year-old patient beginning analysis told his doctor of a   15 dream in which he was soaring over India, apparently under his own power. The landscape was wrapped in blue haze, making individual features hard to distinguish. But on the ground below he saw a broken line, as on a map. Within it were the words "MALARIAL AREA." He couldn't remember how the dream ended; its impressions evidently faded out as mysteriously as they arose.

When the doctor asked him what came to mind about the dream, the patient vaguely recalled reading once about an apparently successful antimalaria campaign in India. He also remembered being fascinated by a particularly attractive poster of an Indian temple in the window of a travel agency. Was it on his way to the doctor's office? He couldn't be sure. So here was the stuff that dreams are made of: maybe, he suggested and the doctor tentatively agreed, the memory had been evoked now that he was embarking on an equivalent psychological journey into the past, stirring up powerful, buried feelings.

In the dream, there was a strong hint that, while he was anxious to make the journey, he was uneasy about one particular area. When the analyst asked the patient if he associated anything with "Malarial Area," he decided, after some thought, that the phrase could be an anagram. At his next session, he brought the analyst more than 30 words he had extracted from the phrase: "male," "realm," "liar" and so on. But the significant ones for him were "ail," "alarm" and "mal-ear," the last a hybrid coinage of his own. These words connected to an experience he could barely remember, a childhood bout of scarlet fever complicated by an acute ear infection that had forced his parents to hospitalize him—leaving him separated from his mother at the critical age of $3\frac{1}{2}$.

There was something a bit too pat about all this, of course. It seems likely there was a deeper structure submerged in the dream, some blue-hazed "India" beyond conscious recall. Not everything in a dream is analyzable. But here, once again, was a scenario that "worked" for the dreamer—in this case, encouraging him to go ahead with the analysis in spite of his apprehensions about it.

Dreams "thrive" on metaphor, as Edward Brennan says. Freed from the inhibitions of verbal communication, it seems, we respond to a visual imagery that may have been our earliest mode of thinking—one reason, perhaps, why the language of poetry can stir us as it does. That may explain, too, why some dreams can haunt us with a power more persuasive even than that of poetry, shimmering in the mind like lost cities or leaving us, for hours afterward, with an unaccountable feeling of terror.

Questions

1. What are the differences between dream images and other kinds of images? In what ways can the image from a dream have a greater impact on us than any other kind of image?

2. Who was Sigmund Freud? What is his relationship to dream analysis? Who was Carl Jung? What do the two quotes at the beginning of the article suggest about the differences between Freud and Jung? You may want to do further research to better understand their differences.

3. Gelman paraphrases psychoanalyst Edward Brennan writing, "Dreams 'thrive' on metaphors" (paragraph 19). What does that mean? What examples of this does Gelman include in article? What other examples of images as metaphors can you think of in your own dreams and experiences?

4. Gelman compares Freud's techniques for understanding dreams to those of Sherlock Holmes. What does he mean by this? What did Freud and Holmes have in common in their methods?
5. Write an essay in which you describe a dream that had an effect on you in some way. Start by describing it in detail, including any emotional impact it had on you. Then try to interpret it. What do you think the dream images mean? What does it say about your personality or the way you felt when you had it? Do you think it is valuable to study dream images the way we study other visual images? Why or why not?

The Inner Savant
Douglas S. Fox

Douglas S. Fox is a professional journalist who writes about advances in medical science and related fields, as well as the researchers who do the work. His articles may be read in various journals, including U.S. News & World Report, The New Scientist, Discover, Scientific American, *and others. His article "The Inner Savant" originally appeared in* Discover *in February 2002.*

Getting Started

Fox describes some of the abilities and talents of people with a condition known as autistic savantism. This is "a rare condition marked by severe mental and social deficits but also by a mysterious talent that appears spontaneously—usually before age 6." One example is provided by Nadia, a 3-year old girl, who is able to draw horses with exquisite detail and sensitivity despite the fact that she has had no training in art. What do the drawings of most 3-year olds look like? Do you think that drawing ability is innate or learned? On what do you base your opinion? What do you know about autism or savantism? What other types of savant ability have you heard about and what do you think connects the different kinds of abilities that savants have? In what ways can images created by untrained artists be powerful?

———————— ✦ ————————

N adia appeared healthy at birth, but by the time she was 2, her parents knew something was amiss. She avoided eye contact and didn't respond when her mother smiled or cooed. She didn't even seem to recognize her mother. At 6 months she still had not spoken a word. She was unusually clumsy and spent hours in repetitive play, such as tearing paper into strips. But at $3\frac{1}{2}$ she picked up a pen and began to draw—not scribble, *draw*. Without any training, she created from memory sketches of galloping horses that only a trained adult could equal. Unlike the way most people might draw a horse, beginning with its outline, Nadia began with random details. First a hoof, then the horse's mane, then its harness. Only later did she lay down firm lines connecting these floating features. And when she did connect them, they were always in the correct position relative to one another.

Nadia is an autistic savant, a rare condition marked by severe mental and social deficits but also by a mysterious talent that appears spontaneously—usually before age 6.

Sometimes the ability of a savant is so striking, it eventually makes news. The most famous savant was a man called Joseph, the individual Dustin Hoffman drew upon for his character in the 1988 movie *Rain Man*. Joseph could immediately answer this question: "What number times what number gives 1,234,567,890?" His answer was "Nine times 137,174,210." Another savant could double 8,388,628 up to 24 times within several seconds, yielding the sum 140,737,488,355,328. A 6-year-old savant named Trevor listened to his older brother play the piano one day, then climbed onto the piano stool himself and played it better. A savant named Eric could find what he called the "sweet spot" in a room full of speakers playing music, the spot where sound waves from the different sources hit his ears at exactly the same time.

Most researchers have offered a simple explanation for these extraordinary gifts: compulsive learning. But Allan Snyder, a vision researcher and award-winning physicist who is director of the Center for the Mind at the University of Sydney and the Australian National University, has advanced a new explanation of such talents. "Each of us has the innate capacity for savantlike skills," says Snyder, "but that mental machinery is unconscious in most people."

Savants, he believes, can tap into the human mind's remark-
able processing abilities. Even something as simple as seeing, he explains, requires phenomenally complex information processing. When a person looks at an object, for example, the brain immediately estimates an object's distance by calculating the subtle differences between the two images on each retina (computers programmed to do this require extreme memory and speed). During the process of face recognition, the brain analyzes countless
5

details, such as the texture of skin and the shape of the eyes, jaw-bone, and lips. Most people are not aware of these calculations. In savants, says Snyder, the top layer of mental processing—conceptual thinking, making conclusions—is somehow stripped away. Without it, savants can access a startling capacity for recalling endless detail or for performing lightning-quick calculations. Snyder's theory has a radical conclusion of its own: He believes it may be possible someday to create technologies that will allow any nonautistic person to exploit these abilities.

The origins of autism are thought to lie in early brain development. During the first three years of life, the brain grows at a tremendous rate. In autistic children, neurons seem to connect haphazardly, causing widespread abnormalities, especially in the cerebellum, which integrates thinking and movement, and the limbic region, which integrates experience with specific emotions. Abnormalities in these regions seem to stunt interest in the environment and in social interaction. Autistic children have narrowed fields of attention and a poor ability to recognize faces. They are more likely to view a face, for example, as individual components rather than as a whole. Imaging studies have shown that when autistic children see a familiar face, their pattern of brain activation is different from that of normal children.

That narrowed focus may explain the autistic child's ability to concentrate endlessly on a single repetitive activity, such as rocking in a chair or watching clothes tumble in a dryer. Only one out of 10 autistic children show special skills.

In a 1999 paper, Snyder and his colleague John Mitchell challenged the compulsive-practice explanation for savant abilities, arguing that the same skills are biologically latent in all of us. "Everyone in the world was skeptical," says Vilayanur Ramachandran, director of the Center for Brain and Cognition at the University of California at San Diego. "Snyder deserves credit for making it clear that savant abilities might be extremely important for understanding aspects of human nature and creativity."

Snyder's office at the University of Sydney is in a gothic building, complete with pointed towers and notched battlements. Inside, Nadia's drawings of horses adorn the walls; artwork by other savants hangs in nearby rooms.

Snyder's interest in autism evolved from his studies of light   10
and vision. Trained as a physicist, he spent several years studying fiber optics and how light beams can guide their own path.

At one time he was interested in studying the natural fiber optics in insects' eyes. The question that carried him from vision research to autism had to do with what happens after light hits the human retina: How are the incoming signals transformed into data that is ultimately processed as images in the brain? Snyder was fascinated by the processing power required to accomplish such a feat.

During a sabbatical to Cambridge in 1987, Snyder devoured Ramachandran's careful studies of perception and optical illusions. One showed how the brain derives an object's three-dimensional shape: Falling light creates a shadow pattern on the object, and by interpreting the shading, the brain grasps the object's shape. "You're not aware how your mind comes to those conclusions," says Snyder. "When you look at a ball, you don't know why you see it as a ball and not a circle. The reason is your brain is extracting the shape from the subtle shading around the ball's surface." Every brain possesses that innate ability, yet only artists can do it backward, using shading to portray volume.

"Then," says Snyder, speaking slowly for emphasis, "I asked the question that put me on a 10-year quest"—how can we bypass the mind's conceptual thinking and gain conscious access to the raw, uninterpreted information of our basic perceptions? Can we shed the assumptions built into our visual processing system?

A few years later, he read about Nadia and other savant artists in Oliver Sacks's *The Man Who Mistook His Wife for a Hat and Other Clinical Tales.* As he sat in his Sydney apartment one afternoon with the book in hand, an idea surfaced. Perhaps someone like Nadia who lacked the ability to organize sensory input into concepts might provide a window into the fundamental features of perception.

Snyder's theory began with art, but he came to believe that all savant skills, whether in music, calculation, math, or spatial relationships, derive from a lightning-fast processor in the brain that divides things—time, space, or an object—into equal parts. Dividing time might allow a savant child to know the exact time when he's awakened, and it might help Eric find the sweet spot by allowing him to sense millisecond differences in the sounds hitting his right and left ears. Dividing space might allow Nadia to place a disembodied hoof and mane on a page precisely where they belong. It might also allow two savant twins to instantaneously count matches spilled on the floor (one said "111"; the other said "37, 37, 37"). Meanwhile, splitting numbers might allow math savants to factor 10-digit numbers or easily identify large prime numbers—which are impossible to split.

Compulsive practice might enhance these skills over time, but Snyder contends that practice alone cannot explain the phenomenon. As evidence, he cites rare cases of sudden-onset savantism. Orlando Serrell, for example, was hit on the head by a baseball at the age of 10. A few months later, he began recalling an endless barrage of license-plate numbers, song lyrics, and weather reports.

If someone can become an instant savant, Snyder thought, doesn't that suggest we all have the potential locked away in our brains? "Snyder's ideas sound very New Age. This is why people are skeptical," says Ramachandran. "But I have a more open mind than many of my colleagues simply because I've seen [sudden-onset cases] happen."

Bruce Miller, a neurologist at the University of California at San Francisco, has seen similar transformations in patients with frontotemporal dementia, a degenerative brain disease that strikes people in their fifties and sixties. Some of these patients, he says, spontaneously develop both interest and skill in art and music. Brain-imaging studies have shown that most patients with frontotemporal dementia who develop skills have abnormally low blood flow or low metabolic activity in their left temporal lobe. Because language abilities are concentrated in the left side of the brain, these people gradually lose the ability to speak, read, and write. They also lose face recognition. Meanwhile, the right side of the brain, which supports visual and spatial processing, is better preserved.

"They really do lose the linguistic meaning of things," says Miller, who believes Snyder's ideas about latent abilities complement his own observations about frontotemporal dementia. "There's a loss of higher-order processing that goes on in the anterior temporal lobe." In particular, frontotemporal dementia damages the ventral stream, a brain region that is associated with naming objects. Patients with damage in this area can't name what they're looking at, but they can often paint it beautifully. Miller has also seen physiological similarities in the brains of autistic savants and patients with frontotemporal dementia. When he performed brain-imaging studies on an autistic savant artist who started drawing horses at 18 months, he saw abnormalities similar to those of artists with frontotemporal dementia: decreased blood flow and slowed neuronal firing in the left temporal lobe.

One blustery, rainy morning I drove to Mansfield, a small farm town 180 miles northeast of Melbourne. I was heading to a day clinic for autistic adults, where I hoped to meet a savant. The three-hour drive pitched and rolled through hills, occasionally cutting through dense eucalyptus forests punctuated with yellow koala-crossing signs. From time to time, I saw large white-crested parrots; in one spot, a flock of a thousand or more in flight wheeled about like a galaxy.

I finally spotted my destination: Acorn Outdoor Ornaments. Within this one-story house, autistic adults learn how to live independently. They also create inexpensive lawn decorations, like the cement dwarf I see on the roof.

Joan Curtis, a physician who runs Acorn and a related follow-up program, explained that while true savants are rare, many people with autism have significant talents. Nurturing their gifts, she said, helps draw them into social interaction. Guy was one of the participants I met at Acorn. Although he was uncomfortable shaking my hand, all things electronic fascinated him, and he questioned me intently about my tape recorder.

Every horizontal surface in Guy's room was covered with his creations. One was an electric fan with a metal alligator mouth on the front that opened and closed as it rotated from side to side. On another fan a metal fisherman raised and lowered his pole with each revolution. And then I saw the sheep. Viewed from the left, it was covered in wool. Viewed from the right, it was a skeleton, which I learned Guy had assembled without any help. Guy didn't say much about himself. He cannot read nor do arithmetic, but he has built an electric dog that barks, pants, wags its tail, and urinates.

During my visit, another Acorn participant, Tim, blew into the room like a surprise guest on *The Tonight Show*. He was in a hurry to leave again, but asked me my birthday—July 15, 1970.

"Born on a Wednesday, eh?" he responded nonchalantly—and   25
correctly.

"How did you do that?" I asked.

"I did it well," he replied.

"But how?" I asked.

"*Very* well," he replied with obvious pleasure. Then he was out the door and gone.

How do calendar savants do it? Several years ago Timothy   30
Rickard, a cognitive psychologist at the University of California at San Diego, evaluated a 40-year-old man with a mental age of 5 who could assign a day of the week to a date with 70 percent accuracy. Because the man was blind from birth, he couldn't study calendars or even imagine calendars. He couldn't do simple

arithmetic either, so he couldn't use a mathematical algorithm. But he could only do dates falling within his lifetime, which suggests that he used memory.

He could, however, do some arithmetic, such as answer this question: If today is Wednesday, what day is two days from now? Rickard suspects that memorizing 2,000 dates and using such arithmetic would allow 70 percent accuracy. "That doesn't reduce it to a trivial skill, but it's not inconceivable that someone could acquire this performance with a lot of effort," he says. It's especially plausible given the single-minded drive with which autistics pursue interests.

Yet Tim, the savant at Acorn, can calculate dates as far back as 1900, as well as into the future. And there are reports of twins who could calculate dates 40,000 years in the past or future. Still, practice may be part of it. Robyn Young, an autism researcher at Flinders University in Adelaide, Australia, says some calendar savants study perpetual calendars several days a week (there are only 14 different calendar configurations; perpetual calendars cross-reference them to years).

But even if savants practice, they may still tap into that universal ability Snyder has proposed. Here it helps to consider art savants. That Nadia began drawings with minor features rather than overall outlines suggests that she tended to perceive individual details more prominently than she did the whole—or the concept—of what she was drawing. Other savant artists draw the same way.

Autistic children differ from nonautistic children in another way. Normal kids find it frustrating to copy a picture containing a visual illusion, such as M. C. Escher's drawing in which water flows uphill. Autistic children don't. That fits with Snyder's idea that they're recording what they see without interpretation and reproducing it with ease in their own drawings.

Even accomplished artists sometimes employ strategies to 35 shake up their preconceptions about what they're seeing. Guy Diehl is not a savant, but he is known for his series of crystal-clear still lifes of stacked books, drafting implements, and fruit. When Diehl finds that he's hit a sticking point on a painting, for example, he may actually view it in a mirror or upside down. "It reveals things you otherwise wouldn't see, because you're seeing it differently," he says. "You're almost seeing it for the first time again."

Diehl showed me how art students use this technique to learn to draw. He put a pair of scissors on a table and told me to draw the negative space around the scissors, not the scissors themselves. The result: I felt I was drawing individual lines, not an object, and my drawing wasn't half bad, either.

Drawing exercises are one way of coaxing conceptual machinery to take five, but Snyder is pursuing a more direct method. He has suggested that a technique called transcranial magnetic stimulation, which uses magnetic fields to disrupt neuronal firing, could knock out a normal person's conceptual brain machinery, temporarily rendering him savantlike.

Young and her colleague Michael Ridding of the University of Adelaide tried it. Using transcranial magnetic stimulation on 17 volunteers, they inhibited neural activity in the frontotemporal area. This language and concept-supporting brain region is affected in patients with frontotemporal dementia and in the art savant whom Miller studied. In this altered state, the volunteers performed savantlike tasks—horse drawing, calendar calculating, and multiplying.

Five of the 17 volunteers improved—not to savant levels, but no one expected that, because savants practice. Furthermore, transcranial magnetic stimulation isn't a precise tool for targeting brain regions. But the five volunteers who improved were those in whom separate neurological assessments indicated that the frontotemporal area was successfully targeted. "Obviously I don't think the idea is so outlandish anymore," says Young. "I think it is a plausible hypothesis. It always was, but I didn't expect we'd actually find the things we did."

Snyder himself is experimenting with grander ideas. "We want to enhance conceptual abilities," he says, "and on the other hand remove them and enhance objectivity." He imagines a combination of training and hardware that might, for example, help an engineer get past a sticking point on a design project by offering a fresh angle on the problem. One method would involve learning to monitor one's own brain waves. By watching one's own brain waves during drawing exercises, Snyder imagines it may be possible to learn to control them in a way that shuts down their concept-making machinery—even the left temporal lobe itself.

Even if further research never fully reveals why savants have extraordinary skills, we may at least learn from their potential. Snyder is optimistic. "I envisage the day," he says, "when the way to get out of a [mental rut] is you pick up this thing—those of us with jobs that demand a certain type of creativity—and you stimulate your brain. I'm very serious about this."

Questions

1. Artists create images for personal expression, to explore their experiences, or to make money. What purpose do you think it served for Nadia to create her drawings? What might make her reasons different from those of other image-makers?

2. What evidence is included in the article to support the idea that "the same skills [as those exhibited by an autistic savant] are biologically latent in everyone" (paragraph 7)? Which researchers are quoted? What kind of research are they conducting?

3. Try doing an exercise mentioned in the article. First, draw a pair of scissors lying on a table. Then create a second drawing of only the space around the scissors. What is the difference in looking and thinking about what you saw in these two approaches? How does this relate to the way in which savants might see the world differently from other people?

4. What might scientists do someday so that we all can experience the ability to perform savantlike behavior? What would one gain from this experience? Would you like the ability of a savant if it meant, as it sometimes seems to, being more isolated and less sociable?

5. Write a paper in which you describe your experience either drawing a ball or looking carefully at a drawing of a ball. What makes the ball in the drawing look solid, look round, look as though it is firmly on the page and not floating? Describe what you observe in close detail. Did writing this essay give you any insights into how you see and how you understand what you see?

In the River of Consciousness
OLIVER SACKS

Science writer, neurologist, and medical researcher, Sacks has been referred to by the New York Times *as "the poet laureate of medicine." Among his many books is the award-winning* Awakenings *(1973), which inspired the Oscar-nominated Hollywood movie "Awakenings," about long-term comatose encephalitic patients who were revived through the use of the then-experimental drug L-dopa. Dr. Sacks has written about patients with a variety of neurological disorders in books, which include* Migraine *(1970);* Seeing Voices: A Journey into the World of the Deaf *(1990);* The Man Who Mistook His Wife for a Hat *(1985); and* Uncle Tungsten: Memories of a Chemical Boyhood *(2001), among others, and in essays for the* New York Times. *"In the River of Consciousness" is excerpted from one of his essays in* The New York Review of Books.

Getting Started

In this article, Sacks explores a very basic aspect of vision. . .our ability to detect motion. Philosophers have long speculated about whether we see the world as continuous and fluid or in discrete snapshots that the brain weaves together. Sacks suggests that the advent of motion pictures changed the way we approach this question. Have you ever experienced life in a kind of stop time as some of his patients have? Have you ever been tricked by the optical illusion of a spinning fan or wheel? What is it like to suddenly become aware of a difference in your visual perception? Do you think that movie techniques like zooming, fading, and dissolving have changed the way we see the world? Can you think of other imaging technologies that not only produce new kinds of images but also change the way we think about vision itself?

————————— ✦ —————————

1.

"Time," says Jorge Luis Borges, "is the substance I am made of. Time is a river that carries me away, but I am the river. . . ." Our movements, our actions, are extended in time, as are our perceptions, our thoughts, the contents of consciousness. We live in time, we organize time, we are time creatures through and through. But is the time we live in, or live by, continuous—like Borges's river? Or is it more comparable to a chain or a train, a succession of discrete moments, like beads on a string?

David Hume, in the eighteenth century, favored the idea of discrete moments, and for him the mind was "nothing but a bundle or collection of different perceptions, which succeed each other with an inconceivable rapidity, and are in a perpetual flux and movement."

For William James, writing his *Principles of Psychology* in 1890, the "Humean view," as he called it, was both powerful and vexing. It seemed counterintuitive, as a start. In his famous chapter on "the stream of thought," James stressed that to its possessor, consciousness seems to be always continuous, "without breach, crack, or division," never "chopped up, into bits." The content of consciousness might be changing continually, but we move smoothly from one thought to another, one percept to another, without interruption or breaks. For James, thought *flowed*; hence his introduction of the term "stream of consciousness." But, he wondered, "is consciousness really discontinuous . . . and does it only seem continuous to itself by an illusion analogous to that of the zoetrope?"

Before 1830 (short of making an actual working model, or toy theater), there was no way of making representations or images that had movement. Nor would it have occurred to anyone that a sensation or illusion of movement *could* be conveyed by still pictures. How could pictures convey movement if they had none themselves? The very idea was paradoxical, a contradiction. But the zoetrope proved that individual images could be fused in the brain to give an illusion of continuous motion, an idea that was soon to give rise to the motion picture.

Zoetropes (and many other similar devices, with a variety of   5
names) were extremely popular in James's time, and few middle-class Victorian households were without one. All of these instruments contained a drum or disc on which a series of drawings—of animals moving, ball games, acrobats in motion, plants growing—was painted or pasted. The drawings could be viewed one at a time through radial slits in the drum, but when the drum was set into motion, the separate drawings flicked by in rapid succession, and at a critical speed, this suddenly gave way to the perception of a single, steady moving picture. When one slowed the drum again, the illusion vanished. Though zoetropes were usually seen as toys, providing a magical illusion of motion, they were originally designed (often by scientists or philosophers) with a sense that they could serve a very serious purpose: to illuminate the mechanisms both of vision and of animal motion.

Had James been writing a few years later, he might indeed have used the analogy of a motion picture. A movie, with its taut stream of thematically connected images, its visual narrative integrated by the viewpoint and values of its director, is not at all a bad metaphor for the stream of consciousness itself. And the technical and conceptual devices of cinema—zooming, fading, dissolving, omission, allusion, association and juxtaposition of all sorts—rather closely mimic (and perhaps are designed to mimic) the streamings and veerings of consciousness.

It is an analogy that Henri Bergson used twenty years later, in his 1908 book *Creative Evolution*, where he devoted an entire section to "The Cinematographic Mechanism of Thought, and the Mechanistic Illusion": We take snapshots, as it were, of the passing reality, and . . . we have only to string these on a becoming, . . . situated at the back of the apparatus of knowledge, in order to imitate what there is that is characteristic in this becoming itself. . . . We hardly do anything else than set going a kind of cinematograph inside us. . . . The *mechanism of our ordinary knowledge is of a cinematographical kind.*

Were James and Bergson intuiting a truth in comparing visual perception—and indeed, the flow of consciousness itself—to such a mechanism? Are the brain mechanisms that give coherence to perception and consciousness somehow analogous to motion picture cameras and projectors? Does the eye/brain actually "take" perceptual stills and somehow fuse them to give a sense of continuity and motion? No clear answer was forthcoming during their lifetimes.

There is a rare but dramatic neurological disturbance that a number of my patients have experienced during attacks of migraine, when they may lose the sense of visual continuity and motion and see instead a flickering series of "stills." The stills may be clear-cut and sharp, and succeed one another without superimposition or overlap, but more commonly they are somewhat blurred, as with a too-long photographic exposure, and they persist for so long that each is still visible when the next "frame" is seen, and three or four frames, the earlier ones progressively fainter, are apt to be superimposed on each other. While the effect is somewhat like that of a film (albeit an improperly shot and presented one, in which each exposure has been too long to freeze motion completely and the rate of presentation too slow to achieve fusion), it also resembles some of E.J. Marey's "chronophotographs" of the 1880s, in which one sees a whole array of photographic moments or time frames superimposed on a single plate.[1]

I heard several accounts of such visual effects while working in the late 1960s with a large number of migraine patients, and when I wrote about this in my 1970 book *Migraine*, I noted that the rate of flickering in these episodes seemed to be between six

10

---

[1]Étienne-Jules Marey, in France, like Eadweard Muybridge in the United States, pioneered the development of quick-fire, instantaneous, serial photographs. While these could be arrayed around a zoetrope drum to provide a brief "movie," they could also be used to decompose movement, to investigate the temporal organization and biodynamics of animal and human motion. This was Marey's special interest, as a physiologist, and for this purpose he preferred to superimpose his images—a dozen or twenty images, a second's worth—on a single plate. Such composite photographs, in effect, captured a span of time; this is why he called them "chronophotographs." Marey's photographs became the model for all subsequent scientific photographic studies of movement, and chronophotography was an inspiration to artists, too (one thinks of Duchamp's famous *Nude Descending a Staircase*, which Duchamp himself referred to as "a static image of movement").

and twelve per second. There might also be, in cases of migraine delirium, a flickering of kaleidoscopic patterns or hallucinations. (The flickering might then accelerate to restore the appearance of normal motion or of a continuously modulated hallucination.) Finding no good accounts of the phenomenon in the medical literature—perhaps not entirely surprising, for such attacks are brief, rare, and not readily predicted or provoked—I used the term "cinematographic" vision for them; for patients always compared them to films run too slow.

This was a startling visual phenomenon, for which, in the 1960s, there was no good physiological explanation. But I could not help wondering then whether visual perception might in a very real way be analogous to cinematography, taking in the visual environment in brief, instantaneous, static frames, or "stills," and then, under normal conditions, fusing these to give visual awareness its usual movement and continuity—a "fusion" which, seemingly, was failing to occur in the very abnormal conditions of these migraine attacks.

Such visual effects may also occur in certain seizures, as well as in intoxications (especially with hallucinogens such as LSD). And there are other visual effects that may occur. Moving objects may leave a smear or wake in the direction they move; images may repeat themselves; and afterimages may be greatly prolonged. I have experienced this myself, following the drinking of sakau, a hallucinogen and intoxicant popular in Micronesia. I described some of these effects in a journal, and later in my book *The Island of the Colorblind:*

> Ghost petals ray out from a flower on our table, like a halo around it; when it is moved . . . it leaves a slight train, a visual smear . . . in its wake. Watching a palm waving, I see a succession of stills, like a film run too slow, its continuity no longer maintained.

I heard strikingly similar accounts in the late 1960s from some of my post-encephalitic patients, when they were "awakened," and especially overexcited, by taking the drug L-DOPA. Some patients described cinematic vision; some described extraordinary "standstills," sometimes hours long, in which not only visual flow was arrested, but the stream of movement, of action, of thought itself.

These standstills were especially severe with one patient, Hester Y. Once I was called to the ward because Mrs. Y. had started a bath, and there was now a flood in the bathroom. I found her standing completely motionless in the middle of the flood.

She jumped when I touched her, and said, "What happened?" "You tell me," I answered. 15

She said that she had started to run a bath for herself, and there was an inch of water in the tub. . .and then I touched her, and she suddenly realized that the tub must have run over and caused a flood. But she had been stuck, transfixed, at that perceptual moment when there was just an inch of water in the bath.

Such standstills showed that consciousness could be brought to a halt, stopped dead, for substantial periods, while automatic, nonconscious function—maintenance of posture or breathing, for example—continued as before.

Another striking example of perceptual standstill could be demonstrated with a common visual illusion, that of the Necker cube. Normally, when we look at this ambiguous perspective drawing of a cube, it switches perspective every few seconds, first seeming to project, then to recede, and no effort of will suffices to prevent this switching back and forth. The drawing itself does not change, nor does the retinal image. The switching is a cortical process, a conflict in consciousness itself, as it vacillates between alternative perceptual interpretations. This switching is seen in all normal subjects, and can be observed with functional brain imaging. But a post-encephalitic patient, during a standstill state, may see the same unchanging perspective for minutes or hours at a time.

The normal flow of consciousness, it seemed, could not only be fragmented, broken into small, snapshot-like bits, but could be suspended intermittently, for hours at a time.[2] I found this even more puzzling and uncanny than cinematic vision, for it has been accepted almost axiomatically since the time of William James that consciousness, in its very nature, is ever-changing and ever-flowing; but now my own clinical experience had to cast doubt on even this. 20

---

[2]Music, with its rhythm and flow, can be of crucial importance in such freezings, allowing patients to resume their suddenly arrested flow of movement perception, and thought. Music sometimes seems able to act as a sort of model or template for the sense of time and movement such patients have temporarily lost, and which they need to regain. Thus a parkinsonian patient in the midst of a standstill may be able to move when music is played. Indeed, they may be completely unable to walk, but able to dance to music. Neurologists intuitively use musical terms here, and speak of parkinsonism as a "kinetic stutter" and normal movement as "kinetic melody." William Harvey, writing in 1627, referred to animal motion as "the silent music of the body."

Thus I was primed to be further fascinated when, in 1983, Josef Zihl and his colleagues in Munich published a single, very fully described case of motion blindness: a woman who became permanently unable to perceive motion following a stroke. (The stroke had damaged the highly specific areas of the visual cortex which physiologists have shown in experimental animals to be crucial for motion perception.) In this patient, whom they call L. M., there were "freeze frames" lasting several seconds, during which Mrs. M. would see a prolonged, motionless image and be visually unaware of any movement around her, though her flow of thought and perception was otherwise normal. For example, Mrs. M. might begin a conversation with a friend standing in front of her, but not be able to see her friend's lips moving or facial expressions changing. And if the friend moved around behind her, Mrs. M. might continue to "see" him in front of her, even though his voice now came from behind. She might see a car "frozen" a considerable distance from her, but find, when she tried to cross the road, that it was now almost upon her; she would see a "glacier," a frozen arc of tea coming from the spout of the teapot, but then realize that she had overfilled the cup, and that there was now a puddle of tea on the table. Such a condition was utterly bewildering, and sometimes quite dangerous.

There are clear differences between cinematic vision and the sort of motion blindness described by Zihl; and perhaps between these and the very long visual and sometimes global freezes experienced by some post-encephalitic patients. These differences imply that there must be a number of different mechanisms or systems for the perception of visual motion and the continuity of visual consciousness—and this accords with evidence obtained from perceptual and psychological experiments. Some or all of these mechanisms may fail to work as they should in certain intoxications, some attacks of migraine, and some forms of brain damage—but can they also reveal themselves under normal conditions?

An obvious example springs to mind, which many of us have seen and perhaps puzzled over when watching evenly rotating objects—fans, wheels, propeller blades—or when walking past fences or palings, when the normal continuity of motion seems to be interrupted. Thus, occasionally, as I lie in bed looking up at my ceiling fan, the blades seem suddenly to reverse direction for a few seconds, and then to return equally suddenly to their original forward motion. Sometimes the fan seems to hover or stall, and sometimes to develop additional blades or dark bands broader than the blades.

It is similar to what happens when, in a film, the wheels of stagecoaches sometimes appear to be going slowly backward or scarcely moving. This wagon-wheel illusion, as it is called, reflects a lack of synchronization between the rate of filming and that of the rotating wheels. But I can have a real-life wagon-wheel illusion even when I look at my fan with the morning sun flooding into my room, bathing everything in a continuous, even light. Is there, then, some flickering or lack of synchronization in my own perceptual mechanisms—analogous, again, to the action of a movie camera?

Dale Purves and his colleagues at Duke University have explored wagon-wheel illusions in great detail, and they have confirmed that this type of illusion or misperception is universal among their subjects. Having excluded any other cause of discontinuity (intermittent lighting, eye movements, etc.), they conclude that the visual system processes information "in sequential episodes," at the rate of three to twenty such episodes per second. Normally, these sequential images are experienced as an unbroken perceptual flow. Indeed, Purves et al. suggest, we may find movies convincing precisely because we ourselves break up time and reality much as a movie camera does, into discrete frames, which we then reassemble into an apparently continuous flow.

In Purves's view, it is precisely this decomposition of what we see into a succession of moments that enables the brain to detect and compute motion; for all it has to do is to note the differing positions of objects between successive "frames," and from these calculate the direction and speed of motion.[3]

2.

But this is not enough. We do not merely calculate movement as a robot might—we *perceive* it. We perceive motion, just as we perceive color or depth, as a unique qualitative experience that is vital to our visual awareness and consciousness. Something beyond our understanding occurs in the genesis of qualia, the transformation of an objective cerebral computation to a subjective experience. Philosophers argue endlessly over how these transformations occur, and whether we will ever be capable of understanding them. Neuroscientists, by and large, are content for the

---

[3]Whether or not this is so, the brain can also create motion on its own: one can "see" motion when, objectively, there is none, as in the well-known waterfall illusion.

moment to accept that they do occur, and to devote themselves to finding the underlying basis or "neural correlates" of consciousness, starting from such elemental forms of consciousness as the perception of motion.

James dreamed of zoetropes as a metaphor for the conscious brain, Bergson of cinematography—but these were, of necessity, no more than tantalizing analogies and images. It has only been in the last twenty or thirty years that neuroscience could even start to address such issues as the neural basis of consciousness.

Indeed, from having been an almost untouchable subject before the 1970s, the neuroscientific study of consciousness has now become a central concern, one that engages scientists all over the world. Every level of consciousness is now being explored, from the most elemental perceptual mechanisms (mechanisms common to many animals besides ourselves) to the higher reaches of memory, imagery, and self-reflective consciousness.

It is now possible to monitor simultaneously the activities of   30
a hundred or more individual neurons in the brain, and to do this in unanesthetized animals given simple perceptual and mental tasks. We can examine the activity and interactions of large areas of the brain by means of imaging techniques like functional MRIs and PET scans, and such non-invasive techniques can be used with human subjects, to see which areas of the brain are activated in complex mental activities.

In addition to physiological studies, there is the relatively new realm of computerized neural modeling, using populations or networks of virtual neurons, and seeing how these organize themselves in response to various stimuli and constraints.

All of these approaches, along with concepts not available to earlier generations, now combine to make the quest for the neural correlates of consciousness the most fundamental and exciting adventure in neuroscience today. A crucial innovation has been "population-thinking," thinking in terms that take account of the brain's huge population of neurons (a hundred billion or so), and the power of experience to differentially alter the strengths of connections between them, and to promote the formation of functional groups or constellations of neurons throughout the brain—groups whose interactions serve to categorize experience.[4]

---

[4]No paradigms or concepts, however original, ever come totally out of the blue. While population-thinking in relation to the brain only emerged in the 1970s, there was an important antecedent twenty-five years earlier, Donald Hebb's famous 1949 book *The Organization of Behavior.* Hebb sought to bridge the great gap between neurophysiology and psychology with a general theory which

(*Continues*)

Instead of seeing the brain as rigid, fixed in mode, programmed like a computer, there is now a much more biological and powerful notion of "experiential selection," of experience literally shaping the connectivity and function of the brain (within genetic, anatomical, and physiological limits, of course).

Questions

1. As Sacks points out, zoetropes and other imaging technologies can change the way we think about thinking because we often use images as analogies for the way the brain works. How do you think that digital photography, to take one modern example, might change our notions of perception and vision? Are there other new imaging techniques that you think will change the way we think about how we see?

2. How do the migraine experiences that Sacks describes (paragraphs 9–11) connect to the importance of our brain in interpreting the information our eye receives? What examples does Sacks provide to support the idea "that there must be a number of different mechanisms or systems for the perception of visual motion" (paragraph 22)? Is there any evidence that examining normal, healthy people might provide further support for the idea? What steps might a medical researcher take to find this out?

3. How have recent technological medical advances improved our ability to visualize and therefore better understand the connection between eye and brain? Go online and look at examples of an MRI or PET scan of the brain. Without being an expert in these technical images, what did you notice about the relationship of them to thinking and seeing?

4. Make a list of the thinkers—philosophers, writers, artists—that Oliver Sacks mentions in the essay. Find out who they are and write a sentence or two about each of them. Why do you think he refers to these people? Why do writers include other thinkers in their essays? Look at some of your earlier essays and notice if, when, and how you refer to other thinkers.

5. Look at the movement of a fan (or wheels) for several minutes. Notice if the blades or wheels seem to reverse movement the way Sacks describes (paragraphs 23–24) or cause any other visual illusions. How long did it take before your perception changed? How did doing this experiment relate to what Sacks has to say about perception?

---

could relate neural processes to mental ones, and, in particular, show how experience could modify, in effect shape, the brain. The potential for modification, Hebb felt, was vested in the synapses which connect brain cells to each other—a single cerebral neuron, we now know, can have up to ten thousand synapses, and the brain as a whole has upward of a hundred trillion, so the capacities for modification are practically infinite. Hebb's original concept was soon to be confirmed, and set the stage for new ways of thinking. Every neuroscientist who now thinks about consciousness is thus indebted to Hebb.

Making Connections

1. The five articles in this chapter were selected because each one refers to a way in which we use images, either personally or culturally. Why do you think each article was chosen; what aspect of the use of an image does each article explore?

2. Fox refers to calendars and how savants "memorize" them in order to predict dates. Calendars are examples of practical image making. What other practical images can you think of that help us make sense of the world—physically, intellectually, and even spiritually?

3. In their articles, Hughes and Carpenter both describe images that are made to be invisible, secret, or transient. Why do you think the creators of such images might want to make them inaccessible or to limit their existence in time? In today's world of instant images, can you think of any that we still want to keep secret or of limited access? How do we do this when the privacy of our images is becoming more difficult to secure?

4. Sacks uses the sophisticated technology of movies as an analogy for the way we see the world while Carpenter discusses images created with very basic tools. Are newer images created with more sophisticated technology necessarily more powerful or is the reverse true? Write an essay in which you explain the reasons for your opinion.

5. The article by Hughes investigates the use of images by Cro-Magnon people who lived thousands of years ago. Pick a familiar image from our time and imagine that it is discovered by archeologists 20,000 years from now. What do you think these future people would make of it and how might they *misinterpret* the way we used it?

6. For a better understanding of the Fox article, you might want to see the film "Rain Man," or the film "Awakenings" in reference to the Sacks article. What is the difference between reading about something and seeing a film of it? Would you rather use text or film to learn about something and what are the reasons that one appeals to you more than the other?

7. Fox and Sacks both explore the role and importance of images by studying extreme examples like savants with remarkable abilities to draw or people with severe motion perception problems. Do you think that images play a different role for such people than they do for other people? How much of the world of the image do we all share? What kinds of images do you think have the broadest appeal or are meaningful to most people? What kinds have the narrowest uses?

8. The introduction to this chapter says that "images emerge from a variety of needs within individuals and even from within cultures as a whole." What needs do you think images fulfilled for some of the image makers described in this chapter—the Cro-Magnon people Hughes discusses, the invisible art makers Carpenter describes, the autistic savants Fox describes, the dreamers Gelman writes about, and the patients Sacks describes. Choose one of these and explain what needs the images seemed to fulfill for these people and why you think this.

CHAPTER 5

Pictures that Prod

"Whoever controls the media, the images, controls the culture."

—Allen Ginsberg

One of the most powerful aspects of images is their ability to affect our attitudes and viewpoints. Images influence our thinking about a wide range of topics, and manipulated by the right people under the right conditions, images can be used as an effective means of directing public opinion. Advertisers, of course, have based an entire industry on this fact; those who manage propaganda know very well how effective images can be. Most of the time, this manipulation is seen as more or less benign, just another proof that images matter to us in significant ways, and a further example of the intimate ways that images inject themselves into our lives. Yet when the poet Allen Ginsberg made the statement above, he was pointing to the most dangerous version of this manipulation: not simple persuasion on the part of image-makers, but a desire for outright control.

In "Once Again, Patriotic Themes Ring True As Art," journalist Deborah Solomon explores the role that patriotic art plays in society, with a special focus on the impact such images have had on us since the attack on New York City's World Trade Center on September 11, 2001. As Solomon points out, patriotic images have always been used to gain support for governments and their wars. Her article also suggests that such images have an important role to play in supporting the values of the culture they represent. But the power of these images raises the question of when support for cultural values shifts subtly (or not-so-subtly) into coercion.

In "Dire Image: The Art of Persuasion," Alan Robbins, one of the authors of this book, discusses one of the most compelling cases of image manipulation in history: the creation of a comprehensive and complete campaign of propaganda by the Nazis in Germany. In his essay, Robbins looks at the ways in which an entire visual style was designed to support a specific ideology and how this relied less on censorship and more on encouraging existing cultural values. These issues have an inevitable implication for the explosion of the image in modern times.

Richard Goldstein in "Cartoon Wars" points out how even the most seemingly benign of images—cartoons—can take on dire meanings in the right context. In his opinion, in the heightened political environment of our time, even cartoons loom large as statements about important issues. The cartoon wars of his title are part of the general culture war and refer to images that figuratively draw lines in the sand, whether they deal with political, racial, or even sexual themes. Because they are so simple and essential, easily seen and grasped, such cartoons can get right to the heart of feelings about controversial issues. Goldstein points to the power of cartoons in capturing essential, and not always positive, notions of the political landscape.

"Reality's Flight" by Nina Willdorf looks at a new type of image that is having profound effects on our visual surround: the amazing popularity of so-called "reality TV." Her article suggests that some form of reality TV has always been with us and, despite predictions, probably always will—thanks to one compelling need that all such images rely on . . . voyeurism. We simply love to know how other people live and act, and the more immediate medium available always takes over this role. Therefore, just as TV displaced film, it is now being replaced by the Web. Contemporary reality shows, in Willdorf's opinion, are popular now because TV must compete with the instant voyeuristic gratification offered by the blogs and webcams of the Internet.

Finally, in "What is Art?", Leo Tolstoy discusses the role of art as a means of the communication of feeling from creator to audience, even speaking of this kind of transmission as an "infection." Most images, he writes, elicit an emotional response and some even overwhelm the feelings. But they only rise to the level of art when the audience is infected by the feeling the creator felt. If it is true that the most powerful images infect us with feelings, Tolstoy's view, expressed in the nineteenth century, has repercussions for the way we negotiate the world of the image now.

Once Again, Patriotic Themes Ring True As Art

DEBORAH SOLOMON

Deborah Solomon is an art critic, biographer, and a regular contributor to the New York Times. *She is also the author of* Jackson Pollock: A Biography *(2001) and* Utopia Parkway: The Life and Work of Joseph Cornell *(1997). She received a Guggenheim Fellowship in 2001 for her work on a biography of Norman Rockwell that is to be published by Farrar, Straus & Giroux. "Once Again, Patriotic Themes Ring True As Art" appeared in the* New York Times *soon after September 11, 2001, and discusses the renewed respect and relevance "to long-discredited images" of patriotic art.*

Getting Started

In this article, Deborah Solomon reports on the resurgence of a particular kind of image she refers to as patriotic art. What is patriotic art? What examples come to your mind? Why do many people turn to such images when there is a war or when their countries are facing serious crises? Why does patriotic art sometimes fall out of favor? Why do some people want to surround themselves with images "that promote American institutions" and why "at times [can such art] prove as enduring as any museum masterpiece?"

---◆---

Patriotic art has never exactly ranked high on the list of aesthetic wonders, but who can doubt its appeal? It is hard to think of a painting in an American museum that can compete for visual immediacy with that famous image of Uncle Sam pointing his finger and sternly admonishing, "I Want You." The World War I recruiting poster is an inadvertent classic of American art, evoking the intense and tragic years when a generation of young men put on uniforms, boarded trains and promised their moms they'd be back soon while knowing they might never be back at all.

Not long after the twin towers fell and the tears started flowing, *New York* magazine ran a humorous cover illustration of Mayor Rudolph W. Giuliani decked out as Uncle Sam. You can glance nearly anywhere these days and see that patriotism has its own look, its own iconography, its own repertory of time-honored images. It is odd to think that my generation, the first for whom avant-garde art was not a moral offense but a subject to be diligently studied in college, now finds itself mesmerized by the landscape of patriotism. We who wrote term papers on Andy Warhol's soup cans and barely bothered to look at any flag that did not bear the signature of Jasper Johns are turning for solace to pictorial representations of honor, country and heroism that were born before we were.

For years, of course, such themes were disdained as artistically incorrect. The "American Century" whose advent was loudly proclaimed after 1945 took its cultural cue not from Peoria, but from Paris: It treated modernism as an assault on bourgeois values and defined the archetypal American artist as a Jackson Pollock sort, a moody genius splashing out abstract pictures. Patriotic art, in the meantime, was presumed to refer to bronze statues of soldiers on horses, as stiff as mannequins and equally oblivious to the temper of the times. To proclaim an unironic interest in such art was to invite sneers from sophisticates, to be written off as a visual illiterate.

Yet the events of Sept. 11 and the weeks since have brought a sudden relevance and even respect to long-discredited images. The most striking example is the picture by Thomas E. Franklin, a 35-year-old staff photographer for *The Bergen Record* that recently appeared on front pages around the world and made the cover of *Newsweek*. By now you have seen it: Three firefighters, their clothes and black helmets shiny with ash, gaze into a squinty-bright sky as they hoist a flag above the rubble of the World Trade Center.

The image became an overnight icon, and not only because it 5 attests to the self-sacrificing courage of the firemen. It also sends us back in time, evoking classic scenes of soldiers in battle. One thinks, in particular, of the photograph of Iwo Jima taken on Feb. 23, 1945, the four marines huddled together as they raise a flag above the island, their bodies and outstretched arms forming a pyramid that itself harks back to the balanced forms of Renaissance sculpture.

Not surprisingly, the photograph of Iwo Jima was later revealed to have been staged; it was taken a short time after the actual event occurred. Some people felt this made it fraudulent and also discredited the statue that was based on it, a mammoth bronze memorial that stands west of Arlington National Cemetery and remains the best-known monument of World War II. But such thinking is foolish. If art is a lie that tells the truth, as Picasso once said, the Iwo Jima Memorial certainly qualifies.

What, exactly, is patriotic art? In contrast to the School of Paris (think Picasso) or the School of New York (think Pollock), patriotic art might be regarded as the school of Washington, confining itself to eye-catching images that promote American institutions. It is commonly maligned as propaganda. It reached an apogee during World War I, when the federal government, seeking to mold opinion in a country where radio and television were not yet available, enlisted visual artists to advertise its cause. What they were selling was not soap or light bulbs, but the war effort and the government itself.

The Division of Pictorial Publicity, which was part of America's version of a propaganda ministry, wallpapered buildings and streets across the country with tens of thousands of posters, the most popular of which depicted Uncle Sam and his pointing finger.

That poster, by the way, was created in 1917 by James Montgomery Flagg, a prodigiously gifted illustrator who in some ways was an unlikely patriot. Flagg was a vivid character, a New York bohemian with striking features and a predilection for blond show girls. Unknown to the American public, he used himself as the model for his Uncle Sam. His recruiting poster takes an amorous come-on ("I want you") and turns it into a patriotic come-on.

Henry James once observed that Americans have "the reputation of always boasting and blowing and waving the American flag." Yet patriotic imagery need not be festooned with stars and stripes. Norman Rockwell, who did more to visualize the aspirations of Americans than any other artist of the 20th century, seldom painted the flag. Instead he painted a country whose spirit remained abundantly intact despite two world wars and the Great Depression. In a time when anthrax attacks only intensify our yearnings to return to normalcy, Rockwell's pictures of kids, dogs and uncranky grandmothers might be viewed as normalcy incarnate.

That's certainly the subject of his "Freedom From Fear" (1943), one in a quartet of wartime paintings based on President

Roosevelt's rousing words. It shows two children snug in bed, their mother stooping to pull up their blanket, their father looking on, holding a newspaper whose partially visible headline announces news of "bombings" and "horror" abroad. To see the painting today is to see six decades slip away. We know now what it means to crave freedom from fear, the freedom to walk kids to school and toss a baseball in a park without feeling a shadow of trepidation darken the face of American democracy.

It would be absurd to pretend that patriotic art can give form to the full range and depth of human emotion. It cannot. It captures mainly one emotion: an appreciation for the values and rituals of American life. A few months ago that may have sounded corny, but it no longer does. As we continue to try to lend shape to feelings of national concern and affection, it would be a mistake to dismiss patriotic art as kitsch. It serves a purpose in the immediate present and—to judge from the example of Uncle Sam, Iwo Jima and two kids tucked into bed—at times can prove as enduring as any museum masterpiece.

Questions

1. How does Solomon define patriotic art? What examples does she provide? What differences do you notice among the various examples she describes? What about them makes them all "patriotic" in some way?

2. Does Solomon think that the art produced by Andy Warhol and Jasper Johns is patriotic? Go online and look at some of the images these artists have created. Why do you think she mentions them in this article?

3. Why do the images that Solomon describes in her article have such power and resonance? What makes a particular kind of image patriotic to you? Find some samples of patriotic images not mentioned in the article and explain your reasons for choosing them.

4. Does it matter to you that some photographs such as the famous Iwo Jima photograph might have been staged? What does Solomon mean when she writes: "If art is a lie that tells the truth, as Picasso once said, the Iwo Jima Memorial certainly qualifies" (paragraph 6)? What do you think Picasso meant?

5. Solomon mentions a number of images that refer to patriotic themes. The paintings of Norman Rockwell, the "I Want You" poster by James Montgomery Flagg, and the photos of Iwo Jima and the 9/11 firefighters raising the flag. Look at some of these online and write an essay about whether you think of them as representing "propaganda" or "patriotism," and what the difference is between these two ideas.

Dire Image: The Art of Persuasion
ALAN ROBBINS

Alan Robbins is the Janet Estabrook Rogers Professor of Visual and Performing Arts at Kean University in New Jersey, where he teaches design and visual studies. He also directs the Design Center at the university, producing exhibitions, publications, and innovative design products. Professor Robbins is a frequent presenter at national conferences on the topics of graphic design, technology, and visual studies. He has published 16 books, including, most recently, two science fiction mysteries: A Small Box of Chaos *(2005) and* An Interlude in Dreamland *(2005).*

Getting Started

The influence of images on our attitudes and beliefs is well-demonstrated by both advertising and propaganda, but the example Alan Robbins presents in this article is one of the most extreme. Has an image ever changed or helped you form your opinion about something. If so, what examples come to mind? Have you ever based your attitude about something solely on images you have seen of it? How do you know a propaganda image when you see one? Is propaganda different from persuasion? When do images designed to convince become dangerous to a society?

———————— ✦ ————————

Images are one of the cherished things we make. Whether using colored powders made from Ice Age plants or pixels on a high-resolution touchscreen, we are image-makers and have always been. Our passion for making and remaking images is undeniable.

But images are unique among our creations in their ability to remake us as well. Whether we see them as windows on the world or mirrors to ourselves, we have a deep and broad investment in them. We create them to express ourselves, to explain the world, to investigate and to communicate. But we also turn around and believe in them, trust them, look to them for clues about how and what to think.

In a very real sense, we become our images. We change our appearance, make decisions, develop our truths and our lies, based on the images we see. Just think of our attitudes about what is going on in the world . . . who we think we are, what our values are, how we should look, who our enemies are. Then consider how much of that comes from images, from pictures on TV, photographs, and movies.

This influence matters because images are more and more the way we know the world and each other. And it matters because it means that anyone who can control images has a unique power over us—not only over what we see but also what we know, how we think, and even who we are.

But it is hard to look at ourselves objectively since we are too   5
caught up in our own drama, our own story. To understand how vulnerable we are to our own pictures, we would have to look at a different time and a place when images were used very powerfully to manipulate the understanding, behavior, and attitudes of an entire country. Not just because it is interesting, although it is. But because it is so *possible*.

The case to study is Nazi Germany, because Adolf Hitler himself had very precise ideas about how to manipulate the masses using images. Hitler was, notoriously, an artist first. In fact, thousands of watercolors, oils, and drawings have been attributed to him. A famous statement in his book *Mein Kampf* says that "art is the only truly enduring effort of human labor." This is a sentiment that could have been made by any devoted artist—but Hitler was no ordinary artist.

There is still plenty of debate about whether he was a good one or not; one theory suggests that his artistic frustration lead to his megalomania. Some critics of his work see cold, stiff renderings devoid of people and life that offer a glimpse into a brutal mind. Others see competent compositions, sensitivity to the play of color and light, and skill in dealing with perspective that are all the result of careful looking.

But talent and skill are the wrong places to search for a lesson. It was his commitment to the power of visual communication that can give us an insight into what came later. Hitler was fundamentally aware of the role that the image could play in the world and he understood its ability to convince and coerce.

So when he writes, also in *Mein Kampf*, that "art is a mighty and fanatical mission," it is the word fanatical that we should take note of. It suggests how committed he was to the role of the aesthetic—the whole look and style—of the Third Reich. After all, it was under his direction that the "Nazi look" became so crystallized. Cutlery, monuments, stamps, tanks, uniforms, stage sets, flags, pageants, mastheads, furniture, exhibits, even the design of the Volkswagen Beetle, in which Hitler had a direct hand, all came to embody this emerging style.

To put it in modern terms, Hitler was the art director of a dire   10
image, the dark visionary behind almost every image produced in
Germany during that time. That makes him one of the inventors
of the politics of the image in the modern age.

Most famously, it was Hitler himself who chose the swastika as
the party logo. The swastika is an ancient symbol found in one
form or another in almost every culture on earth. It is a stable design, self-contained and balanced, but with a sense of motion or ro-
tation. It is therefore normally used to suggest orderly change . . .
like the progression of the seasons or the planting of crops. It was
even popular in the United States before the war where boys and
girls clubs used the symbol as a sign of unity.

The idea of using a swastika was originally proposed by a
dentist named Friedrich Kohn who also studied symbology, but
Hitler instantly understood the raw power of a logo as well as any
art director when he wrote "in hundreds of thousands of cases, an
effective emblem can give the first impetus for the interest in a
movement." Of course he redesigned it to fit his needs and produced a more powerful, bolder symbol, always in black, usually
on an angle, always opening to the right, often in a white circle on
a red background.

These were not random choices, at least not to the designer
himself. In *Mein Kampf* he says "As National Socialists we see our
program in our flag. In the red we see the social idea of the movement, in the white the national idea, in the swastika the mission of
the fight for the victory of the idea, of creative work, which in itself
is and always will be anti-Semitic." In other words, every decision
had a purpose, meant something, and was a symbol of the ideology.

With the help of Joseph Goebbels, minister of propaganda,
and Albert Speer, the national architect, the swastika and its
many uses became the most effective "identity system" ever created. We talk a lot about branding nowadays, how companies
carefully design all their products to fit a very clear message that
can gain lifelong devotees. And branding is, of course, highly effective marketing practice. But there can be a dark side too, and
Hitler in this regard was a master of branding.

After all, no other logo in history carries such an instanta-   15
neous shock of recognition. Half a century later, it still cannot be
shown in public without eliciting the deepest feelings. It is a perfect example of the power of the image to reach profoundly into
the human psyche.

But the logo was only one small piece of the entire dire image. Every major visual communication was carefully designed,
styled, and organized as well. The political rallies, for example,

were designed to be overwhelming visual pageants with choreography from musical extravaganzas, cadences from the liturgy of the Catholic Church, movement and music from the theater, movie lighting. Like rock concerts, like sports events, they were designed to create a mass emotion, to suppress the very idea of the individual and carry viewers off in an ecstasy of mysticism, theater, movement, and even eroticism.

And always at the center of these, of course, was the hypnotic and absurd presence of Hitler himself. His persona at these rallies was no accident, for this too was carefully crafted. It is hard for us now, after a half-century of television, to understand the appeal of his operatic gestures and pounding rhetoric. After all, he took his cues from theatre and from radio drama. He studied the gestures of silent movies. His speeches were not just written for posterity, but rehearsed and performed for their visual impact, their dramatic arc as it might be captured on film. There is a fascinating series of candid shots of Hitler practicing his rhetorical postures in a photographer's studio, not before a mirror, but on film so they could be studied later for their visual power.

But beyond all these basic elements of the Nazi "brand" was a much more profound form of visual coercion. This was accomplished through the Chambers of Culture established in 1933 and placed under the direction of Josef Goebbels, the propaganda minister. They were created to bring political pressure to bear on the arts by turning an existing system of artists' unions and societies into official Nazi institutions.

Separate Chambers were organized in music, theater, visual arts, literature, film, radio, and the press, and these quickly included thousands of professional and amateur artists in all fields throughout Germany. In fact, the chambers were a popular idea at first because, as Goebbels said, they would liberate German artists from the "competitive chaos of the liberal era." In other words, they would free artists and designers to pursue their work because they would have the support and encouragement of the state.

One of the largest of the culture Chambers was called the Visual Arts Chamber and it is a perfect example of how images can be molded towards an ideology. The Visual Arts Chamber included graphic designers, painters, sculptors, and typographers, and it became the role of this Chamber to manage all exhibitions, art collections, publications, and competitions. Artists who worked for the Chamber—and this eventually included most working artists—could count on exemption from military service and on getting work through government-sponsored projects and sanctioned commissions.

In 1937, the Visual Arts Chamber organized the first in a series of "Great German Art" exhibitions. This was an attempt to build a national consensus on the acceptable imagery of the Nazi era. "Art belongs to the whole complex of the racial values and gifts of the People," Hitler announced, and thereby set the tone for this component of the dire image. Artists applied by the thousands to be exhibited, visitors flocked to the museums by the hundreds of thousands, and writers published dissertations and reviews. After all, there was money to be made, reputations to build, prizes to win.

The energy was so compelling that some critics at the time positively gushed about the works: "heroic subjects dominate over sentimental ones," "the life of the state is a new subject which demands new expressions and styles," "clear, strong, full of character," "healthy, fresh, optimistic."

In the same year, 1937, the Visual Arts Chamber purged the German museum collections of what was now considered dangerous and anti-Nazi art. An infamous exhibit was mounted in Munich, called the "Degenerate Art" exhibition to display all that would now be considered unacceptable to the new aesthetic: abstraction, modernism, and experimentation. In fact, the absolute power and influence of the Visual Arts Chamber soon made it possible to reinforce these officially sanctioned ideas relentlessly . . . in every visual product, not just art. It controlled magazine illustrations, children's books, reports, flyers, posters, and even which typefaces would be acceptable and which would be deemed too "Semitic."

This control was systematically pursued through every popular medium of visual communications. It was a comprehensive attempt to influence, compel, and manipulate the national character—but not primarily through censorship. There was a far more powerful method—the manipulation of existing cultural biases.

The themes that emerge from the art and poster design of the   25
time, the most direct of the visual communications, are mostly presented as positive and patriotic. Of course there is the consistent anti-Semitism, sometimes blatant, sometimes subtle. But the visual themes that comprise the dire image tend to draw on the traditions of the national past and rely on notions with deep-seated resonance within the German culture. For example, there is the appeal of the simple country life and the return to the purity of nature presented through images of pastoral landscapes and peasant families and farmers. After all, it was part of the Nazi rhetoric that the strength of the German character came from the soil of the land. Eagles and lions also appear prominently to represent courage and victory.

Family values are conveyed through endless depictions of the Aryan family ideal, which is almost always two parents, three children, and a grandparent all in stereotypical poses of gentility and devotion, models of racial purity and national unity. The family was to be the nucleus of the new state.

The ideal of the body is another common theme in these images, as well as in contemporary movies and at sports competitions and demonstrations. Paintings show nudes as distant, classical forms in country settings, while posters present German athletes in poses of grace, strength, and power.

As in many countries fighting World War II, a large number of posters were produced to support the war effort—either for enlistment or on the home front. The Nazi versions of these were very similar to those of other countries, including the U.S., but they take special care to juxtapose images of ordinary citizens with those of the brave hero-warrior, to drive home the point that every German was a potential soldier.

The call to a mythic past is reflected all throughout the German visual art of this era. Like any totalitarian, Hitler loved the classical style and its echoes of great empires of the past. Monuments, paintings, sculptures, and posters all contain visual references to the wreaths, profiles, eagles, and cornices of ancient Rome and Napoleonic France.

Considering how complete, how total, this manipulation of the image was, one question that emerges is, why did all of those artists and designers participate? For one thing, like every other citizen, they were caught up in the frenzy of change—"the raging water which engulfed everything," as the writer Golo Mann has put it. They were enticed by the art mania that began with Hitler, continued through the Culture Chambers, and spread all the way to the enthusiastic participation of the public.

And perhaps even more compelling is the idea that images are themselves persuasive, the output of compelling cultural dreams. Perhaps all these image-makers were seduced—along with everyone else—by the very image they were creating. They were caught up in the passion of their work, assuring themselves that Germany would continue to be the land of great, heroic art, of Goethe and Dürer and Beethoven.

It is fascinating to think how all this worked—and worked so well. But it should be more than simply fascinating. As the writer Eva Hoffman has said, "At this point, the task is not only to remember, but to remember strenuously—explore, decode, and deepen the terrain of memory. Moreover, what is at stake is not only the past, but the present. In memories, too, begin responsibilities."

We should not take this simply as a history lesson. It should be a warning for us—right here and now—to keep a careful eye on the images of our own time and what they are making of us.

Questions

1. Are there any kinds of images that you think we should not look at or that we should be protected from seeing? Would you be in favor of a law that made it illegal to show certain kinds of images to adults in our country? If so, what kinds of images would fit into this category?
2. Are there any images that you think of as being pure propaganda? Are they found in the news, in entertainment media, in museums? Find a propaganda image on the Web and write an essay explaining what makes you think it is propaganda, rather than another kind of image. Consider in your essay the differences between propaganda images and others.
3. Go to the TV and look at some commercials. Besides the products being sold, what are the values being sold? How are these values communicated? Do you "buy" these values? How does the Internet or news media sell values? which values do they sell?
4. Pick a product brand that you know or like and think about all the ways that the company communicates its message to you (e.g., its logo, ads, campaigns, etc.). What is the message, or messages, of the company you picked? Is this propaganda or something else? Explain your answer.
5. Robbins writes about the "manipulation of existing cultural biases" as a powerful way to influence viewer's opinions and attitudes (paragraph 24). Do you see any of this kind of thing happening in the images of our society? What kinds of cultural biases do you find being manipulated in the media?

Cartoon Wars
RICHARD GOLDSTEIN

Richard Goldstein was an editor at the Village Voice *for many years. He is a contributor to* The Nation *and writes frequently about pop culture, politics, and sexuality. "Cartoon Wars" is excerpted from his article in* The Nation *in February 2005, which questions censorship and explores political uses for cartoons.*

Getting Started

From a very clear political perspective, Richard Goldstein looks at the simplest of images to find that they can have profound effects.

Do you like cartoons or do you find them too simplistic? Do you think cartoons are only for children? Have you ever seen a cartoon that made a political point or thought that there was a "hidden" message in a cartoon? Why is satire acceptable in a cartoon format when it is sometimes unacceptable in other forms of expression? Why can cartoons with a message sometimes be even more inflammatory than other kinds of images?

———————————— ✦ ————————————

O nce upon a time, a psychiatrist named Fredric Wertham went on a tear over Wonder Woman. He detected a vagina in the crook of her cartoon arm, and he thought her superpowers were giving girls "the wrong idea" about women's place in society. As for Batman's ward, Robin, his bare legs and devotion to his guardian were planting homosexual thoughts in boys, or so Wertham believed. His crusade led to Congressional hearings and the "voluntary" censorship of comics.

That was back in the freaked-out fifties; nothing so extreme has happened recently. But at an inaugural banquet [in January 2005], right-wing moralist James Dobson lectured members of Congress on the threat posed by SpongeBob SquarePants. Unlike some, he wasn't bothered by this deep-sea dweller holding hands with his buddy Patrick, a starfish. Nor was he troubled by the porous Mr. Pants appearing in a video promoting tolerance. Dobson's target was the "pledge of tolerance" one of the videos many sponsors had posted on its website. It dared to mention sexual identity among the categories that merit sensitivity. To Dobson, this was "homosexual propaganda" and another sign that cartoon characters are being "hijacked" to move the gay agenda.

It's an old obsession of the religious right. Remember Jerry Falwell's jihad against Tinky Winky, the purse-packing Teletubby? "He is purple—the gay-pride color; and his antenna is shaped like a triangle—the gay-pride symbol," Falwell fumed, adding that such "subtle depictions" of gay sexuality were being deliberately inserted into children's entertainment. Today's right-wing moralists are less bothered by subliminal messages than by the real issue of teaching children that homosexuals are worthy of respect. Dobson and his kind aren't really worried about cartoons turning kids queer. Their aim is to see that homophobia is free to operate, and one way to do that is to keep children from seeing gays as part of the human community.

During the Clinton years, these puritans were preaching mostly to the choir, but now the government too is listening. In late January, the new education secretary, Margaret Spellings, criticized the **PBS** show *Postcards From Buster* because its host, a gregarious bunny, had traveled to Vermont where he encountered, among other residents, a female couple. PBS decided not to distribute that episode (though local stations still may air it).

It's no surprise that kids' stuff looms so large in the culture war. 5 No form of pop culture is more prone to blunt moralizing, whether it's the liberal ideal of inclusiveness in *Postcards From Buster* or the conservative critique of "political correctness" in the animated feature *The Incredibles*. But this struggle involves the medium as well as the message. Cartoons are powerful in a special way, and the less realistic they are the more potent they seem. Children are not the only ones deemed vulnerable to their impact. And you don't have to be a right-winger to see evil between the lines.

· · ·

Take a step back from the particulars and you can sense the anxiety that animates the cartoon wars. Fundamentalists are convinced that pop culture is stealing the souls of their children. Gays are concerned that liberals will abandon them, especially after the talk from leading Democrats about how same-sex marriage lost John Kerry the election. Liberals are caught in a bind, as the same system that thwarts the collective advancement of African Americans bestows considerable power on some of them. Do some progressives resent blacks who rise by embracing conservative values? Do they wish gay rights would go away? Maybe not consciously, but such negative sentiments must exist along with empathy—we wouldn't be human if they didn't. And editorial cartoonists can sniff the emotional wind. The best of them delve into the subconscious.

During the 1996 [presidential] campaign, Bob Dole was often drawn with a withered arm, or shown as a patient on an operating table. This idea was unspeakable in polite society, but it probably played a part in Dole's defeat. Clinton was portrayed as a lubricious bozo with a bulbous phallic nose, while Bush is fitted with a tiny schnoz and giant ears, giving him a distinctly infantile aura. These images work by tapping into hidden feelings, and that is the mandate of editorial cartoonists. They are the *tummlers* of journalism. Of course, their revelations aren't always welcome. Nor are they necessarily wholesome. Sometimes they reveal the fear and loathing behind the smiley face.

My generation will never forget Herblock's vicious rendition of Richard Nixon as an unshaven demento, or David Levine's infamous image of Lyndon Johnson lifting his shirt to show off a surgical scar in the shape of Vietnam. These sketches stick in the mind not just because of their content but because of their formal qualities. They capture something that seems essential, something we have always felt and perhaps feared in ourselves. It wasn't just the sight of a Hasid kissing a West Indian woman on the cover of *The New Yorker* that caused such a furor in 1993. It was the power of this Art Spiegelman image as a cartoon.

The word once referred to a crude model of a more important work, and in a sense it still does. Cartoons have an unfinished look that leaves a lot of interpretive space. Their sparse details and antic distortions are surreal yet recognizable enough to hit the target, whether it's a powerful politician or a basic human type. And because cartoons are the stuff of childhood, they invite us to enter a regressive, dreamy state. Movies do something similar through lighting, framing and the subliminal flicker of film itself. Cartoons work a bit like movies even when they are standing still.

To those who say that sometimes a parrot is just a parrot, I   10
offer this memory of a cartoon that delighted me as a child. It was an animated trip to Africa, replete with nurturing lions, chatty monkeys and bouncy pickaninnies. It ended with a map of Africa, drawn in black. "And so we bid farewell to the dark continent," the narrator intoned. Then a pair of huge white lips burst from the map, crooning "Bah-bye!" This image enchanted me then and embarrasses me now, but the fact that it remains embedded in my imagination says something about the enduring power of cartoons.

With the rise of graphic novels, computer-generated games and other meta-cartoon forms, it's clear that this medium is central to the postmodern sensibility. The price of such authority is that no cartoonist can claim to be in it just for laffs. These unstable images are going to be the subject of intense examination and roiling debate. That can be hard on the creative process, but the good news is that you never know where the argument will lead. After Dobson's remarks, the United Church of Christ announced that it welcomes SpongeBob into its flock, along with Tinky Winky. The cartoon wars continue.

Questions

1. What examples does Goldstein provide to support the idea that cartoons may have a subliminal message? Can you think of some examples of cartoons that seem questionable in some way? Explain.

2. Cartoons are among the most popular and powerful images created in our culture. Goldstein writes that "Cartoons have an unfinished look that leaves a lot of interpretive space" (paragraph 9). Do you think this simplicity is the reason for cartoons' popularity, or is there something else? What makes cartoons different from other kinds of images, like paintings or photos?

3. Video games are a very popular format that also use cartoon images. In what ways do you think that the images in video games can have the effects on us that Goldstein describes?
4. Goldstein uses the word *tummler* to describe political cartoonists. *Tummler,* a Yiddish word, refers to a person who incites someone to action. In what ways might cartoons incite people to action? What examples can you think of when this has happened?
5. Do you think cartoons are a "safer" or a more "dangerous" medium for political expression? Can they go over the line? Should cartoons be regulated or censored? What kinds of cartoons would you be in favor of censoring?

Reality's Flight
NINA WILLDORF

Nina Willdorf is a graduate of Columbia University. She is a staff writer at the Boston Phoenix *and has won two awards from the New England Press Association. She is a frequent contributor to such magazines as* Budget Travel *and* Child *and has written several books, including* Wedding Chic *(2003) and* City Chic *(2005).*

Getting Started

Although written several years ago and referring to a previous television season, the issues Nina Willdorf raises about reality TV are still very much with us. What is your opinion about the whole phenomenon of reality TV that continues to dominate television? What reality TV shows have you watched and what do you think of them? Why do you think they are so popular? What is so compelling about the images they present? Do you agree with some researchers that there is merit to such programs or do you think reality TV is just trash TV?

◆

The Associated Press exuberantly reported that the Miss America Pageant is looking to incorporate elements of the so-called reality-television genre into its competition. If the changes are approved by the individual states, the pageant, which will air next month on ABC, could loosely follow the format of CBS's phenomenally successful *Survivor,* with losing contestants logging votes for the woman they think should win the crown.

Some consider this news yet another sign of the genre's success. Endless reports shrilly herald the arrival of the latest Fabulous New Reality Show—each more over-the-top than the last. *The BBC re-creates life in the trenches of World War I! MTV is casting for* Kidnapped! *Matt and Ben want YOU to participate in their new reality-TV show,* The Runner! (All true.)

And the Nielsen ratings have fed the storm. This past season, *Survivor* beat long-standing favorite *Friends* in its Thursday-night slot. The gross-out fest *Fear Factor* catapulted itself into first place in its time slot for a number of weeks. As Tom Shales at the *Washington Post* recently fretted, both the sit-com and the quality drama are becoming "endangered species" in the wake of the reality-TV boom.

But other critics aren't too concerned. Despite a full roster of shows in the pipeline, scads of reality-inspired books and movies, and rah-rah back-patting in networks' high-rise boardrooms, many critics believe the reality-TV phenomenon of 2001 is like the teen-pop-star trend of 2000 or the Internet craze of 1999: bloated, self-congratulatory, out of touch, and on the fast track to a very necessary shake-out.

Says Mark Crispin Miller, professor of media studies at New   5
York University and the author of *The Bush Dyslexicon* (Norton, 2001): "As the culture has become more saturated by TV, and as the audience has become more blasé, and as the industry has come to be dominated by a few giant, heavily debt-ridden players who have to compete with each other ever more frantically for the high ball, the content of TV has become more titillating." He pauses. "The kind of voyeurism that appeals today tends to be quite naked."

But he's not surprised. "This *always* happens," he says. "[The networks] all try to repeat what succeeded 10 minutes ago. There's a glut and then a number of them fail."

Cultural critic Douglas Rushkoff, author of several books, including the online open-source novel *Exit Strategy,* agrees: "It's over."

But if that's the case, where does television go next?

If you've been listening to the TV hype over the past two years, you might think that what's called reality television is innovative and fresh. But ask your parents: the truth is, the stuff's been around for decades. You can find its roots in shows like *Candid Camera, The National Lampoon Radio Hour,* and *Cops.*

Although the groundwork was laid as far back as the 1950s, to-   10
day's reality shows seem more like bastard children of MTV, which aired the first glorious episode of *The Real World* in 1992. Seven strangers were picked to live in a house, have their lives taped, and start getting *real*—and Americans were glued to their sets. The

formula of intrigue, sexual tension, confession, angry confrontation, and coming-of-age—all on camera—was a winner. But European stations caught on faster than American ones. It wasn't until the honchos at CBS picked up their binoculars, spotted a hit overseas, and created *Who Wants To Be a Millionaire?*—their own version of the British game show *Millionaire*—that the precedent was set for pillaging and appropriating European television shows.

After *Millionaire,* CBS followed by grabbing up and retooling the Dutch show *Big Brother,* and then the Swedish program *Survivor.* Then, in the final hour, perhaps to save face after the failed debacle of the XFL, NBC—under the new direction of TV wunderkind Jeff Zucker—stepped in with grosser, flashier, *realer* programming. In the past year, the network—which Salon.com's Joyce Millman dubbed "Nothing But Cruelty"—has raced to compete, offering reality shows including *Fear Factor* and *Spy TV.*

The predominant theory about the lure of reality TV can be summed up in one word: voyeurism. The problem is, as with anything addictive—sugar, cigarettes, drugs—it's possible to have too much of a good (or, in this case, popular) thing. The tide already seems to be turning. Three weeks after Tom Shales's maudlin elegy for dramas and sit-coms, Nielsen spit out a whole new set of ratings showing that prime time was losing viewers across the board. Just two weeks later, noted *The Hollywood Reporter,* the spoils for all shows, including reality TV, were "meager." UPN's flop of a reality-TV show, *Manhunt,* couldn't even win a respectable number of viewers with a real scandal, when a contestant accused producers of rigging the show's final result and reshooting footage, and filed a complaint with the FCC. Must-see TV? More like who-cares TV.

Viewers weeping into their TV dinners can blame it on the Web. In many ways, reality is the necessary new niche for television in the wake of the Internet. Before the dot-com days, television provided an immediacy that countered film's heavily edited, stylized form. But with its faster headlines, news reports, and up-to-the-minute services, the Net elbowed in on TV's territory, and the tube was forced to redefine itself. So-called reality television—which is in fact a heavily edited, pseudo-documentary format—is the result.

The genre's whole premise is more, more, more. And not surprisingly, what once seemed novel—the delivery of titillating and taboo inside dope—has degenerated. It's like watching someone do a striptease: it starts out sexy, but soon you become as blasé as a gynecologist. *Yeah, she's naked. So what?*

Douglas Rushkoff believes that all the behind-the-scenes 15
access given to viewers of shows like *Big Brother, The Real World,*

and *Temptation Island*—the bathroom cam, the bedroom cam, the watch-me-floss cam—has led the genre to its death cam.

"It's not as much voyeurism as it is about exhibitionism," Rushkoff says. Sure enough, just look at the folks populating the programs: most are media whores hoping to find fame by logging face time on prime time. Many are actors, musicians, or wannabes. One of reality TV's biggest stars, *Survivor* host Jeff Probst, recently eschewed any adherence to "reality" by launching a career as a film director, with an upcoming indie flick, *Finder's Fee*. "Most [people on reality programs] aren't behaving, they're auditioning for work," Rushkoff adds. "It's gotten so boring."

So what's next? Rushkoff, sighing audibly into the phone when asked for his thoughts on the future of reality TV, wearily dismisses the genre. "By the time networks pick up on this stuff, it's already over," he says. "After O.J. and Monica, [viewers] are basically just passing the time until the next big scandal."

But despite the deathwatch, the genre isn't without its merits, or without a future, argues Robert Thompson, director of Syracuse University's Center for the Study of Popular Television, who admits he's "countin' down the days" till upcoming reality program *Love Cruise* starts. A show like *Survivor* synthesizes "the unpredictability from sports" and "catty sexuality from soap operas," yet "ends with narrative steamrollers of voting out," Thompson says. "It's not another doctor, lawyer, detective show."

Thompson believes that shows like *Survivor*, the genre's best, will eventually take their place in TV's ranks without pushing out other forms. "Reality TV of the kind we're seeing now is going to join the sit-com and the drama," he says. "There won't be as much of it on. It will be less exciting. It'll just become . . . just one of the other genres."

Thompson guesses that a show like *Big Brother*, which mixes the   20
Web (live shots are available 24 hours a day), the TV, and the mighty dollar (a show-themed board game, baseball caps, and T-shirts are all available), is paving the way for the future profitability of reality TV. "You can literally stalk these characters," he says. "If I could have followed Farrah Fawcett around 24 hours a day after watching *Charlie's Angels*, that's how money could be made."

Obsessive in its access and not edited enough, *Big Brother* has a long way to go before it can be expected to carry the Future of Television. Even Thompson doesn't think the show is "any good yet." But he believes it has the potential to "clear the real estate for TV and the Internet to become bosom buddies." He pauses. "The history of *that* is still to be written."

Questions

1. What is voyeurism? Why do many see reality TV as voyeuristic? Is voyeurism always a bad thing? Can it be the same as curiosity? According to Willdorf, does reality TV really reflect the "real" world? How does she support her point of view?

2. What relationship does Willdorf try to establish between the Web and reality TV? What can you get by watching the images on the Web that you cannot get from TV programs?

3. Two popular forms of reality TV are the adventure-style programs like *Survivor* and the living-together ones like *Big Brother*. Watch a sample of each and write about whether you think there is a difference between these two types of reality programs in terms of their impact on our society.

4. Which other types of TV programming are mentioned in the Willdorf article? What others can you think of? Which types of programming do you like to watch? What would you like to see more of on TV? What would you like to see less of? Why?

5. Write an essay in which you discuss the position taken by some TV critics that the reality-TV phenomenon is "bloated, self-congratulatory, out of touch, and on the fast track to a very necessary shake-out" (paragraph 4).

What Is Art?

Leo Tolstoy

Count Leo Nikoleyevich Tolstoy (1828–1910) was a Russian novelist who wrote two of the most celebrated novels of all time: War and Peace *(1865–69) and* Anna Karenina *(1875–77). He was a philosophical and spiritual thinker who also wrote books, pamphlets, and articles on religious, moral, and social themes. Among these are* What I Believe *(1884),* What Then Must We Do? *(1886), and* What Is Art? *(1896) from which the following excerpt is taken.*

Getting Started

Translated from Russian and written over a century ago, the writing in this essay may be hard to connect with at first. Yet Tolstoy is exploring the fascinating question of how it is possible that images can affect us in any way at all. He is using the word *art* here but what he suggests can be applied to any image. How do you define art? Are all images art or is art a special category of the image? Why do people create art and what are artists trying to accomplish by making it? Think about a memorable piece of art that had an impact on you in some way. What did it make you feel? Did it seem to create a personal connection between you and the person who made it?

———————— ✦ ————————

E very work of art causes the receiver to enter into a certain kind of relationship both with him who produced or is producing the art, and with all those who, simultaneously, previously, or subsequently, receive the same artistic impression.

Speech transmitting the thoughts and experiences of men serves as a means of union among them, and art serves a similar purpose. The peculiarity of this latter means of intercourse, distinguishing it from intercourse by means of words, consists in this, that whereas by words a man transmits his thoughts to another, by art he transmits his feelings.

The activity of art is based on the fact that a man receiving through his sense of hearing or sight another man's expression of feeling, is capable of experiencing the emotion which moved the man who expressed it. To take the simplest example: one man laughs, and another who hears becomes merry, or a man weeps, and another who hears feels sorrow. A man is excited or irritated, and another man seeing him is brought to a similar state of mind. By his movements or by the sounds of his voice a man expresses courage and determination or sadness and calmness, and this state of mind passes on to others. A man suffers, manifesting his sufferings by groans and spasms, and this suffering transmits itself to other people; a man expresses his feeling of admiration, devotion, fear, respect, or love, to certain objects, persons, or phenomena, and others are infected by the same feelings of admiration, devotion, fear, respect, or love, to the same objects, persons, or phenomena.

And it is on this capacity of man to receive another man's expression of feeling and to experience those feelings himself, that the activity of art is based.

If a man infects another or others directly, immediately, by his appearance or by the sounds he gives vent to at the very time he experiences the feeling; if he causes another man to yawn when he himself cannot help yawning, or to laugh or cry when he himself is obliged to laugh or cry, or to suffer when he himself is suffering—that does not amount to art.

5

Art begins when one person with the object of joining another or others to himself in one and the same feeling, expresses that feeling by certain external indications. To take the simplest example: a boy having experienced, let us say, fear on encountering a wolf, relates that encounter, and in order to evoke in others the feeling he has experienced, describes himself, his condition before the encounter, the surroundings, the woods, his own light-heartedness, and then the wolf's appearance, its movements, the distance between himself and the wolf, and so forth. All this, if only the boy when telling the story again experiences the feelings he had lived through, and infects the hearers and compels them to feel what he had experienced—is art. Even if the boy had not seen a wolf but had frequently been afraid of one, and if wishing to evoke in others the fear he had felt, he invented an encounter with a wolf and recounted it so as to make his hearers share the feelings he experienced when he feared the wolf, that also would be art. And just in the same way it is art if a man, having experienced either the fear of suffering or the attraction of enjoyment (whether in reality or in imagination), expresses these feelings on canvas or in marble so that others are infected by them. And it is also art if a man feels, or imagines to himself, feelings of delight, gladness, sorrow, despair, courage, or despondency, and the transition from one to another of these feelings, and expresses them by sounds so that the hearers are infected by them and experience them as they were experienced by the composer.

The feelings with which the artist infects others may be most various—very strong or very weak, very important or very insignificant, very bad or very good: feelings of love of one's country, self-devotion and submission to fate or to God expressed in a drama, raptures of lovers described in a novel, feelings of voluptuousness expressed in a picture, courage expressed in a triumphal march, merriment evoked by a dance, humor evoked by a funny story, the feeling of quietness transmitted by an evening landscape or by a lullaby, or the feeling of admiration evoked by a beautiful arabesque—it is all art.

If only the spectators or auditors are infected by the feelings which the author has felt, it is art.

To evoke in oneself a feeling one has once experienced and having evoked it in oneself then by means of movements, lines, colors, sounds, or forms expressed in words, so to transmit that feeling that others experience the same feeling—this is the activity of art.

Art is a human activity consisting in this, that one man con- 10
sciously by means of certain external signs, hands on to others
feelings he has lived through, and that others are infected by
these feelings and also experience them.

Art is not, as the metaphysicians say, the manifestation of
some mysterious idea of beauty or God; it is not, as the aesthetic
physiologists say, a game in which man lets off his excess of stored-
up energy; it is not the expression of man's emotions by external
signs; it is not the production of pleasing objects; and, above all, it
is not pleasure; but it is a means of union among men joining them
together in the same feelings, and indispensable for the life and
progress toward well-being of individuals and of humanity.

Questions

1. Tolstoy writes: "Art begins when one person with the object of joining another
   or others to himself in one and the same feeling, expresses that feeling by certain external indication" (paragraph 6). What does this statement mean?
2. Tolstoy states, "If only the spectators or auditors are infected by the feeling
   which the author has felt, it is art" (paragraph 9). Do you agree? What about
   propaganda? According to Tolstoy, can propaganda images be art? What do
   you think about this?
3. Tolstoy makes the point that art "is not pleasure" (paragraph 12). Why is this
   an important idea? Why do most of us prefer that art "be pleasure"—or at
   least pleasurable? What kinds of art make you uncomfortable? Can "uncomfortable art" still qualify as art according to Tolstoy?
4. In the last paragraph of this essay, Tolstoy rejects the idea that art is about
   the search for beauty, the quest for personal expression, or the communication of pleasure and states that it is only about the transfer of feelings. Does
   this idea apply to all images? What images can you think of, whether they
   are considered art or not, that do not fit Tolstoy's theory?
5. Try to apply Tolstoy's definition of art as "infection" to movies, TV, the Web,
   performance art, or any other medium you prefer. Does the definition work
   for these and other new forms of expression? Why or why not?

Making Connections

1. You have read in this chapter about the roles that art, patriotic images, propaganda, cartoons, and reality TV can play in prodding our attitudes and behaviors. What other kinds of images can you think of that have this kind of powerful effect? What visual medium do you consider to be the most powerful and what is it about those particular images that makes them so potent?

2. Tolstoy suggests that art is most effective and beneficial when it is able to create in or "infect" the viewer with feelings like those the artist felt. How do you think Robbins would respond to this, given his essay about the danger of manipulating the viewer's feelings?

3. What is the difference between patriotic and propaganda images? Is propaganda necessarily negative? Can you think of situations when it might be important and even positive to use images to try to convince people of something? How do you think Solomon or Robbins would respond to this?

4. How would Goldstein respond to Tolstoy's comment that art is not about pleasure? Would either think that cartoons that give pleasure through humor can be considered art? Do you think that good art, or powerful images, can be funny? What examples of this can you think of?

5. Do you believe that images should be controlled or limited? Should certain groups of people be protected from certain images? Or should there be a free market of this kind of product? Choose two of the authors in this chapter and, in a short essay, answer this question from each perspective. Then answer it from your own.

6. How would you compare a reality TV program to a program with "real" people as seen on Oprah or Dr. Phil? Think about both of these in terms of the voyeurism that Willdorf describes, the propaganda that Robbins discusses, and even the patriotism that Solomon writes about. How does television itself play into these forces? Write an essay in which you explore these issues.

7. Current images in the media present the United States as a highly polarized society with red states and blue states, right and left wings. Think of the various articles in this chapter and explore the question of the role that the media plays in supporting this notion of a polarized country. Write an essay about how images stress our differences rather than our similarities and think about why such images might be appealing in the current climate.

8. The five articles in this chapter were selected because each one explores a way in which images alter our attitudes. Find an image online that has a clear political message or is clearly meant to convince you of something. Write an essay in which you describe its purpose and message. Explain why the image is effective or not.

The Image as Reality

"You've been living in a dream world, Neo."
—Morpheus in the film "The Matrix"

Images are compelling because, among other reasons, they seem real to us on some level. In the film *The Matrix*, the character Neo discovers that his ordinary everyday life is, in fact, only a sophisticated computer projection and that the real world is something quite different. The movie is science fiction, but the role images play in our world is not far from this speculation.

The world of the image with which we have surrounded ourselves can be seen as a kind of matrix, an artificial creation that we take to be accurate, factual, important, true, and, in many ways, as real as the real world. But it is one thing to cry at the movies, laugh at a TV show, trust in a photo, or get lost in a painting. It is another to believe that the images we see in the media show us the world as it really is.

"The Digital Media Landscape: Liquid Imagery, Shaky Credibility" by Thomas Wheeler examines the role that photography plays in creating the visual landscape. Wheeler points out that, thanks to the democratization of technology, images are no longer under the strict control of the people who created them. And photos, which we have spent two hundred years believing represent the truth of the moment they were taken, are no longer reliable. Digital manipulation makes all photos only the starting point for the final image. To prove his case, Wheeler lists a number of examples of image manipulation that blur the line between reality and the image. This manipulation suggests to him that old assumptions are out and a new flexibility is in. Or as he puts it, "the notion that seeing is believing is under assault."

183

In the second selection, Ada Louise Huxtable examines the relationship between reality and images of it through the prism of architecture. In "Living with the Fake and Learning to Like It," she explores the notion that we have actually lost our interest in distinguishing the genuine from the fake in environments and by implication, in all media. "Surrogate experience and synthetic settings have become the preferred American way of life," Huxtable writes. Her primary example is the appealing false reality that is Las Vegas with its rain forests in the desert and its copies of New York, Paris, and Rome in the heart of the American West. And the same is happening everywhere, even in the world of art, where the distinctions between original, reconstruction, and reproduction are getting increasingly blurry. Huxtable suggests that instant gratification and intensity of experience are taking precedence over subtlety and authenticity.

A well-known astronomer looks at another fascinating aspect of this slippery relationship between images and reality in the third selection. In "Colorizing the Cosmos," Bob Berman directs our attention toward the realm of space photography, where familiar images of the cosmos are routinely retouched and enhanced—colors added or intensified, and other aspects of the image altered. These "touched-up" images call into question what we really know about the cosmos and should make us reconsider how comfortable we have become believing in images that are largely synthetic.

In "Pygmalion's Power," art historian Ernst Gombrich discusses the ways in which art and reality become confused. From the painter who is saddened to find his work somehow less than real, to myths that blur the differences, to theories of art as the "imitation of nature," Gombrich questions whether the distinction between art and reality is as clear as it seems to be. Gombrich challenges the notion that the borderlines between making and imitating are distinct, and he suggests that in creating art—just one of the categories of images—we are not merely copying the world, we are creating a new world with new implications and new effects.

In his essay "The Work of Art in the Age of Mechanical Reproduction," literary critic and philosopher Walter Benjamin draws our attention to film and its ability to reproduce life in such a manner that it seems more real than real. Close-ups and slow motion change our view of the world and allow us to focus on details that were once unimaginable. Even though he was writing in the early twentieth century, prior to the advent of the Internet and cable TV, Benjamin was able to see how images would alter our concept of reality.

The Digital Media Landscape
THOMAS H. WHEELER

Thomas Wheeler is the former Editor-in-Chief of Guitar Player *magazine and author of several books on guitars, including* American Guitars *and* The Stratocaster Chronicles. *In 1991 he joined the faculty of the School of Journalism and Communication at the University of Oregon, where he won the Marshall Award for innovative teaching. His research explores the ethical dimensions of image manipulation in nonfiction media, and he has spoken to numerous ethics and professional groups on these topics. He is the author of a textbook,* Phototruth or Photofiction: Ethics and Media Imagery In The Digital Age *(2002) from which "The Digital Media Landscape: Liquid Imagery, Shaky Credibility" is excerpted.*

Getting Started

If you have ever used a computer to manipulate a digital image, you know how easily and undetectably this can be done. Have you ever altered a photo or video to make a face look better, change the background, or remove someone from the scene? Why do you think these photographic "tricks" are so popular? Can you tell when an image has been altered? What examples of manipulated images in magazines, newspapers, on TV or the Web can you think of? Do you believe that the public needs to be made aware when this is taking place? Should a manipulated image be labeled as such or do you feel that this is unnecessary because in the end "it's only a picture"?

———————— ✦ ————————

High-tech deception is today's technology, not tomorrow's.
—The Dallas Morning News[1]

It may be comforting to cling to old categories of photography, to assure ourselves that whatever happens outside the field of "photojournalism" will have little impact on the credibility of

———————

[1]Jim Wright, "Movie Plot Should Dog Wags in White House," *The Dallas Morning News* (March 1, 1998): 7J.

news photos. However, we will take the opposite view. While our primary concern is journalistic photography, and while people do indeed bring different expectations to different media (a daily newspaper vs. a sci-fi movie, for example), public faith in "photo-truth" is surely affected by everyday experiences with viewing and interpreting visual media in a variety of forms—especially considering the much-decried blurring of lines between news, public relations, advertising, and entertainment. To better grasp the threat to the credibility of still photography in newspapers and magazines, it will serve us well to briefly explore developments in broadcast television, cable, film, computer programs, personal game toys, and so on.

On occasion, we examine even tabloids such as *National Enquirer* and satirical magazines such as *Spy*, not because they are typically included in discussions of serious journalism (obviously, they are not) but because they are part of the digital-media landscape and because the flood of photofiction from myriad sources will likely influence how viewers perceive mass-media images of all kinds—including journalistic photos.

NO GOING BACK

"The digital revolution is over," according to the November/December 1997 issue of *American Photo* magazine, and while the media's adoption of these technologies will evolve for some time, the claim that digital media are here to stay is indeed beyond debate. Professional photographers and publications embrace digital cameras and processes with increasing frequency. That same issue of *American Photo* quoted a commercial photographer as saying, "A couple of years ago I couldn't imagine what I would do with a computer; now I can't imagine what I would do without one." The magazine concluded, "The paradigm *has* shifted, and there's no going back."[2]

Most photographs seen in news magazines and newspapers with substantial circulations are either created by digital processes or converted into digital data during production.[3] What

---

[2]David Schonauer, "The Future of Photography 1997," *American Photo* (November/December 1997): 47.

[3]Edgar Shaobua Huang, "Readers' Perception of Digital Alteration and Truth-Value in Documentary Photographs," submitted in partial fulfillment for a Ph.D. degree, School of Journalism, Indiana University (October 1999): 2–3.

makes this ethically significant is an essential quality of digital data: its susceptibility to easy, unlimited, and virtually undetectable manipulation.

SHIFTS IN AUTHORITY

While recent discussion has understandably addressed dazzling new technologies, another factor in the new age is a shift in authority. People making decisions about how or whether images should be manipulated are increasingly part of what might be called the computer-graphics culture and are not steeped in the traditional values of photojournalism, or journalism of any kind. This is especially true of many communicators who find the Internet better suited to their tastes and goals than established print or broadcast media.[4]

Moreover, while photographers have long lamented their lack of control over how their images are published, their influence has diminished even further in recent years. Because a single image can be fragmented into components more easily than ever (the beach, the palm tree, and the moon can be isolated, sold to separate clients, and perhaps later recombined in different ways), the notion of ownership of a photo faces redefinition; some observers suggest it is already outdated.[5] One complicating factor is

5

---

[4]"Control over [the moment, composition, light, color] has been transferred from the photographer to the photo lab." Donald R. Katz, "Why Pictures Lie," *Esquire* (June 1990): 94; "These people [art directors and designers] have not been taught the traditional, classic values and goals of documentary photojournalism," George Wedding of *The Sacramento Bee* quoted in J.D. Lasica, "Photographs That Lie: The Ethical Dilemma of Digital Retouching," *Washington Journalism Review* (June 1989): 24; see also, Paul Lester, editor, "NPPA Code of Ethics," *NPPA Special Report: The Ethics of Photojournalism* (Durham, NC: National Press Photographers Association, 1990): 130–31.

[5]"In the digital age, when images can be lifted from the Internet or scanned from books and magazines, the notion of copyright is simply antiquated." David Schonauer, "In Camera" column, *American Photo* (July/August 1999): 32. Some people disagree, such as members of the FPG (Freelance Photographers' Guild), which sued *Newsday* because the New York daily scanned a James Porto photo-illustration, then added, deleted, and recombined various elements, and published it without attribution or permission. *Newsday* settled out of court. *Newsday* attorney Bruce Keller said, "This is a simple copyright issue, not a new technology issue," but FPG President Barbara Roberts noted that digital technology had made the theft of images much easier. Akiko Busch, "Stock and Security: FPG vs. *Newsday*," *Print* (November/December 1995): 48.

the Internet, which has made it almost effortless to steal, reproduce, and redistribute copyrighted material—text and images alike.[6]

IS A PHOTO "WHATEVER YOU WANT IT TO BE"?

Even the word "photograph" itself may be on its way to the boneyard of outmoded concepts. Nature photographer Art Wolfe is well known for his "photo" of a zebra herd, some members of which were digitally cloned. He said in 1997, "For me, making a digital photo is like making a watercolor. . . . It's not a painting, and it's not a photo. It's something altogether new."[7] Professor Shiela Reaves reported that the Meredith Corporation's director of production told magazine educators, "I don't consider a photograph to be a photograph anymore. It's something to work with."[8]

Indeed, once a digital image has been altered, the altered version becomes, in a very real sense, the new "original." Roger Ressmeyer sold a photo that was subsequently altered. "People want the altered image, and I don't have it," he reported. "My original is worthless."[9]

However we might define a photograph today, most of us have grown up thinking of a photo as being more fixed, more tangible, more *real* than merely "something to work with." Is the Meredith Corporation production director's quote a glimpse of things to come? Is a photograph no longer a photograph? Is it instead, as Kodak's 1996 advertising slogan promised, "whatever you want it to be"?

---

[6]"The ease at which written material can be copied and distributed on the Internet has made it possible to steal copyrighted works in staggering proportions." Martha L. Stone, "Copyright Questions Abound on the Web," *Editor & Publisher* (December 12, 1998): 44.

[7]David Schonauer, "Showcase: Art Wolfe," *American Photo* (November/December 1997): 56.

[8]Shiela Reaves, "Digital Alteration of Photographs in Magazines: An Examination of the Ethics," a paper presented at the annual convention of the Association for Education in Journalism and Mass Communication (AEJMC), Washington, D.C., August 1989, 8. See also Shiela Reaves, "Photography, Pixels, and New Technology: Is There a 'Paradigm Shift'?" a paper presented at the annual convention of AEJMC, Washington, D.C., August 1989.

[9]Reaves, "Photography, Pixels," 9.

CHANGING ASSUMPTIONS

Larger questions abound. What is the future of photographic   10
credibility and, by extension, the credibility of all visual media, in
an age when even amateur shutterbugs have access to increasingly affordable digital cameras (from 1995 to 1997, sales of these
items increased by about 700 percent) and to software designed
for, as one 1997 advertisement put it, "everything from retouching pimples to removing an ex-spouse"? Signposts in the digital
landscape:

- In the wake of the September 11, 2001, terrorist attacks in
  New York and Washington, D.C., actor/director Ben Stiller
  ordered the digital erasing of the World Trade Center towers
  from scenes of Manhattan's skyline in his film *Zoolander*.
- Aki, the digitally animated female protagonist of the sci-fi
  movie *Final Fantasy*, was selected over real-life models and
  starlets to become the cover girl for *Maxim* magazine's "Hot
  100" supplement in 2001.
- During the 2001 elections in Britain, the Labor Party associated their opponent, William Hague, with Margaret Thatcher
  by distributing composite posters that pictured Hague's face
  with Ms. Thatcher's hair and earrings.
- Telecommunications giant Alcatel produced a TV ad in 2001
  that used footage of Martin Luther King Jr.'s famous "I have a
  dream" speech. A portion of the doctored version (in vintage
  black & white, complete with authentic looking scratches and
  flecks) seemed to show Dr. King speaking not to the familiar
  teeming throng but rather to a deserted Washington Mall.
- At the 2002 Winter Olympic Games in Salt Lake City, downhill
  skiers raced against the clock, one at a time; with new synchro-
  nized replay technology, broadcasters later superimposed
  "ghost" images of two competitors so viewers could compare
  their progress at various stages of their respective runs.
- During speed skating events in the 2002 Winter Olympic
  Games, the nationalities of competitors were identified by
  flags digitally inserted beneath the ice in their respective
  lanes. Two years previously, digital flags on the bottom of the
  pool identified the nationalities of Olympic swimmers; the
  technology is so sophisticated that one could see surface
  waves and shimmering reflections above the flags.
- The *New York Times* reported in 2000 that fictional websites
  were increasingly popular. Some offer no actual services or

products but are graphically indistinguishable from those that do.

- Webbie Tookay posed for a feature in the October 1999 *Details* magazine, pitched Nokia telephones to Latin American consumers, and was slated to join a virtual band; the digital creation of animator Steven Stahlberg, Tookay is "managed" by the Illusion 2K agency, which represents virtual models.
- Yearbook photos are sometimes manipulated by students (or their parents). Aside from cosmetic touch-ups to photos of themselves, a photographer's representative said in 1999 that customers view photos of other people, then say, "I like that smile, that pose, that background or those clothes." Aspects of these details can be incorporated into the customer's own "portrait."[10]
- Hewlett Packard encourages its software customers to "crop and manipulate images—all as creativity dictates."
- Tiger Electronics introduced the Clone Zone and Dear Diary "electronic organizers," boasting that "kids can even morph the photos!"
- With Mattel's Me2Cam digital video camera/CD Rom system, a child "can actually step into the computer"; its features include a "virtual fun house that distorts her image!"
- Software now permits computer operators to add images of new products into old film or live video feeds. Stars in classic movies from bygone eras could appear to be holding or using the latest brand-name products. Signs, billboards or other commercial messages could also be integrated, the results looking as if the inserts had been part of the original scene. In one remarkable example of "virtual advertising," a Blockbuster videocassette box was digitally placed on a table in an episode of the "Seven Days" television series.[11] The March 17,

---

[10]Cree Lawson (AP), "Retouching Yearbook Pictures Catches on," *The Register-Guard*, Eugene, Oregon (June 25, 1999): 11A.

[11]"You are seeing the first glimpse of the future of advertising," according to a spokesman for Aegis Group P.L.C. From an advertiser's point of view, one advantage to the new strategy is that it allows updated or entirely new products to be placed in the same film or video at different times or for different audiences. Stuart Elliott, "Real or Virtual? You Call It: Digital Sleight of Hand Can Put Ads Almost Anywhere," *New York Times* (October 1, 1999): C1.

1999, episode of that series featured the live-video insertion of "electronic product images" for Coca-Cola, Wells Fargo, and other sponsors in background scenes.

- Syndicators of the television show *Law and Order* announced in 2001 they were working on agreements to provide post-production insertion of images of logos, signs, and products into previously filmed scenes. Payments would be in addition to fees advertisers paid for regular ads. A spokesman for Princeton Video Image (PVI) said, "You could sell a box of cereal in the kitchen one [airing], and dish soap in the next." PVI's website explains that the distribution of these "virtual insertions" could also be allocated by region: "For example, the sitcom *Frasier* can have a can of Coke on his living room table in the Northeast region broadcasts, and a can of Diet Coke on his living room table for the West Coast broadcast region. A broadcaster can show a *Seinfeld* rerun with a box of Corn Flakes on Jerry's kitchen table one time and a box of Special K the next time the show aired."
- Racing cars are typically plastered with sponsors' logos, but during portions of the Fox Sports Network broadcast of NASCAR's 2001 Budweiser Shootout, some vehicles looked oddly blank; the network had digitally removed the logos from some of the cars whose advertisers had failed to pay Fox for displaying them.
- With DivorceX software from Canada's Western Pro Imaging Labs, "divorcees can now eradicate their previous partners from photographs without resorting to a scissor job. . . . The technology can also make people thinner, younger, and can remove double chins or scars."
- Do-it-yourself photo portrait booths offer the option of "Foto Fantasy" digital manipulation.
- Kai's Photo Soap software permits amateur photographers to fix their pictures by, among other alterations, removing objects in the background.
- Kodak's Image Magic theater kiosks let moviegoers create digital posters of their "appearances" in Hollywood films.
- Introduced in 1998, the Game Boy Camera costs only $49, is marketed to kids, and invites users to "take snapshots of your friends . . . and make them a part of the action as their faces become the characters."

There may be nothing unethical about these practices, but can even newspaper photography maintain its authenticity in a visual environment where viewers are bombarded with images in which fanciful dreamscapes appear to be as real as any photograph, humans are "morphed" into phantasms, and dead celebrities come back to life to mingle with contemporary actors, to hawk beer, to dance with vacuum cleaners?[12]

DECLINING CONFIDENCE

We may even be approaching a time when the public will assume that unless otherwise specified a journalistic photo is *likely* to have been altered. In the aftermath of its highly controversial—and highly altered—1994 O.J. Simpson cover, *Time's* managing editor felt compelled to assure readers that certain other photos in the magazine had *not* been altered.[13] The statement was among the most revealing of the many comments made in the wake of the Simpson debacle; previously, no such promises had been deemed necessary in the venerable news magazine.

The implications of increasing photofakery are particularly significant in light of a declining confidence in journalism itself. *Newsweek's* July 20, 1998, issue reported, "The public's faith in the press may be at a new low,"[14] and in September 1998 the *American Journalism Review* devoted several feature articles to recent, highly publicized ethical lapses.[15] (Even *60 Minutes* was duped into airing a phony "documentary" featuring actors, misleading locations, and staged events.[16])

Another relevant trend is visual imagery's increasing dominance over the printed word. As NYU professor and critic Neil

---

[12]In television commercials aired in 1997, footage from three Fred Astaire movies was combined with film of Dirt Devil products. Diet Coke ads seemed to capture Paula Abdul dancing with Gene Kelly, and Elton John performing with Louis Armstrong. Sean Means, "Altered Images: Photo Technology Creates a Reality That's Not There," *Salt Lake Tribune* (March 3, 1997): B1.

[13]James R. Gaines, "To Our Readers," *Time* (July 4, 1994): 4.

[14]Evan Thomas and Gregory L. Vistica, "Fallout from a Media Fiasco," *Newsweek* (July 20, 1998): 24. In addition, a July 4, 1999, Associated Press story reported the results of a telephone survey taken by Vanderbilt University's First Amendment Center. The center's ombudsman, Paul McMasters, said, "The news media is in deep trouble with the American public." AP, "Survey Indicates Public Fed Up With News Media," *The Register-Guard*, Eugene, Oregon (July 4, 1999): 5A.

[15]Judith Sheppard, "Playing Defense: Is Enough Being Done To Prevent Future Journalistic Embarrassments?" *American Journalism Review* (September 1998).

[16]AP, December 7, 1998.

Postman said, "The environment created by language, and the printed word, has now been moved to the periphery of the culture . . . and at its center, the image has taken over."[17]

BEYOND PRINT MEDIA

Our challenge extends beyond newspapers and magazines to broadcast, cable, film, video, and online media. All of the image-manipulation techniques available to print media have analogs in digital video and film editing,[18] providing new opportunities not only to Hollywood studios but also to news organizations—or for that matter anyone with access to a digital camera and a computer. On a wintry January day in 1994, bundled-up ABC television correspondent Cokie Roberts was introduced to viewers as reporting "from Capitol Hill"; in fact, she was in a presumably comfy Washington studio, standing before a projected image of the Capitol building (the network apologized).[19]

The ABC/Roberts trickery was decidedly low-tech compared to what's on the horizon. *The Dallas Morning News* reported that with the latest software, "news anchors can do their stuff on camera in a bare, blue room . . . the whole set is dubbed in digitally, to show any kind of style, scenery, furniture, you name it."[20] Producer/writer Andrew Niccol was quoted in 2001 as saying, "Very soon we will be able to turn on our television sets and not know if the presenter is real or fake, and frankly we won't care." In one example, an animated "cyber anchor" named Ananova appeared on a website to read actual news and weather reports. According to the May 7, 2001, *New York Times* (p. B8), "Within weeks after her debut last year, Ananova was besieged by requests for personal appearances, calls from Hollywood agents and record companies asking to sign her."

In his classic work, *1984*, George Orwell offered this description of the ultimate totalitarian state's propaganda mechanism: "There were the huge printing shops with their sub-editors, their

15

---

[17]"Consuming Images," *The Public Mind: Image and Reality in America* (PBS video, 1989).

[18]"Video will go the same way as film as newsrooms turn to new computer technology . . . much of the equipment and technology now exists." Lou Prato, "Coming Up: Digital Pictures at 11," *American Journalism Review* (July/August 1994): 48.

[19]"Darts and Laurels" column, *Columbia Journalism Review* (May/June 1994): http://www.cjr.org/ year/94/3/d_l.asp.

[20]Wright, 7J. See also Prato, 48.

typography experts, and their elaborately equipped studios for the faking of photographs." One wonders what Orwell might have thought of this 1996 announcement for Reality 3-D software (note that the product is directed not to advertisers but to news professionals):

> EarthWatch . . . introduces a revolutionary new product line. Reality 3-D is the next step in graphics, permitting real-time animations for weather and news . . . [providing] a simulated helicopter perspective with a photorealistic Virtual City Skyline. . . . The system will simulate fires, explosions, and permit the user to re-create accidents in near real-time, getting compelling visuals on the air . . . before video arrives on the scene. With a virtual set, your weather or news talent can be in a simulated 3-D landscape, walking knee-deep through fronts, storms, or hurricanes, or walking through your virtual skyline."[21]

Videographers have long been able to restructure raw footage to create new "realities"; now, with computer modeling, vocal sampling, and re-animation techniques they can literally put words in a speaker's mouth. The faces of actors James Garner and Jack Lemmon were digitally "pasted" onto the bodies of stunt men on horseback in the film *My Fellow Americans*.[22] In *Star Wars: Episode I—The Phantom Menace*, nonanimated characters existing only in the digital realm "interacted" with real actors filmed in studios and on location; also, a live actor's expression from one take was digitally grafted onto his face in another take.[23] The technology that allowed Tom Hanks to chat briefly with John F. Kennedy in *Forrest Gump* has been refined; if focus groups decree that the public wants to see a romantic epic starring Leonardo Di Caprio opposite a teenaged Elizabeth Taylor, technicians may soon be able to render it on computers.

Consider the implications of applying these technologies to a faked newscast, political speech, disaster announcement, or declaration of war. "In a few years, anybody will be able to get in

---

[21]Don Fitzpatrick, "Shoptalk," Don Fitzpatrick Associates, http://www.tvspy.com, October 8, 1996.

[22]See Andy Seiler, "Technology Puts Fiction in 'Contact' with Reality," *USA Today* (July 30, 1997): 5D.

[23]"This may be the first step toward a cinematic future in which virtual actors replace flesh-and-blood ones. . . ." David A. Kaplan, "The Selling of Star Wars," *Newsweek* (May 17, 1999): 60.

there and manipulate images," says Ken Ralston, special effects supervisor on the films *Contact* (which seemed to portray President Clinton speaking about events in the film), *Forrest Gump*, and *Who Framed Roger Rabbit?* "It's going to be everywhere, in every facet of our lives."[24]

With the relatively low costs of video gear and easy-to-use software, even individuals working on a shoestring can make reasonably professional looking videos brimming with special effects. Given the Internet, as well as an expected increase in satellite transmissions and the advent of cable modems and multiple digital television channels, those videos will soon be distributed worldwide with ease—and perhaps without whatever ethical safeguards might have been attached had they emerged through conventional channels.[25] Then again, the World Wide Web may facilitate a new kind of photo-based storytelling whose layers of meaning and richness of context are scarcely approached by traditional photojournalism.

SUMMARY

Digital technologies continue to revolutionize all mass media, not only exposing the public to more manipulated images but also giving them more opportunities to do the manipulating themselves, even in their everyday, personal photographic experiences. Some consequences of all this remain unclear, but certainly the assumption that "seeing is believing" is under assault amid this environment of elastic imagery.

Questions

1. Wheeler informs us that since most images in the media are digital, they are susceptible to "easy, unlimited, and virtually undetectable manipulation" (paragraph 4). What do you think is the best example that he provides to make his case? What others do you know about that he does not mention? How do you think these changes affect us as viewers?

2. Imagine watching a news story on television and finding out that the images were digitally created to present the story in a vivid way. Would you find this acceptable because it would help tell the story or unacceptable because it is fake? Explain the reasons for your reaction.

---

[24]Kaplan, 60.

[25]Bruce Haring, "Digital Video: A Movie Star in the Making," *USA Today* (July 1, 1998): 5D.

3. According to Wheeler, what special problems does the Internet present in relation to images? Do you think that images on the Web have a different impact on us than images in print media?

4. Wheeler predicts that "we may even be approaching a time when the public will assume that unless otherwise specified a journalistic photo is *likely* to have been altered" (paragraph 11). When does it matter that you know if an image has been manipulated? Always, sometimes, never? Do images of people in the news as opposed to those in entertainment contexts seem to matter more?

5. Find a picture in a newspaper, news magazine, an e-zine, or in a conventional magazine that you think has been manipulated in some way. Write a brief essay in which you explain what aspects you think have been manipulated and why and whether these alterations matter to you.

Living with the Fake and Learning to Like It
ADA LOUISE HUXTABLE

Ada Louise Huxable is the architecture critic for the Wall Street Journal. *For many years, she held the same position at the* New York Times, *where she won the Pulitzer Prize, the first awarded for distinguished criticism. Among her many articles and books are* Architecture, Anyone? *(1986) and* The Unreal America: Architecture and Illusion *(1997). Her article "Living with the Fake and Learning to Like It," which confronts the issue of fake architecture, originally appeared in the* New York Times *in 1997.*

Getting Started

Have you ever been to Las Vegas, Disney World, a historical village, or a themed adventure park? What is it like to be in an environment that has been designed to give you a certain kind of experience? What is the difference between seeing the pyramid at the Luxor Hotel in Las Vegas and the one in Egypt? What do we mean when we talk about the difference between the real and the fake? Can something that is fake, like a copy or a reconstruction, be as vivid and valuable as the original it is based on? In her essay, Huxtable writes about architecture and interior design. How might you connect the issues concerning artificially created places with those of artificially created images?

———————— ✦ ————————

I do not know just when we lost our sense of reality or our interest in it, but at some point it was decided that reality was not the only option. It was possible, permissible and even desirable to improve on it; one could substitute a more agreeable product. Architecture and the environment as packaging or playacting, as disengagement from reality, is a notion whose time, alas, seems to have come. Give or take demolition and natural disasters, architecture is the most immediate, expressive and lasting art to ever record the human condition. Cities are the containers and generators of our history and culture. We are what we build; stone and steel do not lie. But there has been a radical change in the way we perceive and understand this physical reality.

Surrogate experience and synthetic settings have become the preferred American way of life. Environment is entertainment and artifice; it is the theme park with the enormously profitable real-estate bottom line and a stunning record as the country's biggest growth industry. Build an "enclave" of old buildings moved out of the path of development, and you have the past; build a mall and multiplex, and you have the future. Build a replica of New York in Las Vegas as a skyscraper casino with Coney Island rides, and you have a crowd-pleaser without the risk of a trip to the Big Apple.

Distinctions are no longer made or deemed necessary between the real and the false; the edge usually goes to the latter, as an improved version with defects corrected—accessible and user-friendly. As usual, it is California that sets the trends and establishes the values for the rest of the country. Only a Californian would observe that it is becoming increasingly difficult to tell the real fake from the fake fake. All fakes are clearly not equal; there are good fakes and bad fakes. The standard is no longer real versus phony but the relative merits of the imitation. What makes the good ones better is their improvement on reality.

The real fake reaches its apogee in places like Las Vegas, where it has been developed into an art form. Continuous, competitive frontages of moving light and color and constantly accelerating novelty lead to the gaming tables and hotels. The purpose is clear and the solution is dazzling; the result is completely and sublimely itself. The outrageously fake fake has developed its own indigenous style and life style to become a real place. This is an urban design frontier where extraordinary things are happening.

The Los Angeles architect Jon Jerde, an established master of   5 the modern shopping mall and all its clones and offspring, understands this transformation well. Using a salesman's pitch and psychologist's insights he speaks of "place making," in which advanced technology and programmed perceptions are used for unprecedented solutions and sensations. The dream of pedestrianism, so valiantly and fruitlessly pursued by planners who have looked to the past and overseas for models of historic hill towns and plazas, has been aggressively naturalized; the social stroll has become a sensuous assault. In a Jerde makeover, a 1,400-foot-long, 90-foot high arched space frame spans Las Vegas's Fremont Street—the original, now dated Strip—wrapping the nighttime walker in a computer-generated sound and light show provided by 211 million lights and a 540,000-watt sound system. This "Fremont Street experience" is billed as "a linear urban theater for pedestrians along the city's familiar icon and historic heart."

Yes, Virginia, Las Vegas has a historic heart; you are too young to remember, but Fremont Street was invented and incorporated in 1905. More than 90 years old now, and getting a little tired, it is part of historic America along with Williamsburg and more recent landmarks like Route 66, the Mom and Pop motel and the earliest golden arches of McDonald's.

The street is still evolving in a uniquely American way. It would be a mistake, as the Swiss philosopher and student of American urbanism André Corboz has pointed out, to mistake Las Vegas for Monte Carlo. A singular confluence of desire, flash and the big sell has created its character and destiny. Built to be exactly what it is, this is the real, real fake at the highest, loudest and most authentically inauthentic level of illusion and invention. It must be understood on its own terms.

Since gambling has been renamed gaming (another triumph of still another uniquely American phenomenon, public relations), and thus cleansed of all pejorative connotations and rendered euphemistically harmless, it has emerged at the top of the list of America's favorite pastimes. Today, Las Vegas and Atlantic City (one offers the desert and the other the ocean to those who venture outdoors) are being touted as family vacation spots.

It has finally come together: the lunar theatrical landscape of the Strip and the casino hotels, the amusement park and the shopping mall, all themed and prefabricated and available as a packaged vacation for all. Morris Lapidus's Miami hotels of the

1950's—the unforgettable gilded excesses of the faux-French Fontainebleau and the sluggish crocodiles in the equally faux jungle under the Americana's lobby stairs—have evolved into the breath-stopping extravaganzas of Caesar's Palace with its heroic Styrofoam statuary and the Luxor's Sphinx and mirror-glass pyramid.

The latest drop-dead entry in this pantheon of exuberant termi-   10
nal pretense is New York, New York, a hotel and casino complex de-signed as a pastiche of New York's most famous buildings; a collage of pin-striped towers makes its wonderfully improbable facade.

In front of this mirage-melange of skyscrapers is a dotty row of older New York landmarks, side by side, almost holding hands—Grant's Tomb, Ellis Island, Grand Central Terminal, the Brooklyn Bridge and SoHo's cast-iron Haughwout store (a dead giveaway that some real New York architecture buffs have been at work) all laced together with the airy, looping curves of a giant roller coaster. The architects, Gaskin & Bezanski, working with the firm of Yates-Silverman, seem to have perfected the genre of inspired looniness and outer-edge spectacle of the best of these undertakings.

The family that games together also shops together in the Fo-rum Shops, a 250,000-square–foot addition to Caesar's World, where moving sidewalks take them through six triumphal arches rising from cascading fountains into the streets of stores. "Your typical Roman via," the critic Aaron Betsky reported on the occa-sion of the grand opening in 1992, "where the sun sets and rises on an electronically controlled cycle, continually bathing acres of faux finishes in rosy hues. Animatronic robots welcome you with a burst of lasers, and a rococo version of the Fountain of the Four Rivers drowns out the sound of nearby slots." In Las Vegas, "his-tory repeats itself neither as farce nor as tragedy but as a themed environment."

Once the substitute, or surrogate, is considered the more ac-ceptable experience, remarkable things occur. There are rain forests in Las Vegas that casino guests find infinitely more im-pressive than the South American variety; they prefer the combi-nation of tropicana and silks (the trade name for false foliage) with the added attraction of live white tigers.

In Texas, when movie makers planned a film about the Alamo and found the real landmark small and unprepossessing, they built a bigger and better Alamo in a nearby town. Today both the false and the genuine Alamo are equally popular tourist attractions. (If one is good, two are better. And the new, improved version is best of all.) A start has been made on taking the pressure off national parks by bringing tourists to a high-tech show-and-tell presentation of Zion Park, with a drive-by en route; one can experience it all that way and still get to Vegas by night.

Nor are the fine distinctions between the real fake and the   15
fake fake always clear. The surrogate version is rarely sublime; more often it is a reduced and emptied-out idea based on what Corboz has called the "poverty of the re-invention of the not known." Surprisingly, it is only in the freewheeling and not too fussy commercial world that the substitute comes off. At a higher level, confusion is encouraged in a much more subtle and insidious and dangerous way. In the world of art and scholarship, where they really know the difference, there is a growing interdependence of the real and the fake, with a disturbing identification of the values of the original and the copy. The slippage is taking place at institutional and cultural sources that have always been the defenders and keepers of authenticity.

Museums, dependent on tourism, must compete for attendance with entertainment-geared attractions. That takes a lot of hype and high-class souvenirs in the gift shop.

The art, science and culture museum of the University of California at Berkeley, located not in Berkeley but in the affluent suburb of Blackhawk, augmented a 1991 show of New Guinea artifacts with a "science theater," where an experience called Nature's Fury produced a rocking earthquake simulation from a mini-volcano, going a step further for "lifelike" relevance appropriate to the community, a suggested survivor's kit was displayed in the trunk of a BMW. Life-size scenes in narrative settings subordinate the thing itself to a dramatic recreation. With nothing to recommend them except their often shabby authenticity, the real objects simply have less appeal than snappy simulations.

While art museums are more removed from the tourist track where "the world's great masterpieces" are re-created in everything from living tableaux to glow-in-the-dark copies on velvet, even the primary citadels have not escaped the trend. High art has been "contaminated"—this is the semiotician and novelist Umberto Eco's word; no one else would dare use it—by the "blurring of the boundaries" of original and reproduction. It is common practice for originals, reconstructions and reproductions to be mingled in an effort to bring museum displays "to life"; one must read the exhibition labels to know what is real and what is not.

The leveling of the works of art with copies for sale in the museum shop is omnipresent. The ostensible purpose of the reproduction, to make one want the original, has been supplanted by the feeling that the original is no longer necessary. The copy is considered just as good and, in some cases, better; Eco and the French philosopher Jean Baudrillard both argue that the simulation replaces the original to become the reality in most minds, even if this is not overtly expressed, and even in those places meant to guard the uniqueness and the meaning of the work of art.

According to the American cultural historian Margaret   20
Crawford and Richard Sennett, the novelist and sociologist who specializes in the philosophical and symbolic aspects of urbanism, there is a relationship between the museum shop and that feature of mall salesmanship called "adjacent attraction." In both the commercial and the cultural setting, there is a transfer of values, from real objects of esthetic and historical validity to lesser products.

Even when direct copies are not involved, the frequent use of real objects as promotional devices raises the price and perception of the thing for sale, through the kind of association that "blurs the boundaries," as Eco expressed it. But the process also works both ways. The commodity (for a price) becomes identified with the qualities of the object (no price, or even, in the case of artworks, priceless), so that the same value is given to both.

The blurring of the boundaries has now become a constant in scholarship and connoisseurship. The computer substitutes the picture on the screen for the original work of art. Because the computer and the camera have made available an incredible array of research sources, arcane problems can be explored as never before; scholars can deal with masses of data and remote collections of awe-inspiring completeness and diversity. This is one of the seductive miracles of the electronic age. Entire dissertations can be written without ever seeing the originals. Access is increasingly limited to the fragile drawings, documents and rare books that are primary resources.

Since this is the point of scholarship where the eye is trained, the loss of direct contact is incalculable. It is through the immediate visual and sensory response engendered by repeated exposure to the actual work of art that connoisseurship is created—the related sequence of close knowledge and informed taste by which works of art can be accurately understood, compared, defined, judged and enjoyed. There is no replacement for this primary experience—the direct connection with the hand of the artist in the actual touch of the pen or the stroke of the brush—no matter how technically perfect the reproduction.

Eco of the impeccable, bemused and outraged eye has given the subject of authenticity an unexpected and very important spin. Rather than liking reality or the real thing too little, he says, Americans love it too much. We are obsessed with reality, with the possession of the object, determined to have it at any cost, in the most immediate and tangible form, unconcerned with authenticity or the loss of historical, cultural or esthetic meaning. This pervasive attitude, established through a massive popular network, has "spread to the products of high culture and the entertainment industry," Eco notes, where the relationship among values, judgment and authenticity has virtually ceased to exist.

The theme park has no such problem of degenerative authenticity. Nothing in it is admired for its reality, only for the calculated manipulation and simulation of its sources. It is not surprising that much of the most popular and profitable development of the genre is spearheaded and bankrolled by the masters of illusion; the movie and entertainment businesses have become the major innovators and investors in theme parks and related enterprises.   25

An entire industry has sprung up to serve themed entertainment, providing those erupting volcanoes and fiberglass rock formations on the grounds of Las Vegas casinos; according to an industry spokesman "you get a very artificial appearance with real rock." Those who wonder what happened to American know-how have just not been looking in the right places.

With reality voided and illusion preferred, almost anything can have uncritical acceptance. For those without memory, nostalgia fills the void. For those without reference points, novelties are enough. For those without the standards supplied by familiarity with the source, knockoffs will do. Escalating sensation supplants intellectual and esthetic response.

For all of the above, the outrageous is essential. There must be instant gratification; above all, one must be able to buy sensation and status; the experience and the products must be for sale. The remarkable marriage of technologically based and shrewdly programmed artificial experience with a manufactured and managed environment, for a real-life substitute of controlled and pricey pleasures, is a totally American product and the real American dream.

Questions

1. Huxtable writes: "All fakes are clearly not equal; there are good fakes and bad fakes. The standard is no longer real versus phony but the relative merits of the imitation. What makes the good ones better is their improvement on reality" (paragraph 3). What does she mean by this statement? What is an example of a "good fake" or a "bad fake"? How can something artificial improve on reality?

2. Is Huxtable a fan of replicas and reproductions in architecture? Is her tone in this article serious, humorous, ironic, sad, or annoyed? What in her writing tells you how to assess her approach and where in the article do you find her attitude about this subject?

3. Make a list of the places Huxtable mentions. What do they have in common? Which ones have you seen? What is your opinion of them?

4. Make a list of the people Huxtable mentions. Who are they? Why are their opinions important to Huxtable's point of view? Why do writers refer to other thinkers when they want to make a point?

5. What is the function of the museum shop or the visitor store in contributing to the blurring of the distinction between real and fake? Why do people buy replicas or reproductions as souvenirs? Why do many people prefer to visit the theme park or replica village rather than go to the "real" place or see the "real" thing?

Colorizing the Cosmos
BOB BERMAN

Bob Berman is the director of the Overlook and Cobb-Matthieson Observatories near Woodstock, New York, and adjunct professor of astronomy at Marymount Manhattan College. He is the astronomy editor of The Old Farmer's Almanac *and writes monthly columns for both* Discover *and* Astronomy *magazines, and he has appeared on* The Today Show *and* Late Night with David Letterman. *His previous books include* Secrets of the Night Sky *(1995);* Cosmic Adventure: Other Secrets Beyond the Night Sky *(2000); and* Strange Universe: The Weird and Wild Science of Everyday Life on Earth and Beyond *(2003, 2005).*

Getting Started

In this very short and succinct article, astronomer Berman discloses a little-known fact that is startling to most people when they hear it—the images of space with which we are so familiar are almost all digitally altered. What color do you think the planets are? What color do you associate with galaxies and nebulae? Do you think scientific photos must be accurate and, if so, what do you mean by accuracy in images? What are the "real" colors of things we cannot see without instruments or computers? Why might space photos or any images from the world of science be altered or enhanced?

─────────────── ◆ ───────────────

What color is the cosmos? Planets, nebulae, and galaxies appear wan and faint when eyed through a backyard telescope. But researchers using imaging techniques show us a much more chromatic view.

That's right, the colors in many familiar photographs of the cosmos are fake. For more than 20 years, space agencies have embellished images of the heavens. Some of the images *have* to be enhanced: Photos assembled from wavelengths beyond the eye's perception have no color, so researchers paint them any way they choose. Venus, for example, has invisible cloud patterns that show up in infrared photos; NASA depicts them in orange and blue. Similarly, X-ray detectors reveal invisible galactic structures. Researchers color-code these features according to wavelength or temperature.

False color, for the sake of drama, got a lot of reinforcement when the giant outer planets were photographed during the Voyager mission in the late 1970s and 1980s. Researchers intensified color and contrast to maximize detail, and the media fell in love with the brilliant images.

When *Voyager 2* reached Neptune in 1989, the previously pale planet was promoted to sky blue with red tinges. Uranus was—and still is—presented as lime green. No scientific principles justify these embellishments; Uranus is featureless. Without detail to enhance, the planet needed a rich new color to get the attention of the press. Likewise, Mars has been painted circus red instead of pale pumpkin. And Jupiter's yellow-white bands and light pink Red Spot have been tweaked to orange and candy-apple red.

Colorization is not confined to images from deep-space probes. Consider the celebrated 1995 Hubble photo, dubbed Pillars of Creation, by Jeff Hester and Paul Scowen of Arizona State University. This vivid image of the Eagle nebula's spirelike columns has graced the covers of astronomy magazines and has been made into a hit poster. 5

Through amateur telescopes these faint gas clouds appear gray and unexciting. Larger instruments sometimes show such nebulae as pale green because the retina responds to that tint in dim light. By contrast, photography brings out a dominant red emitted by the Eagle's hydrogen atoms. The universe is well stocked with these lovely cherry-red nebulae, thanks to hydrogen's omnipresence.

But such unvarying red can become tiresome after the first few thousand light-years of cosmic inventory. To avoid such monochromaticity, astronomers took separate pictures of the Eagle through different filters. Coloring each image with brilliant tints and bleeding them together yielded the spectacular hues of the Pillars of Creation.

Hester says his celebrated Hubble picture was merely intended to bring out scientific detail. The real Eagle nebula, he surmises, would look ghostly faint with pale, feeble colors. He calls his work an "artistic rendering of what the scientist sees."

Such artistic license is so commonplace that the presented universe bears little resemblance to the real thing. Instead, we have a cosmos in designer colors.

Questions

1. The full title of this article is "Colorizing the Cosmos: Sorry, the Real Universe Isn't That Dramatic." Why do you think Berman includes an apology in the title? Were you disappointed by the realization that the colors in photos of the cosmos are not entirely accurate? Why or why not?

2. Why do the colors in the photos of the cosmos often *have* to be enhanced? Should there be a statement at the bottom of each photo stating that the colors have been enhanced or altered in some way? Why or why not?

3. This article is about the manipulation of color, a highly emotional and personal aspect of images. What feelings do you associate with the colors of the planets—the blue Earth, the gray moon, the red planet Mars? How important do you think colors are to our understanding of the skies or to our experience of any image?

4. Do you think the images presented to us by scientific organizations like NASA should be thought of differently from those published by news or entertainment media? Do you expect any kinds of images to be more "real" than others?

5. There is a difference between things that can be seen with the naked eye—like the moon—and things that can only be seen with instruments—like distant stars, which are too faint to see. Does the image of something you can

see unaided seem more "real" in some way than something you cannot see without technology? Are you more comfortable with the altering of images of things that cannot be seen naturally or those that can be? Why?

Pygmalion's Power
ERNST GOMBRICH

Ernst Gombrich (1909–2001) was born in Vienna and moved to England in 1937. Most of the members of his family, who remained in Austria during World War II, were killed during the Holocaust. Gombrich was a prominent art critic whose first book, The Story of Art *(1949), has been translated into more than 20 languages. Among his many publications is the classic text* Art and Illusion *(1960), from which "Pygmalion's Power" was excerpted.*

Getting Started

Unlike some of the other writers in this book, Gombrich is a critic and historian not a journalist and his writing can therefore be a bit harder to understand. Yet he is focusing on a key aspect of all images—is art just a pale copy of reality or is it as real and vivid as reality itself? What do you think about this question? Do images seem like imitations of nature to you? Or do you think that images are just as real as anything else you see? If you laugh at a movie or cry at a television show, does that mean you are being fooled into thinking that you are watching real life? Or are art and other sorts of images a kind of alternate reality?

———————— ✦ ————————

> *Once there was an old man whose name was Nahokoboni. He was troubled in his mind because he had no daughter, and who could look after him if he had no son-in-law? Being a witch doctor, he therefore carved himself a daughter out of a plum tree. . . .*
>
> —A fairy tale of the Guiana Indians

Ever since the Greek philosophers called art an "imitation of nature" their successors have been busy affirming, denying, or qualifying this definition. . . . They try to show some of the limits of this aim toward a perfect "imitation" set by the nature of the medium on the one hand and by the psychology of artistic procedure on the other. Everybody knows that this imitation has ceased to be the concern of artists today. But is this a new departure? Were the Greeks right even in their description of the aims of the artists in the past?

Their own mythology would have told them a different story. For it tells of an earlier and more awe-inspiring function of art when the artist did not aim at making a "likeness" but at rivaling creation itself. The most famous of these myths that crystallize belief in the power of art to create rather than to portray is the story of Pygmalion. Ovid turned it into an erotic novelette, but even in his perfumed version we can feel something of the thrill which the artist's mysterious powers once gave to man.

In Ovid, Pygmalion is a sculptor who wants to fashion a woman after his own heart and falls in love with the statue he makes. He prays to Venus for a bride modeled after that image, and the goddess turns the cold marble into a living body. It is a myth that has naturally captivated the imagination of artists. . . Without the underlying promise of this myth, the secret hopes and fears that accompany the act of creation, there might be no art as we know it. One of the most original painters of England, Lucien Freud, wrote: "A moment of complete happiness never occurs in the creation of a work of art. The promise of it is felt in the act of creation, but disappears towards the completion of the work. For it is then that the painter realises that it is only a picture he is painting. Until then he had almost dared to hope that the picture might spring to life."

"Only a picture," says Lucien Freud. It is a motif we find in the whole history of Western art; Vasari tells of Donatello at work on his Zuccone looking at it suddenly and threatening the stone with a dreadful curse, "Speak, speak—*favella, favella, che ti venga il cacasangue!*" And the greatest wizard of them all, Leonardo da Vinci, extolled the power of the artist to create. In that hymn of praise to painting, the "Paragone," he calls the painter "the Lord of all manner of people and of all things." "If the painter wishes to see beauties to fall in love with, it is in his power to bring them forth, and if he wants to see monstrous things that frighten or are foolish or laughable or indeed to be pitied, he is their Lord and God."

Indeed, the power of art to rouse the passions is to him a token of its magic. Unlike the poet, he writes, the painter can so subdue the minds of men that they will fall in love with a painting that does not represent a real woman. "It happened to me," he continues, "that I made a religious painting which was bought by one who so loved it that he wanted to remove the sacred representation so as to be able to kiss it without suspicion. Finally his conscience prevailed over his sighs and lust, but he had to remove the picture from his house."

. . .

And yet Leonardo, if anyone, knew that the artist's desire to create, to bring forth a second reality, finds its inexorable limits in the restrictions of his medium. I feel we catch an echo of the disillusionment with having created only a picture that we found in Lucien Freud when we read in Leonardo's notes: "Painters often fall into despair . . . when they see that their paintings lack the roundness and the liveliness which we find in objects seen in the mirror . . . but it is impossible for a painting to look as rounded as a mirror image . . . except if you look at both with one eye only."

Perhaps the passage betrays the ultimate reason for Leonardo's deep dissatisfaction with his art, his reluctance to reach the fatal moment of completion: all the artist's knowledge and imagination are of no avail, it is only a picture that he has been painting, and it will look flat. Small wonder that contemporaries describe him in his later years as most impatient of the brush and engrossed in mathematics. Mathematics was to help him to be the true maker. Today we read of Leonardo's project to build a "flying machine," but if we look into Leonardo's notes we will not find such an expression. What he wants to make is a bird that will fly, and once more there is an exultant tone in the master's famous prophecy that the bird *would* fly. It did not. And shortly afterward we find Leonardo lodging in the Vatican—at the time when Michelangelo and Raphael were there creating their most renowned works—quarreling with a German mirror maker and fixing wings and a beard to a tame lizard in order to frighten his visitors. He made a dragon, but it was only a whimsical footnote to a Promethean life. The claim to be a creator, a maker of things, passed from the painter to the engineer—leaving to the artist only the small consolation of being a maker of dreams.

This fateful distinction goes back to the very period when the "imitation of nature" was first discovered and defined by the Greeks of the fourth century. There are few more influential discussions on the philosophy of representation than the momentous passage in the *Republic* where Plato introduces the comparison between a painting and a mirror image. It has haunted the philosophy of art ever since. To re-examine his theory of ideas, Plato contrasts the painter with the carpenter. The carpenter who makes the couch translates the idea, or concept, of the couch into matter. The painter who represents the carpenter's couch in one of his paintings only copies the appearance of one particular couch. He is thus twice removed from the idea.

. . .

In the world of the child there is no clear distinction between reality and appearance. He can use the most unlikely tools for the most unlikely purposes—a table upside down for a spaceship, a basin for a crash helmet. For the context of the game it will serve its purpose rather well. The basin does not "represent" a crash helmet, it *is* a kind of improvised helmet, and it might even prove useful. There is no rigid division between the phantom and reality, truth and falsehood, at least not where human purpose and human action come into their own. What we call "culture" or "civilization" is based on man's capacity to be a maker, to invent unexpected uses, and to create artificial substitutes.

To us the word "artificial" seems immensely far removed from art. But this was not always so. The works of cunning craftsmen in myth and story include precious toys and intriguing machines, artificial singing birds, and angels blowing real trumpets. And when men turned from the admiration of artifice to the worship of nature, the landscape gardener was called in to make artificial lakes, artificial waterfalls, and even artificial mountains. For the world of man is not only a world of things; it is a world of symbols where the distinction between reality and make-believe is itself unreal. The dignitary who lays the foundation stone will give it three taps with a silver hammer. The hammer is real, but is the blow? In this twilight region of the symbolic, no such questions are asked, and therefore no answers need be given.

When we make a snowman we do not feel, I submit, that we are constructing a phantom of a man. We are simply making a man of snow. We do not say, "Shall we represent a man who is smoking?" but "Shall we give him a pipe?" For the success of the operation, a real pipe may be just as good or better than a symbolic one made of a twig. It is only afterward that we may introduce the idea of reference, of the snowman's representing somebody. We can make him a portrait or a caricature, or we can discover a likeness to someone and elaborate it. But always, I contend, making will come before matching, creation before reference. As likely as

10

not, we will give our snowman a proper name, call him "Jimmie" or "Jeeves," and will be sorry for him when he starts to slump and melt away.

But are we not still matching something when we make the snowman? Are we not at least modeling our creation after the idea of a man, like Plato's craftsman who copied the idea of the couch? Or, if we reject this metaphysical interpretation, are we not imitating the image of a man we have in our mind? This is the traditional answer, but . . . it will not quite do. First of all, it makes the created image into a replica of something nobody has ever seen, the snowman we allegedly carry in our heads before we body it forth. Moreover there was no such pre-existent snowman. What happens is rather that we feel tempted to work the snow and balance the shapes till we recognize a man. The pile of snow provides us with the first schema, which we correct until it satisfies our minimum definition. A symbolic man, to be sure, but still a member of the species man, subspecies snowman. What we learn from the study of symbolism, I contend, is precisely that to our minds the limits of these definitions are elastic.

Questions

1. What is the purpose of the fairy tale quoted at the beginning of the Gombrich piece? How does it connect with Gombrich's ideas?
2. Who is Pygmalion? What does he do and what are the consequences of his act? Have you ever seen any modern interpretations of this myth? Why does this story still have power for us today?
3. Gombrich refers to "the power of art to rouse the passions" (paragraph 5). Thinking about this in the broadest sense to include images in print, movies, and on the Web, what examples can you find of images that rouse the passions? What are the positive aspects of this? The negative aspects?
4. Gombrich's essay challenges the idea that art merely imitates reality, as suggested by Plato and others. In what ways do you question the reality of the images you see in print media or on television? Do you automatically believe the images in the news for instance, or do you doubt them and, if so, under what circumstances? How do you decide what is real?
5. Gombrich suggests that the question of how well art imitates life is not that important in responding to art, but that we should instead approach art on its own terms and not compare it to real life. How does his example of building a snowman illustrate this idea?

The Work of Art in the Age of Mechanical Reproduction
WALTER BENJAMIN

Walter Benjamin (1892–1940) was a German literary critic and philosopher. As a literary scholar, he translated works written by Marcel Proust and Charles Baudelaire, and his essay "The Task of the Translator" is one of the seminal writings on literary theory. This excerpt from "The Work of Art in the Age of Mechanical Reproduction" deals with film and its impact on our sense of reality.

Getting Started

Translated from German and written in the 1930s, this essay may require some work to understand. But the effort is worthwhile because Benjamin is responding to movies as a brand new medium and foresees how profound their impact on us will be. How does the technology of film change the way we see the world? In what ways do movie images seem real and in what ways do they seem fake? Are the new images created with new techniques always better or more important than older ones? Think of movies or movie images that had a profound effect on you. In what ways do images tell us more about life than direct observation, as Benjamin suggests?

───────── ✦ ─────────

The shooting of a film, especially of a sound film, affords a spectacle unimaginable anywhere at any time before this. It presents a process in which it is impossible to assign to a spectator a viewpoint which would exclude from the actual scene such extraneous accessories as camera equipment, lighting machinery, staff assistants, etc.—unless his eye were on a line parallel with the lens. This circumstance, more than any other, renders superficial and insignificant any possible similarity between a scene in the studio and one on the stage. In the theater one is well aware of the place from which the play cannot immediately be detected as illusionary. There is no such place for the movie scene that is being shot. Its illusionary nature is that of the second degree, the result of cutting. That is to say, in the studio the mechanical equipment has penetrated so deeply into reality that its pure aspect freed from the foreign substance of equipment is the result of a special procedure, namely, the shooting by the specially adjusted camera and the mounting of the shot together with other similar ones. The equipment-free aspect of reality here has become the height of artifice; the sight of immediate reality has become an orchid in the land of technology.

Even more revealing is the comparison of these circumstances, which differ so much from those of the theater, with the situation in painting. Here the question is: How does the cameraman compare with the painter? To answer this we take recourse to an analogy with a surgical operation. The surgeon represents the polar opposite of the magician. The magician heals a sick person by the laying on of hands; the surgeon cuts into the patient's body. The magician maintains the natural distance between the patient and himself; though he reduces it very slightly by the laying on of hands, he greatly increases it by virtue of his authority. The surgeon does exactly the reverse; he greatly diminishes the distance between himself and the patient by penetrating into the patient's body, and increases it but little by the caution with which his hand moves among the organs. In short, in contrast to the magician—who is still hidden in the medical practitioner—the surgeon at the decisive moment abstains from facing the patient man to man; rather, it is through the operation that he penetrates into him.

Magician and surgeon compare to painter and cameraman. The painter maintains in his work a natural distance from reality, the cameraman penetrates deeply into its web.[1] There is a tremendous difference between the pictures they obtain. That of the painter is a total one, that of the cameraman consists of multiple fragments which are assembled under a new law. Thus, for contemporary man the representation of reality by the film is incomparably more significant than that of the painter, since it

---

[1] The boldness of the cameraman is indeed comparable to that of the surgeon. Luc Durtain lists among specific technical sleights of hand those "which are required in surgery in the case of certain difficult operations. I choose as an example a case from otorhinolaryngology; . . . the so-called endonasal perspective procedure; or I refer to the acrobatic tricks of larynx surgery which have to be performed following the reversed picture in the laryngoscope. I might also speak of ear surgery which suggests the precision work of watchmakers. What range of the most subtle muscular acrobatics is required from the man who wants to repair or save the human body! We have only to think of the couching of a cataract where there is virtually a debate of steel with nearly fluid tissue, or of the major abdominal operations (laparotomy)."—Luc Durtain.

offers, precisely because of the thoroughgoing permeation of reality with mechanical equipment, an aspect of reality which is free of all equipment. And that is what one is entitled to ask from a work of art.

. . .

The characteristics of the film lie not only in the manner in which man presents himself to mechanical equipment but also in the manner in which, by means of this apparatus, man can represent his environment. A glance at occupational psychology illustrates the testing capacity of the equipment. Psychoanalysis illustrates it in a different perspective. The film has enriched our field of perception with methods which can be illustrated by those of Freudian theory. Fifty years ago, a slip of the tongue passed more or less unnoticed. Only exceptionally may such a slip have revealed dimensions of depth in a conversation which had seemed to be taking its course on the surface. Since the *Psychopathology of Everyday Life* things have changed. This book isolated and made analyzable things which had heretofore floated along unnoticed in the broad stream of perception. For the entire spectrum of optical, and now also acoustical, perception the film has brought about a similar deepening of apperception. It is only an obverse of this fact that behavior items shown in a movie can be analyzed much more precisely and from more points of view than those presented on paintings or on the stage. As compared with painting, filmed behavior lends itself more readily to analysis because of its incomparably more precise statements of the situation. In comparison with the stage scene, the filmed behavior item lends itself more readily to analysis because it can be isolated more easily. This circumstance derives its chief importance from its tendency to promote the mutual penetration of art and science. Actually, of a screened behavior item which is neatly brought out in a certain situation, like a muscle of a body, it is difficult to say which is more fascinating, its artistic value or its value for science. To demonstrate the identity of the artistic and scientific uses of photography which heretofore usually were separated will be one of the revolutionary functions of the film.[2]

---

[2]Renaissance painting offers a revealing analogy to this situation. The incomparable development of this art and its significance rested not least on the

(*Continues*)

By close-ups of the things around us, by focusing on hidden   5
details of familiar objects, by exploring commonplace milieus under the ingenious guidance of the camera, the film, on the one
hand, extends our comprehension of the necessities which rule
our lives; on the other hand, it manages to assure us of an immense and unexpected field of action. Our taverns and our metropolitan streets, our offices and furnished rooms, our railroad
stations and our factories appeared to have us locked up hope-
lessly. Then came the film and burst this prison-world asunder by
the dynamite of the tenth of a second, so that now, in the midst of
its far-flung ruins and debris, we calmly and adventurously go
traveling. With the close-up, space expands; with slow motion,
movement is extended. The enlargement of a snapshot does not
simply render more precise what in any case was visible, though
unclear: it reveals entirely new structural formations of the subject. So, too, slow motion not only presents familiar qualities of
movement but reveals in them entirely unknown ones "which, far
from looking like retarded rapid movements give the effect of sin-
gularly gliding, floating, supernatural motions."[3] Evidently a different nature opens itself to the camera than opens to the naked
eye—if only because an unconsciously penetrated space is substi-
tuted for a space consciously explored by man. Even if one has
a general knowledge of the way people walk, one knows nothing of a person's posture during the fractional second of a
stride. The act of reaching for a lighter or a spoon is familiar
routine, yet we hardly know what really goes on between hand
and metal, not to mention how this fluctuates with our moods.
Here the camera intervenes with the resources of its lowerings
and liftings, its interruptions and isolations, its extensions and
accelerations, its enlargements and reductions. The camera introduces us to unconscious optics as does psychoanalysis to unconscious impulses.

---

integration of a number of new sciences, or at least of new scientific data. Renaissance painting made use of anatomy and perspective, of mathematics,
meteorology, and chromatology. Valéry writes: "What could be further from
us than the strange claim of a Leonardo to whom painting was a supreme goal
and the ultimate demonstration of knowledge? Leonardo was convinced that
painting demanded universal knowledge, and he did not even shrink from a
theoretical analysis which to us is stunning because of its very depth and precision. . . ."—Paul Valéry, *"Pieces sur l'Art"*, *Autour de Corot*, Paris, p. 191.
[3] Rudolf Arnheim, *Film als Kinst*, (Berlin, 1932), p. 138.

Questions

1. Benjamin mentions the work of Sigmund Freud because he believes that movies, like psychoanalysis, can reveal things to us that we would not have noticed before. In some ways, they may seem more real than real. Do you agree with this idea? Do movies reveal reality or create their own reality? In what ways does a movie image seem "real" to you? Is the reality based on visual effects, movie devices, emotional content, or something else?

2. Benjamin compares the way a surgeon literally "gets inside" the patient to the way movies get inside real life. Have you ever seen a documentary that shows animals or nature in a way you could never see outside the movies? Pick a film like this and think about what techniques unique to movies, such as close-ups and slow motion, helped you "get inside" the natural experience.

3. Visit a Web site like http://www.youtube.com or any other site that presents short films that people have made. What is so compelling, fascinating, or appealing about these small, noncommercial films? Write an essay exploring this issue and try to refer to some of the ideas Benjamin presents to support your analysis.

4. Movies can communicate many things, but there are limits too. Have you ever tried to make a movie or been in a movie? What did you want to show that you couldn't because of the technology? What were you able to communicate that fulfilled your need as a moviemaker? How has the technology changed so that ordinary people can easily make movies? How do you think Benjamin would respond to these changes?

5. What differences have you noticed among the following three types of films: commercial films, independent films, and documentaries? Which seem more real to you? Explain your answer. Which type of film do you usually prefer to see? Why?

Making Connections

1. Imagine that there was a Matrix-like technology that could create experiences that were completely indistinguishable from reality. How would the various authors in this chapter feel about this? How would you? Would your response differ if it was used purely for entertainment as opposed to reporting the news?

2. Both Gombrich and Benjamin discuss our need to create "reality" in our art. What do they mean by this? What makes an image seem real or not? Is it all about the technical tricks or is there an emotional or psychological component as well? What is the most realistic art form you can think of?

3. Huxtable suggests that the entertaining fake can be more appealing to us than the original while Berman shows how NASA creates more vivid images by manipulating the original. What response do you think Wheeler, who is concerned about undetectable fakery, would have to their positions? Are you willing to accept entertaining fakes or vivid manipulations as the real thing? Write an essay explaining your answer and referring to these authors.

4. How do horror movies fit into Huxtable's idea of "living with the fake and learning to like it"? Why do we enjoy the fake effects of movies? Do we think of them as fake or more real than reality? How would some of the writers in this chapter respond to the popularity of horror movies today?

5. Benjamin writes that although the apparatus or technology of film makes it highly artificial, it can reveal reality to us more than theater or painting. How do you think Gombrich who applauds the power of painting or Berman who questions the manipulation of scientific images would feel about this?

6. Berman, Huxtable, and Wheeler seem cautious about the ability of technology to create images of reality. Gombrich and Benjamin seem to celebrate this very ability, at least in the selections chosen here. What do you think? Should we be wary or accepting of the images we make with new technologies? According to these authors, what should our role as consumers of images be?

7. Thinking about the selections you have read in this book, pick ten images from a variety of media that had an important impact on you. What is it about the images you selected that makes them stand out? Write an essay explaining the reasons for your choices and include quotes from any two authors in this book to support your choices.

8. The readings in this book have been divided into the act of seeing, mirroring ourselves, the visual surround, images and their uses, pictures that prod, and the image as reality. What overall themes about the world of the image do all these readings suggest to you? What other questions about images do you think need to be asked?

Credits

Ann Marie Seward Barry. "Media Images and Violence." From *Visual Intelligence: Perception, Image, and Manipulation in Visual Communication* by Ann Marie Seward Barry. Copyright © 1997 State University of New York Press. Reprinted by permission of the State University Press, State University of New York. All rights reserved.

Walter Benjamin. "The Work of Art in the Age of Mechanical Reproduction." From *Illuminations* by Walter Benjamin. In the public domain.

Bob Berman. "Colorizing the Cosmos." This article first appeared in *Discover* September 1999. Copyright © 1999 Bob Berman. Reprinted by permission of the author.

Susan Bordo. "Never Just Pictures." From *Twilight Zones: The Hidden Life of Cultural Images from Plato to O.J.* by Susan Bordo. Copyright © 1997 by The Regents of the University of California Press. Reprinted by permission of the University of California Press.

Thomas J. Campanella. "Eden by Wire: Webcameras and the Telepresent Landscape." Originally appeared in *The Robot in the Garden: Telerobotics and Telepistemology in the Age of the Internet* edited by Ken Goldberg. Copyright © 2000 by Thomas J. Campanella. Reprinted by permission of the author.

Edmund Carpenter. "Silent Music and Invisible Art." From *Natural History* 1978. Copyright © 1978 by Natural History Magazine, Inc. Reprinted by permission of Natural History Magazine, Inc. 1978.

Deborah Curtiss. "Seeing and Awareness." From "Introduction to Visual Literacy" in *A Guide to Visual Arts and Communication*